# MR. CHURCHILL

MR. CHURCHILL

# Mr. Churchill

*by*

## PHILIP GUEDALLA

*Arms, and the man I sing*

DRYDEN'S VIRGIL

*I may be a little irregular at the start
but I am quite regular on the finish*

WILLIAM E. BORAH

REYNAL & HITCHCOCK · NEW YORK

# CONTENTS

# LIST OF ILLUSTRATIONS

# VICTORIAN

*"The soldiers of the Queen, my lads."*

OLD SONG.

# 1

ENGLAND in 1874 stood on the threshold of the last quarter of the Nineteenth Century. Men of seventy, born before Trafalgar and able to remember Waterloo with some distinctness, had lived half their lives before the age of railways and were inclined to think that the last vestige of the past, upstanding and equestrian, had vanished with Lord Palmerston. Men of fifty, more attuned to the world in which they found themselves and fairly evenly divided as to the competing merits of Gladstone and Disraeli, surveyed the future with less misgivings. Men of twenty . . . but nobody minded very much what young men of twenty thought in 1874.

Three-quarters of the century were past. The first quarter had been consumed by war and the uneasy aftermath of war, the second in the steady growth of the new forces—steam locomotives, manufacture by machinery, public opinion as expressed by the new electorate created by the Reform Bill, and (in its last decade) Free Trade. The Nineteenth Century at its meridian turned hopefully towards an era of unlimited expansion; and, so far as England was concerned, its next quarter saw almost all the brightest expectations of the Great Exhibition in process of fulfillment. Cheap food, cheap raw material, and a welcome absence of foreign competition laid the world at its feet;

and while misguided Continental nations rose and fell in the scales of European war, the more judicious subjects of Queen Victoria minded their own (and a major portion of the world's) business. With growing assiduity and extremely satisfactory results they concentrated on production.

The normal growth of the United States was interrupted by the tragic controversy of the Civil War; and Europe reeled through a decade of four successive conflicts, as the French liberated Italy from Austria and Prussia liberated parts of Denmark from the Danes and ousted Austria from Germany and finally effaced the French. These martial vicissitudes were watched with varying emotions by British onlookers in ringside seats, whose business was not interrupted more than absolutely necessary. Business, indeed, was improving steadily. Their chimneys smudged the English skies; and England did not seem to mind, because a large majority of Englishmen could still remember just how far the antecedent age of unmitigated agriculture had fallen short of the idyllic. Meanwhile their towns were growing almost as quickly as their profits in an era of successful common sense, self-help, and enterprise rewarded. This might be uncongenial to lyric poets. But it was precisely what the vast majority of their fellow-countrymen appeared to want in the third quarter of the Nineteenth Century; and as the wheels revolved still faster, advancing streets of red brick cottages steadily engulfed more of the countryside, a new Reform Bill created still more electors, and there was every reason to suppose that the last quarter of the century was going to be much the same, only more so.

Not that the world was stationary in 1874. Quite the reverse. Facetious pencils were busy with the devastating march of female education; and while Man was humorously relegated to a life of petted idleness, du Maurier's young goddesses were seen discussing the differential calculus to the confusion of their athletic beaux. At the same time a threat of more exacting standards in domestic decoration occasioned some alarm among the cheerful Philistines. For Mid-Victorian England knew how to be disrespectful towards anything that it did not respect. That year Tenniel depicted the Catholic hierarchy without sympathy, and the Pope himself without excessive reverence. Towards the Crown he maintained a fair standard of courtliness, especially on the occasion of royal weddings or when a reputedly Republican Mayor of Birmingham named Chamberlain was honored with a royal visit and could be drawn as an obliging lion having his claws trimmed by a charming Princess, and—

> . . . put his red cap in his pocket, and sat on his Fortnightly article,
> And of Red Republican claws or teeth displayed not a particle.

But the Victorians were not above poking robust fun even at the Monarchy. For if they had believed in it a little less, they might have been rather more indulgent of its imperfections, of the royal heir's apparent levity and the Queen's sorrowing retirement. The Prince of Wales, already sternly cautioned in *The Coming K——*, was amiably lampooned that year; while his royal mother scolded him because—

> You seem to think these relatives intrude,
> And to dear Christian you, I fear, are rude.
> This is not right; I love the German race,

and a sequel commented with point and freedom on—

> . . . our Court-select, sedate, demure,
>    Bound in the virtuous chains Victoria forges;
> So good, so dull, so proper, and so pure,
>    And O! so different from her Uncle George's.

The Victorians were not yet Victorian in the full sense, and the satirist of 1874 could deal without embarrassment with—

> . . . the admission
> Of menial Scotchmen to the royal favor,

and felt no difficulty in deploring publicly—

> . . . The luck of Ballater and Braemar Glen;
> How there our Sovereign for half the year
>    Retires from midst the haunts of Englishmen,
> And spends her morning dropping the sad tear,
>    And building Albert cairns on every Ben—
> Then courts reaction in the afternoons,
> By hearing Willie Blair play Scottish tunes.

There were still the fixed stars of derision—excursion steamers, Volunteers, intoxicated gentlemen, the Tichborne claimant, omnibus conductors, conceited artists, courtship, clergymen, and lady novelists. It was,

*Culver*

*FATHER*—"Lord Randolph Churchill was above the average of youthful noblemen . . . and seemed capable of varying the uneventful chronicles of Blenheim Palace," the Marlborough ancestral home.

*Pictures, Inc.*

*MOTHER*—"Miss Jeannette Jerome was dark and lovely. Her mother lived in Paris for her health; and her father . . attended to his business in New York," where he had owned and edited the *New York Times*.

on the whole, a comfortable age which knew where it was going and was comparatively undismayed by a change of Government en route, especially when it replaced the restless Gladstone with the more sedative Disraeli. This substitution was highly welcome to the Queen, who had been losing sympathy with Mr. Gladstone. He was tiresome on the subject of her private time-table and on the public duties which could safely be entrusted to the Prince of Wales; and though she had suppressed a human tendency to tell him that the Government's defeat was largely due to his own unpopularity, there was a suspicious alacrity in her acceptance of his resignation.

So Gladstone had departed and Disraeli ruled in his place. It was the year of the old *condottiere's* triumph. He had been waiting forty years for such an opportunity. Now he had the country with him, to say nothing of the House of Commons and the Queen. For his sovereign was captivated by his romantic manners, by a Prime Minister who dropped on one knee to kiss the royal hand with a murmur of "I plight my troth to the kindest of *mistresses*" and wrote her such daring letters, which dramatized the dull debates at Westminster, or informed her airily of a maiden speech by a duke's younger son, who "said many imprudent things which is not very important in the maiden speech of a young member and a young man; but the House was surprised, and then captivated, by his energy, and natural flow, and his impressive manner. With self-control

7

and study, he might mount. It was a speech of great promise . . ."

## 2

The maiden speaker, though Disraeli was apt to be impressed by the younger sons of dukes, was not unworthy of his praise. Just twenty-five and newly married, Lord Randolph Churchill was above the average of youthful noblemen. It would be flattery to suggest that in the century or so which had elapsed since the eclipse of the great Duke of Marlborough the nation's annals had been appreciably enriched by the house of Churchill. (A similar, and even more prolonged, hiatus could be observed among the Cecils between their Elizabethan flowering and a late revival only recently effected by Lord Salisbury, the most intelligent of Disraeli's colleagues.) But Lord Randolph seemed capable of varying the uneventful chronicles of Blenheim Palace. A younger son, he startled his contemporaries at a preparatory school by his vehemence in declamation and "a distinct, if indefinite, sense of vigor, fluency, masterfulness and good-nature." These were accompanied by "a determined bull-dog type of face," which was remembered at Eton for occasional conflicts with discipline and a slight intemperance of dress.

Oxford brought him nearer to his home; and the Blenheim Harriers competed seriously with the Schools for his attention. But though his studies were a trifle intermittent, he was not averse from reading on his own lines; and an observant friend recalls that "his main literary passion was Gibbon. To Gibbon's immortal work he gave what leisure of reading he had to give, and this literary devotion lasted to the end." This sporting undergraduate of noble family was not readily distinguishable from other undergraduates of sporting tastes except by his pugnacious aspect and an unusual acquaintance with the *Decline and Fall of the Roman Empire.* But, unlike many of the type, he took a degree and then, conforming to his type once more, went off on the Grand Tour.

At twenty-four he fell in love. The scene was Cowes, the season August, and the occasion a ball in honor of a foreign prince on board a British cruiser. Someone introduced him to a young lady from New York, who lived in Paris with her mother. They sat and talked, because he hated dancing; and the next evening he was asked to dine with them on shore. There were three charming sisters, and that night he told a friend that he intended to marry "the dark one." A man of swift decisions, he took her for a walk next day, dined with her once again, proposed, and was accepted.

Miss Jeannette Jerome was dark and lovely. Her mother lived in Paris for her health; and her father, whom he had not met, attended to his business in New York. This gentleman, who at one time owned and edited the *New York Times,* had founded in the course of his career two race-courses adjacent to the city. But besides this honorable claim to rank with Mr. August Belmont as a father of the American turf his interests were highly varied. Since graduating from Princeton he had made and lost considerable sums of money in projects so diverse as shipping, journalism, and the transatlantic cable. In addition, he enjoyed a brief spell of unwelcome quiet as United States consul at Trieste, a port whose foreign representatives often inclined to the unusual, since not long after Mr. Jerome's departure its consular corps was enriched by the arrival of Sir Richard Burton. Always enterprising, he raced with the same ardor as he drove his four-in-hand in Jerome Park, while his family exchanged their town residence in Madison Square with fashionable punctuality for the milder pleasures of a villa at Newport and a steam yacht. Indeed, in moments of unpopularity the spirited New Yorker was quite capable of defending his newspaper office against mob violence with small-arms, if not with artillery.

But his future son-in-law, to whom this pugnacity would have been congenial, was rather hazy on the subject, and intimated vaguely to a ducal parent that "Mr. Jerome is a gentleman who is obliged to live in New York to look after his business. I do not know what it is." This was accompanied by reassuring information as to his finances and the social standing of his wife and daughters (which was fully justified by the fact that they had been honored with invitations to the Tuileries and Compiègne in the dying splendor of the Second Empire), a panegyric on Jeannette, a delicious photograph, and a touching announcement that he loved her "better than life itself, and that my one hope and dream now is that matters may be so arranged that soon I may be united to her by ties that nothing but death itself could have the power to sever," as well as by a tentative request for a small increase in his allowance.

His dream came true, but not at once. For dukes rarely act on impulse; and the Duke of Marlborough was slightly shocked by his son's precipitancy. Besides, New York was a long way from Blenheim Palace. Mrs. Jerome might have been received by Napoleon III and Princess Mathilde. The Persignys were intimates of the Jeromes; and when they were at Cowes in the dark days after Sedan, the Emperor himself called and took them all out sailing. But however they might rank in Paris, a Churchill was a Churchill. After all, transatlantic weddings were something of a novelty in 1873; and there is no plant in the whole world of more cautious growth than Anglo-American negotiation.

At the bare suspicion of reluctance on the British side the Jeromes drew back. Jennie was carried off to Paris; and the young couple had to wait, while the elderly authorities submitted their affection to the test of time. But it came through with flying colors. In the interval Lord Randolph was safely launched in politics. A Radical had ventured to intrude his candidature in the borough of Woodstock, hallowed by the proximity and influence of Blenheim. But the electoral air of 1874 was unfriendly to such outrages, and Lord Randolph Churchill was returned to Parliament by a large majority. These laurels duly won, he ran across to Paris and married Miss Jerome at the British Embassy in a blaze of family approval; and when he brought her home, delighted tenants and supporters duly took out the horses and dragged Lord Randolph and his bride through Woodstock to the house. It was his *annus mirabilis*. For 1874 had brought him a seat in Parliament, a bride, a successful maiden speech, and finally an heir.

Soon London learned to know the dark vivacity of Lady Randolph. After her Parisian apprenticeship she dressed a good deal better than the English. Besides *la belle Américaine* was still something of a novelty for London. Their parties ranged from the royal affability of the Prince of Wales to Disraeli's airy impersonation of a *gourmet*, as the old valetudinarian sat over his one glass of weak brandy and water and then wound up the evening by exclaiming to his host with false, inimitable gusto: "My dear Randolph, I have sipped your excellent champagne; I have drunk your good claret; I have tasted your delicious port—I will have no more." But Society failed to absorb them. There was the cheerful round of the West End, of Blenheim (for the hunting), of Ascot, Newmarket and Goodwood (for the racing), and of Cowes (for remembrance). But the young couple had wider interests—their runs to Paris for visits to the Jeromes and their French friends, and a trip to Philadelphia for the Centennial. Besides, they were not wholly free from money worries; their social life was slightly complicated by the head-long loyalty with which Randolph had taken sides in an unhappy controversy and incurred august displeasure; and in the nursery upstairs there was a lively infant upon whom they had bestowed the names of Winston Leonard—the first for Blenheim, and the second for New York.

The young family's next move was to Dublin. It was an age before the competence of dukes for responsible positions was generally doubted. Besides, Disraeli had a weakness for a duke. He had written books about them when he was young; it gave him peculiar satisfaction to create one when he was old; and if he needed a Lord-Lieutenant of Ireland, why not send a duke? One invitation had already been declined at Blenheim. But now he was an earl himself; and what could be more fitting for an Earl of Beaconsfield in Downing Street than a Duke of Marlborough at Dublin Castle? The invitation was renewed by the Prime Minister, with an added intimation that Lord Randolph might find himself at liberty to accompany his father as secretary (unpaid). It was an age when family affection was not yet excluded from administrative life; and this arrangement might well afford his younger son a welcome retreat. So, at the second time of asking, the invitation was accepted; and shortly after Master Winston's second birthday they were installed at "The Little Lodge" in Phœnix Park.

Irish administration in 1876 had not yet put on the depressing colors familiar in later years. A cautious gentleman named Butt, who led the Irish in the House of Commons and occasionally dined with the Churchills, put forward tentative demands for something in the nature of Home Rule. But nobody took them very seriously, and they were presented with a strictly constitutional appeal. The grim era of Parnell had not yet arrived; and though there were such things as Fenians, they seemed very far from a small boy riding his donkey over the green spaces of Phœnix Park. (Once they thought the Fenians were coming, and his donkey bolted.) Yet within two years of their return to England a gentleman named Burke, who had once given him a drum, was stabbed to death by Irish knives not many yards from "The Little Lodge."

Their life was uneventful though, his lovely mother ennobling castle drawing-rooms with the dark radiance of her beauty and the diamond star in her hair, or sitting the big Irish hunters in the tightest riding-habits of a small boy's recollection. Her husband hunted, shot, fished, caught lobsters, sailed, played chess, and occasionally helped to govern Ireland. Indeed, his wanderings about the country taught him the beginnings of a sympathetic understanding of the Irish and some of their demands, which might conflict dangerously with his party loyalties. But Lord Randolph was never a good party man. For at a time when all good Conservatives had learned to fear the Slav and love the Turk, he was in close correspondence with so formidable a Radical as Dilke upon the subject of autonomy for Greeks, Bulgarians, and Bosnians. These were strange leanings for the secretary (unpaid) of a leading member of Lord Beaconsfield's administration, with the Prime Minister about to bring home "Peace with Honor" from the Congress of Berlin in spite of Bulgarian atrocities, and Mr. Gladstone starting on his "pilgrimage of passion" in Midlothian to denounce the Turk, to denounce the Treaty of Berlin, to denounce unnecessary Zulu wars and superfluous operations on the Northwest Frontier of India, to denounce anything that Lord Beaconsfield might happen to have done, and finally to bring a majority not only of Midlothian electors, but of his fellow-countrymen at large into full agreement with him, and to put the Conservatives out of office, and to bring the Churchills home from Ireland.

Home with vague memories of Fenians and Phœnix Park, a small boy brought with him his first verbal recollection, of his Viceregal grandfather unveiling a military monument at Dublin with the terrific sentence: ". . . and with a withering volley he shattered the enemy's line." Nor was the martial infant, aged four, unaware of the nature of a volley, since distant musketry practice had been the normal accompaniment of his morning walks in Phœnix Park. England was less sensational for Winston, but far more interesting for Randolph.

The Parliament of 1880 was to Lord Randolph Churchill what the campaign of Italy was to the young Napoleon—or, if there is something inherently ridiculous about comparisons between military operations and the Parliamentary exploits of gentlemen in middle life and complete physical security, what the Parliament of 1906 was to Mr. F. E. Smith. In both instances a large Liberal majority returned to Westminster in the state of high moral exaltation peculiar to Liberal majorities. Only in 1880 their fervor was enhanced by the presence at their head of an incomparable leader. Mr. Gladstone was just seventy-one. He had entered Parliament in the reign of William IV and held minor office in the same Government as the Duke of Wellington; Peel's favorite disciple and Palmerston's most trying colleague, he had remade the political ideas of the Liberal Party in his own image, at once generous and austere. His reforming ardor (he was not called "the People's William" for nothing) and his meticulous pursuit of economy presided over six exacting years of a beneficent administration; and when it finally succumbed to the unpopularity that waits for all reformers, he had withdrawn composedly at sixty-five for "an interval between parliament and the grave." But Disraeli and the Turks were too much for him; and his busy pen was soon predicting that "their Zaptiehs and their Mudirs, their Bimbashis and their Yuzbachis, their Kaimakams and their Pashas, one and all, bag and baggage, shall, I hope, clear out from the province they have desolated and profaned."

Lord Beaconsfield responded savagely at a great London demonstration (Lady Randolph was there in an armchair next to the Duchess of Wellington) with his cruel riposte on the subject of "a sophisticated rhetorician, inebriated with the exuberance of his own verbosity." But his invective, which had dragged down Peel, was powerless against Gladstone. For he had a moral issue and a large middle-class electorate; and

16

in 1880 he emerged victorious from the last tournament to the profound discomfiture of the Queen, Lord Beaconsfield, and the Conservatives.

This champion at the head of an obedient majority was now confronted with an impudent and puny adversary in the person of Lord Randolph Churchill. The young nobleman, with three cheerful friends, engaged the venerable Premier in almost nightly combat, which a lifetime of Parliamentary conflict disinclined him to refuse and his more agile adversaries used to considerable effect. At first sight the challenge bore a stronge resemblance to the encounter of David and Goliath with the difference that in the present instance those moral advantages, which had been David's principal resource, appeared to have been transferred to Goliath. In these circumstances the prospects of the combat were, to say the least, one-sided. But the British public has a weakness for the weaker side; and presently the spectacle of the unequal combat at Westminster endeared Lord Randolph to a wider circle. Indeed, his temerity in challenging Mr. Gladstone in the fullness of his powers seemed to combine the dramatic interest of Landseer's "Dignity and Impudence" with something of the gallantry with which Lord Charles Beresford presently became his country's darling by defying the forts at Alexandria in the gun-boat *Condor*.

These sharpshooting activities were not exclusively directed against Mr. Gladstone. For his own leaders were inclined to be a little shocked by such irreverence.

17

Not, perhaps, Lord Beaconsfield himself, since Lord Beaconsfield could recognize that youth, especially noble youth, must have its fling. Besides, he found it easy to forgive anybody who teased Mr. Gladstone. Indeed, he was not above giving a few hints himself. But the party leaders in the House of Commons were less indulgent of Lord Randolph's gay skirmishing; and he was often left to conduct his operations without his party's sanction. Insubordinate to Mr. Gladstone's massive rule, he was almost as insubordinate to his own less enterprising leaders. This led the cheerful *guerrillero* and his trio of supporters to view themselves as an addition to the three existing groupings of Liberals, Conservatives, and Irish under the impressive nickname of "the Fourth Party." Never a good party man, Lord Randolph indulged in a good many private (and not so private) flings at the expense of the more venerable and bearded occupants of the Conservative Front Bench, known for derisive purposes as "the Goats." They found Lord Beaconsfield himself "anything but Goaty." But his more unbending deputies inspired in them a strong distaste for party orthodoxy; and when death removed Lord Beaconsfield, the young bravoes of the Fourth Party were more than ever their own masters.

Independent in their tactics, they were independent in their thought as well; and Lord Randolph was presently enunciating an up-to-date improvement upon current party doctrine under the attractive name of Tory Democracy. Embellished with a few Disraelian oracles, this interesting amalgam was warranted to make electors think like Liberals and vote Conservative. Its author candidly confessed, when answering the fundamental question, What is Tory Democracy? "Tory Democracy is a democracy which supports the Tory party." Nothing could be more disarming. As Lord Rosebery discerned in the exquisite prose elegy which he devoted to Lord Randolph's memory, "it was in reality a useful denomination or resource for anyone who found himself with Radical opinions inside the Tory party, and who did not wish to leave it."

It may be too severe to call it, with Lord Rosebery, "an imposture, an honest and unconscious imposture no doubt, but none the less an imposture." Yet we can recognize Lord Randolph in his assertion that "there are and always have been men who believe that so long as they call themselves Tories, they may blamelessly and harmlessly preach what doctrines they please." That was Lord Randolph Churchill's case. His busy mind was far too active for the dreary negatives of which contemporary Toryism was largely composed, just as his eager temper was unsatisfied by its half-hearted Opposition tactics. The latter drove him to the irregular warfare of the Fourth Party in an endeavor to galvanize Sir Stafford Northcote, while the former inspired his effort to modernize Lord Salisbury by inoculation with the elastic ideals of Tory Democracy. Both contributions can easily be underrated. Yet in assessing his political achievement it may be admitted without injustice that Lord Randolph Churchill was something more than a gadfly, but something less than a Major Prophet.

As practical embarrassments in the insistent form of Irish and Egyptian problems accumulated in the path of Mr. Gladstone's Government, Tory hopes began to rise and Lord Randolph's prospects rose with them. His privateering exploits in the House of Commons had earned him national celebrity. Caricaturists delighted in his perky bellicosity and the fierce challenge of his large mustache; and while they depicted him in a variety of uncomplimentary, diminutive, and mostly animal disguises, he was known to the public by assorted nicknames, of which "Yahoo Churchill" was the least favorable and "Little Randy" the most affectionate. He was in wide demand as a platform speaker, and listeners enjoyed his rich invective. The phrase-making sometimes recalled Disraeli; but there was something in his passages of sustained derision which came directly from his lifelong passion for the *Decline and Fall*.

In Lord Rosebery's diagnosis, "Randolph's humor may be fairly defined as burlesque conception, set off by an artificial pomp of style; a sort of bombastic irony, such as we occasionally taste with relish in an after-dinner speech. Sometimes it is what one could imagine that Gibbon might have uttered had he gone on the stump . . ." One day that manner would be richly echoed by his son. For it is not easy to say which of them was speaking, when an orator proclaimed:

The path of Britain is upon the ocean, her ways lie upon the deep, and you should avoid as your greatest danger any reliance on transcontinental communication, where, at any time, you may have to encounter gigantic military hosts.

That was Lord Randolph Churchill, in his Edinburgh trilogy of 1883 (which he sent, carefully prepared, to the London press before delivery and then had sleepless nights in case they printed his orations in the wrong order). His contemporaries termed it "Randolphian"; but their sons may recognize it as Winstonian. For either of them might have uttered his famous mockery of Mr. Gladstone's performances in wood-cutting—"The forest laments in order that Mr. Gladstone may perspire, and full accounts of these proceedings are forwarded by special correspondents to every daily paper every recurring morning"—no less than his elegant derision of "the lords of suburban villas, of the owners of vineries and pineries"; while prophetic echoes of a later orator linger in his asservation that "to their yells for the repeal of the Union you answer an unchanging, an unchangeable and a unanimous 'No,' " and even in his summary disposal of the resourceful organizer of Mr. Chamberlain's electoral triumphs at Birmingham with a grim phrase about "the dark and evil deeds of Mr. Schnadhorst."

His prospects were improving. A sustained performance as the *enfant terrible* of politics had earned Lord Randolph an assured position in a party which appeared to be on the road back to office. His lovely wife ranked with those fabulous divinities, the "Professional Beauties," although her interests were far more than photographic and she had carried her national aptitude for interior decoration into their new London house, which was arrayed in clean white paint long before its time and bore the added distinction of being the first private house in London to have electric light.

Visitors to Connaught Place in 1883 were confronted with these marvels, to say nothing of a celebrated hostess and a coming man. The same, perhaps, was scarcely true of their son, Winston. A red-headed urchin, he had given a fair amount of trouble under the mild rule of governesses and been packed off to school at the ripe age of seven. But his brief experience as an *alumnus* of St. George's, Ascot, was strikingly unsatisfactory. This pretentious establishment, preparatory for Eton, divided its attentions between corporal punishment and the classics; and its latest pupil did not take to either. Nor were its attractions materially heightened by compulsory cricket and football. After all, he was just seven; and happiness was still represented by games in the nursery with his magic lantern and his toy theater and his real steam engine and his collection of lead soldiers, which had nearly reached a thousand strong. But now he was confronted with the sharp angles of an imitation Public School, where there was nothing to be done by a talkative small boy, whom his contemporaries knew as "Carrots," but to dream of the holidays and count the hours to his next review on the nursery floor, varying the monotony by singing slightly unusual songs on a table in the matron's room. He could still take refuge in a book. How he enjoyed *Treasure Island,* when his father gave him a copy on its first appearance. But his disappointed pedagogues were unfavorably impressed both by the range and variety of his vocabulary and by his apparent eagerness to read anything except the unpalatable matter with which they presented him; and this unfavorable impression was energetically transferred from the teacher to the pupil.

The rôle of lonely little boy in insurrection against authority is detrimental to the health, and Winston's suffered accordingly. At eight he was transferred to Brighton, where his father's doctor could have an eye on him and two ladies kept a school of less masculine rigidity. Here he was permitted to learn things that interested him—French, history, and a good deal of poetry by heart. He seemed to enjoy acting, and he produced a single issue of a school paper. He learned to ride, he learned to swim; but when Miss Eva Moore arrived to teach him how to dance, she found "a small, red-headed pupil, the naughtiest boy in the class; I used to think he was the naughtiest small boy in the world!" Even an aunt described him as "a very interesting being, *though temporarily uppish."* (Had he not won his battle against the masters of St. George's?) But he was doing pretty well at Brighton, learning things he liked and, what was more, learning them in a way that he enjoyed.

Fifty years later he remembered Sunday afternoons

at his preparatory school, when they were permitted to explore old *Punch* cartoons. There are worse methods of learning modern history; and Master Churchill's fancy was regaled with Tenniel's pictorial embodiments of the European nations—those "tribal gods," upon whose deleterious influence Mr. H. G. Wells has commented adversely—in the picturesque vicissitudes of Nineteenth-Century politics. He learned to know Britannia and the British lion and John Bull and the stricken beauty of France in her defeat—"Golly! how I sympathized with France"—and Germania, a less attractive female figure, who left one small, contemporary reader with a vague notion that it would be a fine thing if some day the lovely lady with the broken sword could have her revenge upon her fattish rival.

The small boy was something of an individualist, with a tendency to court martyrdom in his Brighton pew by public demonstrations of the Low Church principles imbibed from his nurse. He also had an aptitude for pert repartee. But this was scarcely to be wondered at in one who was half Randolph Churchill's son and half American small boy. The wider freedom accorded by the New World to its youth produced a type which was just bursting on the Old. It was not so many years since Henry James' refinement had been abraded by a terrific urchin from Schenectady, N. Y., who did not think much of old castles and devastated his relations by vociferating publicly that his pretty sister's real name was not so much *Daisy Miller* as Annie P., as well as by an alarming insistence upon sitting up all night talking to foreign waiters. His face was pale, his eye was sharp, his utterance distinctive; and he was wholly untroubled by any form of diffidence. That formidable type supplied one element in the make-up of the small, red-headed boy upstairs in Connaught Place. The rest was Churchill—Randolph Churchill, though, a livelier species of that stately genius.

For Lord Randolph showed few signs of growing up. There was an element of sacrilege about opposing Mr. Gladstone. But as it was his firm conviction that the duty of an Opposition was to oppose, he set about it with a brisk irreverence; and at thirty-five Lord Randolph was the rising hope of the Conservatives. He had helped to form the Primrose League; he captured the National Union of Conservative Associations by a deft and well-timed resignation; and when Mr. Gladstone's Government was finally defeated in the House of Commons, Lord Randolph's handkerchief was waved, Lord Randolph's figure leapt upon his seat, and Lord Randolph's voice was raised in the view-halloo.

Now he was Secretary of State for India and duly sensible of his responsibility for "that most truly bright and precious gem in the crown of the Queen, the possession of which, more than that of all your Colonial dominions, has raised in power, in resource, in wealth and in authority this small island home of ours far above the level of the majority of nations and of States —has placed it on an equality with, perhaps even in a position of superiority over, every other Empire either of ancient or of modern times." Deploring Parliamentary indifference to Indian affairs, he called on his successors "to watch with the most sedulous attention, to develop with the most anxious care, to guard with the most united and undying resolution the land and the people of Hindostan"; and at least one of them, then ten years old, eventually caught both the substance and the style of his appeal. But Randolph was still irrepressible. For when he caught his venerable Premier and his still more venerable Queen in the act of putting a royal prince into the Bombay command without reference to the Secretary of State for India, he promptly resigned and got his way again. This was a trifle awkward for Lord Salisbury. But he could scarcely face the loss of their best platform speaker on the eve of a General Election.

His greatest triumph waited. For when Mr. Gladstone failed to carry the first Home Rule Bill and the Conservatives returned to office, Randolph Churchill's natural pre-eminence made him Chancellor of the Exchequer and Leader of the House of Commons. This promotion was inevitable, since "he *was* the leader at that moment—natural, inevitable and, as it seemed, indispensable." He had overcome obstructive mediocrities as well as grave suspicions of his orthodoxy—or had he? Mediocrities are not easily defied in politics; and in six months Lord Randolph Churchill had resigned again. This time it was for good. The method had succeeded in 1884 and 1885; but when he tried it once again to win his point in 1886, it failed. For this time the mediocrities, secure in office and quite confident

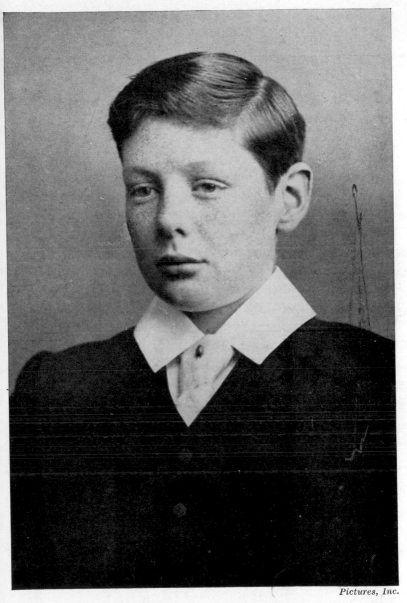

*SCHOOLBOY*—"A small, red-headed pupil, the naughtiest boy in the class."
At Harrow he rose no further than the modest dignity of Head of the Fags,
emerging with the Public Schools fencing championship and a conviction
that he was "all for the Public Schools but I do not want to go there again."

of staying there without his lively aid, accepted it with almost audible relief. The tragedy was swift; and Randolph Churchill remained "a Chancellor of the Exchequer without a Budget, a Leader of the House of Commons but for a single session, a victor without the spoils" and with (what was worse) a reputation of being slightly unaccountable. For Randolph Churchill, it appeared, could not grow up; and in default of a more solid destiny he became the Peter Pan of politics.

The tragedy of 1886 was swift; but in the empty years that followed it began to drag. His speeches were as trenchant as before; his thought was no less daring, with its taste for Radical solutions. Many of his friendships lay on that side of politics. Perhaps he should have become a Liberal. That appears to be his son's conclusion; but when Winston Churchill wrote his father's *Life,* he was a Liberal himself. Between Lord Randolph and the Liberals, however, lay the dividing gulf of Home Rule; and as to that he was committed beyond compromise and with deep sincerity to the view that "Ulster will fight, Ulster will be right." So there was nothing for it but to remain a Unionist and to work for a distant day when "the Tory Party will be turned into a Liberal Party, and in that transformation may yet produce a powerful governing force. If not, G.O.M., Labby, anarchy, etc., are triumphant." At intervals there was a cry among Conservatives that "Randolph must return." At odd moments he had dreams of a "National Party," that elusive avatar which haunts politicians' dreams (as his son searchingly remarked) "at times when ordinary party machinery is not at their disposal." But it was all too difficult; and he lingered on, a disappointed Tory whose bright prospects had been shipwrecked by a fatal weakness for resignation.

His son was growing through those empty years. He grew into Harrow and grew out of it, rising no further than the modest dignity of Head of the Fags and emerging with the Public Schools fencing championship and a strong conviction that he was "all for the Public Schools, but I do not want to go there again." He went there in the year of Queen Victoria's first Jubilee and, remaining in the lowest form three times as long as anybody else, learned more English grammar and less classics than his contemporaries. He showed proficiency in verse recitation and, still dynamic, committed the grave error of precipitating from behind into the swimming-bath someone who looked small enough to render this assault rewarding and secure. But when the victim turned out to be a boy named Amery, of immense strength and vast athletic eminence, young Churchill was reduced to nervous propitiation. "I am very sorry," he remarked, "I mistook you for a Fourth Form boy. You are so small." ("Tactfulness," as Lord Rosebery remarks, "has not perhaps been considered the strongest element in his Corinthian composition; but tact was the first requisite of his enterprise, and it has not failed him"—either in the composition of his father's *Life,* to which Lord Rosebery alluded, or in a difficult encounter with the moist, indignant Amery.) "My father," he resumed, "who is a great man, is also small."

His prospects were now definite. Lord Randolph had decided that his son was to go into the Army, reaching this conclusion either because Winston was not bright enough for the Bar or by reason of a particularly impressive display of his toy soldiers on the floor upstairs in Connaught Place. So he was in the Army class at Harrow, developing a base tendency to trade English essays (which he dictated fluently, if permitted to walk up and down the room) for Latin translations. For the classics still presented insuperable obstacles. So, at the first two attempts, did Sandhurst, although it was hoped that its walls would fall before the more artful summons of an Army crammer's trumpet. But an accident delayed this happy consummation. When boys of eighteen, skylarking in the Christmas holidays, elect to fall off trees from a height of nearly thirty feet, the consequences are far from negligible. The patient was unconscious for three days; his father came racing home from Ireland; and an eminent surgeon diagnosed a ruptured kidney. Transported to London, the invalid saw more than usual of his political surroundings.

It was 1893, when Gladstone led the last rally for Home Rule at eighty-four, and Winston watched him from the gallery. He met his father's friends—Balfour, Chamberlain, Rosebery, Asquith, Morley, and Carson. Not all of them were Tories, since Lord Randolph followed his own line in politics. The crowds still recognized him in the street, and cheered him when he spoke. He always gave them good sport, and they liked the schoolboy quality which distressed his older colleagues. (A young journalist named Barrie, not long from Kirriemuir and lately leader-writer on the *Nottingham Journal,* introduced Lord Randolph in a Stevensonian extravaganza and depicted him enjoying an elementary booby-trap with peals of laughter.) But, though he still played the game, the intervals were longer now, and he seemed to know that he could never win. He had written to his wife, when Arthur Balfour (an old playmate in the Fourth Party) slipped gracefully into his place, that he had "had quite enough of it. I have waited with great patience for the tide to turn, but it has not turned, and will not now turn in time. . . . All this confirms me in my decision to have done with politics and try to make a little money for the boys and for ourselves."

But politics were just beginning for his son. Winston had read every word his father spoke. He knew the ripe, Gibbonian style, and "thought of Austen Chamberlain who was allowed to fight at his father's side, and Herbert Gladstone who had helped the Grand Old Man to cut down the oak trees and went everywhere with him." At this time he dreamed "of comradeship with him, of entering Parliament at his side and in his support." But there seemed little prospect that he would be permitted to help his father in that way, though Randolph once bared the bitterness of his defeat and begged his son to make allowances, because "things do not always go right with me. My every ac-

tion is misjudged and every word distorted." For when
he offered to assist with his father's correspondence, the
offer was declined.

Sandhurst was quite hard enough; and when it
yielded at the third attempt, he found himself a cavalry
cadet. Here was another disappointment for Lord Randolph, who had hoped to see his son in the 60th Rifles.
But now he was reading hard and digging trenches
and making demolitions and mapping the neighborhood of Camberley. The work interested him. At intervals he came up to London and went to the Empire
with his father, who sometimes took him racing or to
political confabulations. Once, indeed, his ardor for
unlikely causes entangled him in a high-spirited attempt to preserve the freedom of the individual from
earnest feminine attempts to purge the Empire Promenade. He prepared a speech, which remained unde-
livered; he traveled up to London; he pawned his
watch to raise expenses; and on a fateful Saturday
night he harangued the Promenade itself in a scene of
some disorder and the very first of Winston Churchill's
public speeches.

Sandhurst was coming to an end, and an accommo-
dating colonel was prepared to take him into the 4th
Hussars. He was twenty now; his father, who was failing fast, consented; and a last weak murmur asked
about his horses. For Randolph's tragedy was ending.
He could fight the mediocrities no longer. Mediocrities
were comforted for years by the swift completeness of
Randolph Churchill's political eclipse. A rash resigna-

31

tion had ruined him; and perhaps he should have changed his party, when he changed his views, instead of staying on with the Conservatives in disappointed captivity. (Those might be the lessons of his career for anyone who studied it—no rash resignations; a change of party when it seemed desirable; and whole-hearted intolerance of sound party mediocrities.) But ill-health completed what political misfortune had begun. There had been a pitiable effort to continue the active struggle of public life, of which one witness has written with somber eloquence, "He was the chief mourner at his own protracted funeral, a public pageant of gloomy years. Will he not be remembered as much for the anguish as for the fleeting triumphs of his life? It is a black moment when the heralds proclaim the passing of the dead, and the great officers break their staves. But it is a sadder still when it is the victim's own voice that announces his decadence, when it is the victim's own hands that break the staff in public. I wonder if generations to come will understand the pity of it, will comprehend the full tragedy of Randolph's married life." He was barely forty-six; and his race was run. To Lord Rosebery it seemed that "he left behind him no great measure. Nor did he found a school or inaugurate a policy." But Randolph Churchill left a son.

3

The world in which Winston Churchill came of age was vastly different from that into which he had been born. For in the intervening twenty years the country had advanced from the Mid-Victorian into the more adventurous Late Victorian age; and 1895 was worlds away from 1874. There were not so many people left in England who could recall a time before the Queen sat on the throne; and the happy accident of her survival gave the Monarchy an almost hieratic character quite unlike anything that Englishmen had ever known before. Now she remained for her respectful and devoted subjects a tiny, venerated figure embodying nearly sixty years of progress, mechanical invention, and empire-building, while her armed forces stiffened at the sight of—

> . . . the Widow at Windsor
> With a hairy gold crown on 'er 'ead.
> She 'as ships on the foam—she 'as millions at 'ome,
> An' she pays us poor beggars in red.

People in middle life looked back with conscious pride upon a time in which they had got their novels written by Dickens and Thackeray, their songs sung by Tennyson and Browning, their politics conducted by Gladstone and Disraeli, and even their beliefs unsettled by Darwin and Huxley. But nearly all of them had vanished now. The Queen lived on; and a few gallant veterans still wore their medals, while Mr. Gladstone (though still good for an explosion on Armenian atrocities) had retired at last. Young people in 1895 dared to look forward to a strange exciting future when the Nineteenth Century itself would follow all its children

33

into history and their letters would be unbelievably dated 1900. But for the moment they were living almost consciously in the end of a great age, deliberately *fin de siècle*. That consciousness led some of them to draw precisely what their predecessors would not have drawn, to write exactly as they would not have written.

Young Mr. Beardsley entertained subscribers to the *Yellow Book* with fancies diametrically opposite to those with which Sir John Millais adorned the Royal Academy; young Mr. Bernard Shaw wrote studiously unromantic plays; still younger Mr. H. G. Wells alarmed the readers of domestic fiction by indicating that its boundaries might be enlarged to include the marvels of science. But these were a spirited minority; and England two years before the Diamond Jubilee was comparatively unaffected by minorities. Home Rulers, Socialists, and Decadents might be unpleasant portents of a less comfortable future. But in 1895 they did not represent the majority of the Queen's subjects, either in politics (as the Liberals found out at the General Election that year) or in other matters of taste and opinion.

Well-connected subalterns of cavalry are rarely unresponsive to the prevailing mood. Young men in such positions are apt to be the children of their age; and Winston Churchill was deeply marked by the ideals and beliefs of his countrymen in 1895. It was an age still fortified in most of its beliefs by the Victorian certainties. Right would prevail, because (since 1837, at any rate) it generally had. Morality had nearly al-

34

ways been victorious; and there were gratifying signs
of a divine purpose in the recent progress of the human
race. This, perhaps, was more apparent in the wide
territories reigned over by Queen Victoria than among
the

> . . . lesser breeds without the Law,

a circumstance affording one more reason for main-
taining their present boundaries, if not for extending
them. Englishmen believed, with a fair show of reason, that they were the Lord's anointed.

> Fair is our lot—O goodly is our heritage!
> (Humble ye, my people, and be fearful in your mirth!)
> > For the Lord our God Most High
> > He hath made the deep as dry,
> He hath smote for us a pathway to the ends of all the
> > Earth!

That was how it struck their latest minstrel; and the
same exalted mood inspired a leading statesman of the
day to write almost gaily that "we have in hand difficulties of the most serious character with France,
Russia, and Germany. We are engaged in an important
expedition in the Soudan; and it is uncertain as yet
whether the war on the North-west frontier of India
has been finally concluded."

This mood of confidence was less unreasoning than
it might seem at the first blush, since economically
their prosperity appeared to be unchallengeable (Galsworthy defined it as "a gilt-edged period"), and there
were solid guarantees of British security. For the Royal
Navy rode supreme on the seven seas; and if Great

Britain had enemies, they were safely situated on the mainland. Afridis and Dervishes could hardly count; and on the Continent the military power of the German Empire was not yet aligned against her, while the French were given over to an ecstasy of paralyzing politics. There was always Russia; but though Russian agents perpetually haunted the dreams of the Government of India, nothing came of it. Serenely confident and with sound reasons for their confidence, the loyal subjects of the Queen held on their course. Even a rebuff in South Africa (attributable to the activities of Cecil Rhodes, who held the prevalent belief even more forcibly than his contemporaries) elicited such brave newspaper headlines as "Hands Off" and "England Yet," and led Joseph Chamberlain to the conclusion that "what is called an 'Act of Vigor' is required to soothe the wounded vanity of the nation. It does not much matter which of our numerous foes we defy, but we ought to defy someone."

Few men escape the influences of the time in which they come of age; and Winston Churchill's life at home, at Sandhurst, or in the 4th Hussars was not secluded. Cavalry subalterns do not live in ivory towers. Besides, his mother was an eager ally now. In former years her life had been almost too crowded for much space to be reserved for his affairs. There had been Society and politics and the vicissitudes of her husband's swift career; and as a little boy he had adored her from a distance. The radiant vision, exquisitely gowned, had been a shade remote; and as it is not easy to confide in Homeric goddesses, the story of his school-boy hopes and fears had been reserved for an admirable nurse. But now his mother entered into all his plans. There was barely twenty years between them; and, as he recalled it, they "worked together on even terms, more like brother and sister than mother and son." Lady Randolph moved (and he moved with her) at the very center of her age. It was a comfortable epoch, when Lord Salisbury was wise, and Lord Rosebery was eloquent, and Joseph Chamberlain saw visions, and Cecil Rhodes dreamed dreams; and not long afterwards the Diamond Jubilee evoked its anthem.

> God of our fathers, known of old,
> Lord of our far-flung battle-line,
> Beneath whose awful Hand we hold
> Dominion over palm and pine—
> Lord God of Hosts, be with us yet,
> Lest we forget—lest we forget!

But, though confident, it was not sedentary. A strong sense of the British destiny preserved it from inactivity. For it knew its duty; and if it listened to its favorite bard, it could not say that it had not been warned, when he looked forward to

> . . . the day of Armageddon, at the last great fight
> of all,
> That Our House stand together and the pillars do
> not fall,

or proclaimed in retrospect that

> If blood be the price of admiralty,
> Lord God, we ha' paid in full!

37

That was the purposeful temper of the epoch in which Winston Churchill came of age; and he bore its imprint beside his natural inheritance from two unusual parents and the haunting memory of his father's failure.

Besides, he had ambitions; and most men's ambitions are fixed upon the type admired by the world in which they come of age. The ideal Englishman of 1895 was not a cloistered type. He might, perhaps, be silent; but he must be strong. More than a decade of savage warfare had consecrated a long calendar of heroes in the public mind—Chard and Bromhead at Rorke's Drift, Burnaby at Abu-Klea, Gordon at Khartoum. Their operations were not crowned with uniform success; but their patriotic purpose was undoubted, and its rays illumined the ambitions of large numbers of young Englishmen in the last years of Queen Victoria. They believed unquestioningly in their country; and if its destiny was rashly challenged, they would wish to know the reason why. Perhaps they did not inquire too closely into their means of doing so. But the visible resources of the British Empire were immense, and, sure of their beliefs, they were no less sure that they would be able to enforce them, if the need arose. In that day patriotism was unquestioned and, perhaps, a shade unquestioning. But skies were clear in 1895, when Winston Churchill first put on the Queen's uniform; and since young men inevitably bear the stamp of their time, he was a child of his age.

## 4

He received the Queen's commission at twenty and, gazetted to the 4th Hussars, went off to Aldershot sporting the gold lace, striped pantaloons, and tiny pill-box forage cap accorded to her mounted troops and privileged to learn the regimental mysteries, the last refinements of military equitation, and the taste of dust in the Long Valley. For he was in the Army now—Queen Victoria's and Kipling's Army. His, like *Captain Gadsby's* (also a Hussar), the privilege of leading on occasion "the best squadron of the best regiment of cavalry in all the world," to know "the soothin', jingle-bump-an'-clank" of Horse Artillery, to watch red-coated infantry go by to the *"rowdy-dowdy-dow!"* of the big drum,

> Eight 'undred fightin' Englishmen, the Colonel, and the Band.

But not his the heart-broken confession of *Captain Gadsby* that he "felt every hoof of the squadron in the small of my back every time that I've led." For, undemoralized by matrimony, young Churchill positively enjoyed "the stir of the horses, the clank of their equipment, the thrill of motion, the tossing plumes, the sense of incorporation in a living machine, the suave dignity of the uniform." He savored "that greatest of all cavalry events—the Charge"; and, in his happy retrospect, "when the line was finally formed and the regiment or brigade was committed to the charge, one could hardly help shouting in joyous wrath."

39

With such proclivities it was small wonder that their latest subaltern found his existence in the 4th Hussars "a gay and lordly life." He learned his soldiering from an unexceptionable source. For Colonel Brabazon combined the qualities of one of Ouida's heroes (which included a small, but trim, imperial worn in defiance of the Queen's Regulations, imperturbable insouciance, and a fashionable inability to pronounce the letter "r") with more solid qualities. His record as a fighting soldier was impressive, and he had at his command a wide range of English literature. But even this Admirable Crichton and the attractions of the Mess could not occupy Lieutenant Churchill's winter leave. Since all his money had been spent on polo ponies, he could not afford to hunt. In these circumstances adventure beckoned; and as the soldiers of the Queen were not engaged in any operations of serious significance, he was reduced to seeking a brief experience of active service with foreign troops.

A Spanish army was conspicuously failing at the moment to absorb the lessons of *guerrilla* warfare from the conscientious hands of Cuban patriots; and as one of his father's oldest friends was ambassador at Madrid, affairs were easily arranged. Sailing for New York, he saw his mother's native shore in November, 1895, and hurried on to Havana. Presently the blue waters of the Caribbean gave way to the rocky hills of Cuba; the Morro frowned across the harbor; and he went ashore to unlimited cigars, oranges, and official courtesies.

En route for the front, he entered his first armored

train and arrived at headquarters. A veteran of Spain's interminable and frequently unsatisfactory wars against Moors, Mexicans, and other Spaniards received him with distinction and consigned him to a flying column, which was understood to be in contact with the enemy. He duly reached it and was initiated in the merits of a rum cocktail (known to later amateurs of such things as a Bacardi) and in the high value, for military and administrative purposes, of the siesta. (That lesson stayed with him for life, and he has testified that "when I was at the Admiralty in the War, I found I could add nearly two hours to my working effort by going to bed for an hour after luncheon.")

The war, so far as he could see, consisted of interminable marches through impenetrable jungle to uncertain destinations, punctuated by stray rifle shots from an elusive enemy. By a happy augury he heard them for the first time on his twenty-first birthday. But apart from this heartening experience and an ability to distinguish the sharper Mausers of his own side from the deep note of Remingtons, with which the Cubans fought, his military education was not notably enriched. Spanish operations were conducted without undue precipitation and in accordance with a dignified convention by which the general and his staff, including their distinguished English guest, sat calmly on their horses just behind the firing-line, a practice whose results might well prove less rewarding (as it did later in South Africa) if practiced against enemies of higher marksmanship or lower chivalry than Cuban patriots.

It would be inelegant to term proceedings of such dignity rough-riding. But it is interesting to observe that two years before Colonel Roosevelt arrived in Cuba as a Rough Rider, he was anticipated in the field by Winston Churchill. Imagination falters at the possibilities of an encounter on the same terrain. But, New Yorkers both—though one of them was only half a New Yorker—their careers present strange parallels. Of the two, Winston Churchill left Cuba with fewer laurels. But he had been under fire, discovering with some relief that the noise exceeds the casualties; and his first campaign in Cuba began to satisfy a lifelong passion for active service and cigars.

Returned to England, he shortly found the regiment at Hounslow and under orders for India,

> Troopin', troopin', troopin' to the sea:
> 'Ere's September come again . . .

The endless cycle of the War Office consigned them to the East. But before his troopship sailed, he had a delicious interlude of life in London with his mother, of polo at Hurlingham and Ranelagh, of the Season when it was still a brilliant reality rather than a delusion fostered by West End tradesmen for the benefit of unfashionable debutantes. He looked back on it from later years as "almost the only idle spell I have ever had"; and the London Season of 1896 lived in his memory as something incomparably brilliant and exclusive. Perhaps it was not quite so exclusive as it seemed to an eager subaltern that summer. For the con-

*FLYER*—The First Lord of the Admiralty explores a new medium in 1914. Here he has just landed after a flight with Major Gerard in a French plane.

*HORSEMAN*—Even in his later life, Mr. Churchill has never lost his zest for polo, which he learned as a subaltern of cavalry in Kipling's India.

summate English system assimilates new elements so swiftly that they are soon indistinguishable from the old. True, the historic families whose names recur in Cabinets and on race-cards were there. But so were the additions which they had received from West Indian plantation fortunes and the wealthy Nabobs of British India; coal and iron had arrived; nor was liquid refreshment unrepresented. American duchesses were not unknown. But that would hardly alarm this cadet of a noble house, who was half American himself.

At any rate, he thoroughly enjoyed himself, dined out extensively, played a great deal of polo, and was asked to week-end parties honored by the presence of Albert Edward, Prince of Wales. Indeed, his constitutional unpunctuality earned a royal rebuke, presently effaced by royal affability. Not that he neglected his opportunities, since he cornered a distinguished soldier one Sunday morning at a country house and extracted something in the nature of a promise that he might come with him on the next expedition he commanded on the Northwest Frontier. In his mother's house he met all that was beautiful in London and much that was bright. Indeed, the catholicity of Lady Randolph's entertainments once supplied him with the supreme embarrassment of parting a Jameson Raider, who was just then on trial at Bow Street for that grave offense against the Foreign Enlistment Act, from a Liberal ex-minister, who had been one of its severest critics. For Randolph Churchill had never been a strict party man, and the tradition lasted in his home. But

43

his son, at twenty-one and under orders for the East, had few thoughts of politics.

5

Embarked in one of Kipling's troopships late in 1896, the subaltern duly arrived in Kipling's India. Though it was nearly ten years since their time, the India of *Soldiers Three* received him rather than the less restricted boundaries inhabited by *Kim*. For subalterns of British cavalry rarely penetrate far beneath the surface of that astonishing sub-continent, which a century of steady nerves and sound administration had entrusted to the Queen-Empress. His, to be more precise, was the India of polo-ponies, pegs, and *Captain Gadsby*. For Lieutenant Churchill, proficient with the first already, learned the merits of the second and associated freely with the third.

His first entry on the scene was impulsive and not unlike him. For the rather backward little boy with a slight difficulty in his speech was now swift and extremely talkative. Sometimes, indeed, he was too swift and, perhaps, too talkative. This time he was too swift. For one bright afternoon his troopship anchored at its destination, and he was confronted by the inviting spectacle of Bombay. A shore-boat brought him in; and as it rose and fell against the dock wall, he grasped eagerly at India in the form of a large iron ring. Then the boat dropped away again, leaving him to scramble into Asia as best he could with a dislocated shoulder, which retained a lifelong disability for tennis and a chronic tendency to go out of action at odd moments (including an unduly expansive gesture at the House of Commons). But he had arrived in India, and the 4th Hussars passed on by way of Poona to the cantonments at Bangalore.

Once more life was "gay and lordly," supported on his pay, an allowance of £500 a year, and the timely aid of local money-lenders. Its leading interest was polo; and the regiment began to do extremely well. But an unending cycle of morning parade followed by evening polo and Mess conversation was not quite enough. He could not subsist, it seems, upon an undiluted course of *The Maltese Cat* with *Captain Gadsby* to follow.

Each day there was an interval about six hours long in which the sun beat down on Southern India; and in the daily interval Lieutenant Churchill began to read. Things interested him, and he made up his mind that he was going to find out about them—things like history and economics and philosophy. There was so much they had not taught him anything about at Harrow and Sandhurst. So he resolved to educate himself on the hot afternoons at Bangalore. His mother sent him out the books he asked for, and Winston Churchill sat down to learn things for himself. He began with the *Decline and Fall,* because Gibbon had been his father's favorite author, and was promptly captivated by the vast sweep of his majestic narrative and the stately measure of his style. This was the source at which his father had imbibed the rich Randolphian compound of derision and false gravity; and though Lieutenant Churchill was not thinking yet of forming his own style, it was formed imperceptibly by Gibbon through the long afternoons at Bangalore.

But he had other guides as well, as he explored the past. For after Gibbon he pursued Macaulay, who had been highly spoken of by his nurse's brother-in-law, a retired prison warder in the Isle of Wight. That author's lyrics already commanded his favorable notice; and he now embarked upon the *History*. The hard glitter of its prose compelled his admiration, and a young Churchill was distressed to read Whig strictures on the great Duke of Marlborough. Now he was reading steadily four hours or so a day. From history he passed on, untutored and intrepid, to navigate the uncharted seas of philosophy. Plato's *Republic* and Aristotle's *Politics* (in suitable translations) afforded him a sort of home-made Greats; and, thus fortified, he faced the more immediate problems raised by Malthus' *Essay on Population* and Darwin's *Origin of Species*.

His mind was soon directed to the riddle of his own position in the universe. Depressed by Schopenhauer and disillusioned by *The Martyrdom of Man,* his pristine faith was now endangered by Gibbon's skepticism and Professor Lecky's milder, though more reasoned, doubts; and the young searcher after truth reacted sharply against the religious teachings of his nursery and school. But presently his faith returned, when his profession brought him into acute danger and he found that prayers for safety received a satisfactory answer. Illogical, perhaps, and unexciting as religious experience, it left him with a sensible conviction that "the practice was comforting and the reasoning led nowhere."

Topping up his reading with the fine, confused feeding of a dictionary of quotations ("The quotations when engraved upon the memory give you good thoughts. They also make you anxious to read the authors and look for more"), he faced the slow unfolding of his professional career. Early in 1897 he sailed home on leave, meeting on board a slim Colonel Ian Hamilton, who hoped prophetically for a chance to serve against the Turks in the Greek War. The young Hussar, as a good Tory, favored the Turkish side and had vague notions (undiscouraged by the circumstance that he had not yet written anything except an unpublished answer to some aspersions on the British Army by Mr. Bernard Shaw) of becoming a war correspondent. But the war collapsed before they could get there; and he was reduced to a brief tour of Italy with Gibbon in his hand.

Then he passed on to one more London Season—London in the brilliant weeks before the Diamond Jubilee, when Joseph Chamberlain was entertaining Colonial Premiers and Society in fancy dress filled Devonshire house and awed the watching crowds in the Green Park outside. He saw the Season out, attending the last fixture of the social calendar at Goodwood. But his racing was interrupted by the discovery of a newspaper paragraph announcing that there was trouble on the Northwest Frontier and that a general he knew— the very general, in fact, who had once promised him a chance of active service—was in command. He promptly wired him and left for Brindisi to catch the boat for India. Arrived there, he discovered that he had no chance of campaigning, unless he could contrive to go as a war correspondent. A newspaper in India obliged forthwith; and the *Daily Telegraph* at home surrendered at discretion to Lady Randolph by accepting him as a contributor. He dashed half the length of India to Bangalore, got leave from his regiment, turned north again, traveled a round two thousand miles to rail-head, posted forty more by *tonga,* and found himself at headquarters.

This was better than Havana. The wild race from Goodwood had been distinctly worth it. For here he was on a September evening in 1897 at the headquarters of the Malakand Field Force and on the point of seeing British troops go into action. He would go into action with them; and war correspondents on the frontier were not necessarily confined to a spectator's rôle. For a gallant officer, who acted as *The Times* correspondent, had just won the Victoria Cross. Indeed, Lieutenant Churchill earned himself a mention in despatches with the honorable record of having "made himself useful at a critical moment." It was an uncomfortable moment, too, in the best tradition of frontier warfare, where Bengal Lancers were apt to lead the way while infantry worked cautiously across a vertical landscape in the disturbing presence of—

> The flying bullet down the Pass,
> That whistles clear: "All flesh is grass."

A British subaltern and five Sikhs dropped to a sudden volley, and the little party began to fall back. Lieutenant Churchill, who had been shooting tribesmen with a borrowed rifle, was carrying a wounded Sikh. But they were rushed; the adjutant was killed; and as a big tribesman hacked at the body, Lieutenant Churchill "forgot everything else at this moment except a desire to kill this man." His first resolve was the heroic expedient of "personal combat *à l'arme blanche*." He had his sword; he had once held the Public Schools fencing championship. But he thought better of it, as his enemy stood waiting for him with the *tulwar,* and took several shots at him with his revolver instead. Then he rejoined his friends at speed. It was a typical example of the poet's timely warning—

> A scrimmage in a Border Station—
> A canter down some dark defile—
> Two thousand pounds of education
> Drops to a ten-rupee *jezail*—
> The Crammer's boast, the Squadron's pride,
> Shot like a rabbit in a ride!

Lieutenant Churchill did not fall strictly within either category; and he escaped their fate. The retreat down the Mamund Valley was resumed. They were still hard pressed; and when the colonel ordered him to go back

49

and hurry up the Buffs, he insisted cautiously upon a written order to this effect, having little taste for arriving at headquarters well in advance of his companions and without satisfactory evidence of the official reason. For Lieutenant Churchill did not always act on impulse.

After this honorable episode he was posted to the 31st Punjab Infantry, with a Hindustani vocabulary confined to the invaluable words for "get on" and "kill," assisted by gestures of unusual eloquence and cries of "Tally ho!" But the remainder of his service with the Malakand Field Force was less eventful. His leave expired; and when operations on the frontier broadened into the wider aims of the Tirah Expeditionary Force (which took the Gordon Highlanders—and Piper Findlater—to the heroism of Dargai), he was unable to accompany it. He tried his hardest; and at home Lady Randolph "left no wire unpulled, no stone unturned, no cutlet uncooked," even carrying her operations to the Olympian heights on which Lord Roberts and Lord Wolseley presided over military destinies. But all was vain; and he was back at Bangalore with polo and the 4th Hussars.

He had other interests as well, since his letters from the front had been favorably received on their first appearance in the newspapers. This mild success encouraged him to make a volume of them and to write a book about the whole campaign. He had a taste for words; and presently his afternoons were occupied in the enjoyable exercise of composition, accelerated by intelligence that *The Times* correspondent was engaged in doing the same thing. His mother found a London publisher; his uncle read the proofs; and *The Story of the Malakand Field Force* appeared in 1898.

A lucid study of frontier warfare, it was strongly influenced in its more impressive passages by the *Decline and Fall,* since subalterns of twenty-three are not, of themselves, prone to reflections which "the philosopher may observe with pity, and the philanthropist deplore with pain." On this Gibbonian foundation he reared a structure of clear and lively narrative bearing a slight resemblance to the writings of a patriotic clergyman of military tastes, whose work enjoyed a wide contemporary popularity and adorned school prize-givings with awards of *How England Saved Europe* and *Fights for the Flag.* Its chapter-headings, with a selection of assorted mottoes, bore witness to the author's reading, when drawn from Kipling, Tennyson, Omar Khayyam, Sir Alfred Lyall, Shakespeare, and Byron (on the subject of their common *alma mater*), and possibly to his *Familiar Quotations,* when retrieved from such more recondite sources as Lucretius and Burke.

But the book's significance lies in its revelation of the author. He was all for action.

> How different are the scenes. The club on an autumn evening—its members grouped anxiously around, discussing, wondering, asserting; the noise of the traffic outside; the cigarette smoke and electric lights within. And only an hour away along the wire, the field, with the bright sunlight shining on the swirling muddy waters; the black

forbidding rocks; the white tents of the brigade a mile up the valley; the long streak of vivid green rice crop by the river; and in the foreground the brown-clad armed men. I can never doubt which is the right end to be at. It is better to be making the news than taking it; to be an actor rather than a critic.

That is a fair specimen of his descriptive manner, and a good sample of Winston Churchill. Nor is he absent from the young author's strong distaste for foreign names—"One unpronounceable name is as good as another . . . Another pestilent tribe, whose name alone is an infliction"—bright foretaste of a later statesman's gift for delighting his fellow-countrymen with sturdy mispronunciations of the misshapen titles of another breed of foreign savages. His views are stoutly Imperialist, and he writes pityingly of Liberals. But the tone is not vainglorious; and his insistence upon supplies of chocolate for military occasions is admirably practical. It is refreshing to discover Lieutenant Churchill on the side of *Captain Bluntschli* rather than in the prancing ranks of romance with *Major Sergius Saranoff;* but one could hardly campaign on the Northwest Frontier and remain a *beau sabreur.*

The book succeeded, in spite of a phenomenal number of misprints admitted by his indulgent uncle (a weekly called it "Napier punctuated by a mad printer's reader"). The reviews were highly favorable; the Prime Minister read it; the Prince of Wales wrote to the author. This was success. He heard the pleasant notes of praise for the first time. His school reports had not found very much to praise him for. But now the praise was almost universal. His evocation of the realities of frontier warfare came at a good moment after the great pageant of the Diamond Jubilee, when patriots viewed such encounters as watch and ward upon the marches of the Empire and romantics thrilled to their echoes as a later generation to the Foreign Legions. (For in 1898 *Bengal Lancer* was a surer draw than *Beau Geste*.) Lieutenant Churchill got his due share of this appreciation. Even the Prince wrote hopefully about his military career and, as became a royal soldier, hoped that he would not follow the sad example of the gallant *Times* correspondent, who was going into Parliament: "You have plenty of time before you, and should certainly stick to the Army before adding M.P. to your name." But the book's success showed him that a few crowded weeks on the frontier, followed by a few more of writing which he quite enjoyed, could earn him as much money as a subaltern received in two years and infinitely more public notice. Here was a fresh and hopeful prospect; and perhaps this easy triumph did more than any other single fact to change his life's direction. For Winston Churchill learned from *The Story of the Malakand Field Force* that one day he might be able to look beyond the Army.

## 6

For the moment there was still Bangalore, the 4th Hussars, and polo, mitigated by his new discovery, the pen. That provided a good occupation for the hot silence of the afternoons. If he could write history, there seemed to be no reason why he could not write a novel. It was done by large numbers of his fellow-creatures; and if they could do it, he was not inclined to flinch from the task. For, like the celebrated pianist, Winston Churchill has always been prepared to try. He might be only twenty-three; but, after all, he had seen real fighting, traveled a good deal, and knew something about politics. The book took him about eight weeks to write, with unsolicited assistance from his brother officers who "made various suggestions for stimulating the love interest which I was not able to accept." But every man is not so unlucky as to find a publisher for his first novel; and perhaps it is unfriendly to linger over Mr. Churchill's.

Yet, *Savrola, a Tale of the Revolution in Laurania,* is not without its interest. The style is undistinguished; the characters, with the exception of an old and faithful nurse, are strikingly unreal; and the setting bears a strong resemblance to those fictitious territories with which Anthony Hope had recently enriched the map. Laurania, one feels, was bounded on the north by Ruritania; but the author's trip to Cuba endowed it with a good deal of rich, Castilian nomenclature (including an Elder Statesman bearing the singularly inappropriate name of Godoy), and his active service supplied a wealth of street-fighting and a duel between coast batteries and warships described with considerable gusto. The central figure is a young democratic hero with an old nurse and a course of reading which largely (and rather touchingly) coincides with his creator's. The *Decline and Fall* is there, with Darwin, Schopenhauer, Lecky, and Macaulay's *Essays*. But when the author turned from letters to the platform, his father's carefully prepared successes taught him that "nothing good can be obtained without effort. These impromptu feats of oratory existed only in the minds of the listeners; the flowers of rhetoric were hothouse plants." He was not making speeches yet; but that would be his method, if he ever did.

Meanwhile, his novel (though it had a year or two to wait) ultimately ran through *Macmillan's Magazine*, reappeared in book form with a becoming dedication to "the Officers of the IVth (Queen's Own) Hussars, in whose company the Author lived for four happy years," and earned him about £700. The experiment was not repeated, though; and modesty impelled him to confess in later years that "I have consistently urged my friends not to read it." But the pen, though mightier than the sword, was less agreeable than the polo-stick. He helped the regiment into the final for the Cup, and then resumed his efforts to return to active service on the frontier, where the Tirah Expeditionary Force was still campaigning. The authorities remained unfavorable; but his friend Ian Hamilton advised a personal assault with his "push and persuasiveness." The attempt involved a long journey north entailing grave risk of absence from his unit without leave. But it succeeded; he received a minor staff appointment, wore red tabs, and consorted with his seniors. Presently he volunteered some sound advice upon the subject of newspaper controversy about the expedition. This won his spurs; and, admitted to staff confidences, he was in a good position to see something of the next campaign. But unhappily the campaign of 1898 on the Northwest Frontier failed to materialize.

That summer British soldiers had something better to look forward to than Indian frontier warfare of the standard pattern. For Sir Herbert Kitchener, Sirdar of the Egyptian Army, was moving south with six brigades in the Sudan to end the Mahdist nightmare and avenge Gordon. Here, plainly, was an opportunity Lieutenant Churchill should not miss. His first application for attachment to the Egyptian Army was refused (though other officers of equal rank and service were accepted) in circumstances which appeared to indicate Sir Herbert as the author of this refusal. But Lieutenant Churchill's operations were rarely broken off at the first rebuff. Indeed, his rare persistence, Lady Randolph's social pull, and the swift emergence from a subaltern's becoming chrysalis of a military historian with unusual opportunities of active service and a tendency to pass judgment on his seniors inspired a rising murmur in less enterprising circles.

Undeterred, he went home on leave and worked every oracle that he or his mother knew in order to get out to Egypt. But all was vain. She even wrote to the Sirdar himself, eliciting a bland repetition of his first refusal. After all, the Army List was full of officers all clamoring to serve with the strongest force that Britain had put in the field for a generation. But only one of them had written *The Story of the Malakand Field Force;* and only one of them received a note from Downing Street, informing him that the Prime Minister had read his book and wished to meet its author. (The reference was naturally to his military history rather than his novel, which had not yet appeared; though if it had, Lord Salisbury's nephew and successor, Mr. Balfour, who regaled his intellectual leisure with the works of Phillips Oppenheim, might have been more attracted by *Savrola*.)

He set off in high spirits to meet the old man by whose obstinacy his father had been ruined. Lord Salisbury was gracious, praised the book, its style and content, informed his visitor how strongly he reminded him of Randolph Churchill, and offered to assist in any way. Lieutenant Churchill knew a way; and soon a telegram from Downing Street to Kitchener elicited a third, and not less firm, refusal.

One last resource remained. The War Office, it seemed, was slightly nettled by the Sirdar's rather autocratic choice of officers, and viewed the British units of his force as lying in its own jurisdiction. The way to Pall Mall lay through Lady Jeune, a friend both of the Churchills and of Sir Evelyn Wood. This potentate, discreetly informed that Kitchener had positively overruled the Prime Minister in the matter of Lieutenant Churchill, promptly attached him to the 21st Lancers for the campaign, with orders to report at once in

Cairo. As this privilege carried the cautious proviso that "you will proceed at your own expense and that in the event of your being killed or wounded in the impending operations, or for any other reason, no charge of any kind will fall on British Army funds," he filled the financial gap by an arrangement to send letters from the front to the *Morning Post*. No less prescient, the President of the Psychical Research Society secured his undertaking to communicate on less remunerative terms, should the worst happen.

Seen off by Lady Randolph at the station, he was in Cairo six days later, just too late to command the troop which had been reserved for him. A happy rival wrote gleefully that he had "got the troop that would have been Winston's." Then they all moved up the Nile, hoping that the Dervishes would not have disappeared before they got there, and Lieutenant Churchill practicing assiduously with a Mauser pistol, which he meant to use instead of trusting to a sword on account of his uncertain shoulder.

They joined the army in the breathless interval before the final march against Omdurman; and one September morning the Lancers on reconnaissance in full view of the great pale yellow dome of the Mahdi's tomb discerned the moving masses of the Khalifa's host, a line of white ruled on the brown plain outside the city and moving to the tap of distant drums. Lieutenant Churchill was detached to take the news to Kitchener. He rode across six miles of desert, where the Nile Expeditionary Force was marching twenty thousand strong in the blazing sun, flanked by the gleaming river and the green islands and the gunboats and the white sails of the river craft. At their head rode Kitchener, a brick-red face barred with an immense mustache, three lengths ahead of two mounted standard-bearers with the Union and Egyptian flags and his headquarters staff. Slightly intimidated (and not altogether sure of his welcome), Lieutenant Churchill made a brief report, answered a question, and effaced himself. Someone asked him to lunch; the army backed against the Nile and settled into its position; and as the sun was going down, an enterprising naval officer named Beatty, moved by a noble impulse, first tendered as largesse to the thirsty cavalry and then flung ashore from his gunboat a large bottle of champagne, which Lieutenant Churchill waded knee-deep in the river to retrieve.

The next day was the most exciting in his life. The Lancers were out reconnoitring before dawn; and as the darkness faded, he made out the vague blur of a moving host and the shimmer of their spears, and caught a distant roar that rose as the sea rises. It was the voice of fifty thousand men affirming their devotion to a leader and a faith. Mahdism had always been victorious en masse. They had swarmed over Hicks' exhausted remnant at El Obeid and through Gordon's crumbling parapets at Khartoum. Sheer numbers broke Stewart's square at Abu Klea; and when the Mahdi slept beneath his pale yellow dome, the Dervish empire was awed into subjection by the massed pageantry of the Khalifa Abdullahi—one hundred thousand armed and marching men on the great plain beyond Omdurman, the thunder of their drums, the flat roar of the *ombeyas,* and the unconquerable folds of the Black Flag.

Force, pageantry, and faith held the Sudan in dull subjection to a dismal tyranny. The faith was shared by all outside his prisons—faith in the fighting creed of Islam entangled with faith in a self-appointed leader (first the Mahdi, the expected one, and then his heir), at whose word victories were won. But a wary policy confined force and the means of exercising it to his most convinced adherents, the red-slippered Baggara whom he brought into Omdurman to rob there as a master-race, and the black army which governed the masters of the capital.

One man controlled the Dervish empire. For one man allotted guns and cartridges. He gave them to his armies on the distant frontiers and to his bodyguard; and this judicious distribution of fire-arms in a population equipped with swords and spears and united by a common faith ruled the Sudan. His leadership was quite unchallengeable; his word was their command; and when he preached in the mosque at Omdurman, twenty thousand listened to his word. Addressing them at length, as Kitchener moved slowly south, he had announced a revelation that English and Egyptian bones would surely whiten in the desert. Then he drew a sword and called for victory; and in the great quadrangle twenty thousand swords went up and twenty thousand voices roared assent.

That was the force of blind obedience, of massed bigotry, of tribal pride aligned against the Sirdar's army, as the sun came up that morning in September, 1898. Lieutenant Churchill on reconnaissance stared at the moving masses and reported direct to Kitchener. Here was a thrill that stayed with him for life. "Talk of Fun," he wrote after thirty years, "Where will you beat this! On horseback, at daybreak, within shot of an advancing army, seeing everything, and corresponding direct with Headquarters." The dervish banners looked like something he had seen in pictures of the Bayeux Tapestry, as the great array came slowly on. There must have been more than fifty thousand of them. Some Baggara—"dark, cowled figures, like monks on horseback"—came near the Lancers. But the British cavalry withdrew discreetly before the great attack was blasted into shreds by the steady fire of British and Egyptian rifles and artillery. The Dervish banners tilted and went down; and the black dream of Mahdism vanished on the drifting smoke of well-drilled musketry.

But the day was not over for the 21st Lancers. As the army moved off towards the city, the cavalry were ordered out to clear the ground. It looked clear enough at first. But the brown plain disclosed a line of Hadendowa riflemen; the riflemen became an army of three thousand men; and the plain split across, revealing suddenly a twelve-foot gully right in their path and filled with hopefully expectant Dervishes. The trumpet sounded; sixteen troops of Lancers wheeled into line; and Lieutenant Churchill was plainly in for something unusual. His regiment was charging, knee to knee, with leveled lances—three hundred men launched at three thousand.

On his gray Arab polo-pony Lieutenant Churchill sheathed his sword and drew his Mauser pistol. Behind him a long line of lances raced towards the enemy. He rode at the gap between two riflemen, scrambled across the gully, fired two shots at a swordsman before he could hamstring his pony, rode down another, shot at a mounted figure, and found himself alone. Fifty yards away two or three crouching figures on a background of huddled Dervishes were aiming at him. This unpleasant solitude alarmed him, and he galloped hard after his troop. Most of them were there.

A solitary Dervish emerged from nowhere with a spear, survived several lance-thrusts, and got within a yard of him before Lieutenant Churchill shot him dead. Then he asked a sergeant if he had enjoyed himself. "Well," said the Lancer, "I don't exactly say I enjoyed it, Sir; but I think I'll get more used to it next time." Everybody laughed; but happily the next time never came. For in three crowded minutes the 21st Lancers had lost about a quarter of their strength. The troop of which Lieutenant Churchill so nearly got command had struck the worst part of the gully and came out with ten killed and eleven wounded and without its officer. Perhaps it was as well that he had been a little late in Cairo.

The victory was won. Kitchener's long preparation had prevailed against the brute force and hysteria of Mahdism. The squalid tyranny and frantic preachings were over now. One leader was a fugitive far to the south, the other a headless body in the Nile close to his desecrated tomb. The false magic of Mahdism had been broken, and Gordon was avenged. The victory had been won by careful planning and smooth execution. But the strange operations of the public mind at home delighted in the charge of the 21st Lancers, which had not very much to do with it. For it recalled the heroic silliness of the Light Brigade at Balaklava or French dithyrambs upon the charge of the Cuirassiers at Waterloo. One rueful chronicler of the campaign wrote that "what the street applauds, the War Office is compelled at least to condone," adding irreverently that "the blunders of British cavalry are the fertile seed of British glory." There could be little doubt about the glory, and Lieutenant Churchill shared it to the full. He retained his own opinion as to the wisdom of launching cavalry with swords and lancers against unshaken infantry with firearms. For he was no romantic, when it came to practical affairs. But, whatever his estimate of its utility, he valued the experience. After all, there are not many men in public life who have ridden in a cavalry charge.

7

Within a week of the battle of Omdurman the 21st Lancers started for home, and Lieutenant Churchill went with them. On the way he visited a friend in hospital at Cairo and left a modest portion of his skin to repair the patient's needs. Thus scarred, he found himself in England once again with his experiences and the prospects of a subaltern. He had been wondering if these were good enough for Randolph Churchill's son. However bright his prospects of promotion (and they were not yet conspicuous), he saw none of solvency.

Four years in the Army had shown that his expenditure was permanently in excess of his receipts and likely to remain so. This unbalanced budget was uninviting, since he was particularly anxious to relieve his mother from the strain of providing his allowance. Manifestly that could never happen so long as he was in the Army. But was there any other line in which he could do better? His books and journalism seemed to provide the answer. For they were infinitely better paid than soldiering; and if his future work was equally successful, he should be able to support himself and to dispense with his mother's contribution. So he made his plans, as the remaining weeks of 1898 stretched out before him. He would go back to India, discharge his duty to the regiment by helping them to win the Polo Tournament of 1899, and then send in his papers. His war correspondence on the Omdurman campaign could be enlarged into a book; and he would make a contract with a newspaper in India to supply them with a London letter. Thus fortified, he could face the world as a civilian supported by his pen.

By way of further interest and added status he proposed to enter Parliament. That should not be too difficult for Randolph Churchill's son. He knew the ropes; he had a relative who worked in the Central Office; and one day he lunched with a group of young Conservatives, of whom Lord Hugh Cecil was most intelligent and Lord Balcarres the most ornamental. All young, all educated at ancient universities, and all in the House of Commons, they rather overawed him. He might shine in Army conversation; but this was quite another matter. Their airy dialectics made quick work of his homemade opinions; and he emerged from the ordeal with a stern resolve to go up to Oxford, when he came home from India, in order to improve his mind. For Winston Churchill had no illusions about his educational equipment. It was quite evident that self-taught reading on hot afternoons at Bangalore was not enough; and he was likely to do better in his new career as a civilian, if he could compete on equal terms. That pointed plainly to the university.

He made inquiries on the subject; but they revealed that the road to Oxford was barred by a more formidable obstacle than a line of Dervishes. Undiluted classicism still held the gate, and the university authorities exacted a full toll of compulsory Greek and Latin. He knew some Latin; but it was too much to embark upon Greek grammar at twenty-four. Cato had faced the task at eighty. But he was not Cato; and the harsh exigencies of Responsions denied him the experience of Oxford and deprived Oxford of the experience of Winston Churchill.

Something might be done, before he left for India, about his political ambitions. Calling at the Central Office, he saw its chief whose enthusiasm waned perceptibly at the news that the prospective candidate would be unable to pay more than his own expenses; but they might still be able to do something for Randolph Churchill's son, to say nothing of a young man with his military record. As he left, they booked him to address a garden-party in the neighborhood of Bath. This modest entry into public life was rendered more impressive by the *Morning Post,* which was now his organ and undertook to report his speech in full. As he had been told to speak for fifteen minutes, he prepared twenty-five and learned it all by heart. There was one phase about "the rising tide of Tory Democracy," contrasted favorably with "the dried-up drainpipe of Radicalism," with which he was particularly pleased. For he meant to fight under his father's banner of Tory Democracy; even in *The Story of the Malakand Field Force* he had alluded to "the Imperial Democracy of England." On the fatal day he went to Bath, surveyed the garden-party, with the jaundiced eye of orators at garden-parties, and let off his speech. The *Morning Post* obliged with a full report, and a brief leading article announcing the appearance of a new figure in politics. Then the world went on again, and he went off to India.

The polo tournament at Meerut was clouded for him by an accident. Four days before it opened he slipped down some steps and put out his shoulder. This meant that No. 1 would have to play with his elbow strapped to his side, precluded from hard hitting and confined to clever riding. That handicap, however, did not prevent the 4th Hussars from winning two successive victories; and in the final Lieutenant Churchill scored two goals, and the tournament was duly won. This was his *Nunc dimittis;* and when he left the regiment, they drank his health. He was going home to finish off his book about the last campaign and to write for the newspapers. For having entered India by way of Poona, he left by way of Fleet Street.

A chapter of his life was over. He was a civilian now, engaged upon a spacious composition in two volumes entitled *The River War, an Account of the Reconquest of the Soudan.* It was to be more than a mere record of the last campaign and had become a study of the whole episode of Mahdism. This entailed inquiries on his way through Egypt. He broke his journey for a fortnight, collecting information and meeting leading actors in the long piece for which Kitchener had contrived a happy ending at Omdurman. Everyone was most obliging, and Lord Cromer even consented to read his earlier chapters in manuscript. This privilege was not without its burdens, since though the great proconsul's knowledge of Egyptian affairs was encyclopædic, his tastes in writing were severely classical. His blue pencil pruned the novice's exuberance unmercifully. But Winston Churchill bowed the head and earned Lord Cromer's blessing.

He was writing hard on board the ship that took him on the next stage of his homeward journey and saw a good deal of the best descriptive writer of his day. The flair of Alfred Harmsworth despatched the vivid observation and sure rendering of G. W. Steevens anywhere that seemed to merit observation and retailed it in his new phenomenon, the *Daily Mail*. Half Kipling and half Balliol, Steevens had just written *With Kitchener to Khartoum,* was now completing his latest survey *In India,* and would soon be etching with his sharpest acids the strange blend of high principles and base behavior presented by elderly French generals in the retrial of Captain Dreyfus.

The promising beginner writing hard in the saloon interested him. Steevens knew his Gibbon too, and they made friends. His book was getting on, and he enjoyed writing it. Perhaps it was a defect of his education that he would not do things which he did not enjoy. But as he found pleasure in his present occupation, that did not greatly matter. At any rate, it was enjoyable to exercise his art, to try out picturesque comparisons of the Nile to "a thread of blue silk drawn across an enormous brown drugget," to comment with perfect freedom on the course of history and the operations of his seniors. (There are compensations for ex-subalterns who take to writing military history.) He

had modified his style. Too much Gibbon on an empty
stomach is an awkward diet for young authors; and the
draught was now diluted with astringent doses of Macaulay. But it was still a potent brew. The blend was
apt to be a little grandiose; the pace was often slow,
since military history carries too much detail to move
swiftly; and the author was occasionally oppressed with
an undue sense of the dignity of history. (So, for that
matter, were his great originals.) But history in 1899
was a full-dress affair. Historians were all expected to
be solemn; and as he was only twenty-four, solemnity
came easy. The scale was generous; but since it was a
spacious age, it seemed appropriate that he should take
two volumes of about four hundred pages each with a
great many maps and illustrations to narrate some two
years of military operations with their historical pre-
liminaries.

*The River War* was a first-rate performance. Indeed,
considering the author's youth, it was phenomenal.
The writing was, perhaps, as good as any that he ever
did, because he had not yet acquired the excessive em-
phasis that comes with public speaking. Its copious material was lucidly arranged, and he missed little of the
drama. His treatment of the central figure avoided
hero-worship. For Kitchener's appeal—"usually un-
gracious, rarely impatient, never unreasonable"—was
strictly unromantic. Winston Churchill's tastes inclined towards romance; and there were moments
when he seemed to crave for a more sympathetic hero

than "the Sirdar, stern and sullen, equally unmoved by fear or enthusiasm."

After all, Kitchener had been markedly unfriendly to his own appearance on the scene of war; and the gruff, Wellingtonian inadequacy of his remark, after shattering a host of fifty thousand men and inflicting thirty thousand casualties, that the enemy had been given "a good dusting" somehow failed to satisfy the young historian's sense of drama. Yet he was unimpressed by Kitchener's one noble lapse into straightforward drama on that Sunday morning two days after Omdurman, when the flag ran up once more above the blind windows of Gordon's ruined palace at Khartoum and the Sirdar called for "Three cheers for the Queen!" and then the minute-guns boomed slowly from the gunboats as four bare-headed Army chaplains ranged themselves between the Sirdar and the place that Gordon died and, after prayer, the pipes of a Sudanese battalion wailed out "Abide with me." Then his commanders stepped forward to shake hands with Kitchener in turn.

He had been fourteen years on the road to Khartoum; and that morning he was not dry-eyed. But the historian, repelled perhaps by this magnificently obvious denouement, did not attend the ceremony; and though his first edition noticed it, subsequent revision removed all echoes of the guns, the cheers, and Gordon's hymn. For he preferred to find the culmination of the long tragedy in the silent circle of dead Emirs on their sheepskins in Kordofan a few months later.

His chivalry was deeply shocked by the desecration of the Mahdi's tomb and the Sirdar's unceremonious treatment of Mohammed Ahmed's head, the head that in life had spread black misery across almost a million square miles of Africa and, venerated after death, was the unholy symbol of all that England had gone into the Sudan to end.

He even found time to make a speech about it after his return to England, which commanded the approval of those enlightened persons whose undoubted loyalty to their own country is often complicated by a perverse affection for its enemies; and Winston Churchill (whose views upon false prophets may have grown sterner since) listened in the House of Commons gallery, while his opinions were reproduced below by the chilly rectitude of Morley and the unbending principle of Mr. C. P. Scott.

This was a strange beginning for a young Conservative. But he got his chance to enter Parliament, though not a very good one. A Lancashire Conservative, who sat for the two-member seat of Oldham, seemed to take a fancy to him and suggested that they should fight the seat together. A meeting was arranged to introduce him to the voters. But before it could be held, his kindly introducer died; and his supporters promptly invited his young friend, Winston Churchill, to fight the by-election. They had never heard him speak; but the Central Office, which did not expect to hold the seat, endorsed their choice. For Toryism was at a discount in the North that summer; and his prospects were a little complicated by running in double harness with a Tory working-man, who combined advanced opinions and the tenure of a Trade Union secretaryship with candidature as a Conservative. This combination might appear to harmonize with the mixed aspirations of Tory Democracy. The pair of candidates were jointly known as "The Scion and the Socialist"; but their complex charms failed to attract the stern democrats of Oldham, who rejected them in favor of two Liberals whose political position was easier to understand.

So Winston Churchill had endured his first defeat, while Mr. Walter Runciman and Mr. Emmott went to Westminster. But the young knight had scarcely won his spurs. For in the heat of battle he had thrown over the Government's Tithes Bill to loud Nonconformist cheers in Oldham and grave Tory frowns in London. This maneuver came of thinking for himself on complicated subjects upon which the party much preferred to think for candidates. At headquarters it left a sad impression of independence. Randolph Churchill had always been unorthodox; and it looked as if his son was going to be much the same. Mr. Balfour, who filled Lord Randolph's place and led the party in the House of Commons, said something scathing on the subject, although he wrote amiably to the candidate about his political career.

That was not ended by his first defeat. The Oldham by-election had been a mere overture played by a beginner's hand; and he had already been the subject of a

grand explosion of publicity in the *Daily Mail,* where
G. W. Steevens wrote him up as "The Youngest Man in
Europe," credited with "qualities which make him, almost at will, a great popular leader, a great journalist,
or the founder of a great advertising business . . . At
the rate he goes, there will hardly be room for him in
Parliament at thirty or in England at forty." At the
moment there appeared to be no room for him in Parliament, although he spent a most instructive summer
day up the river listening to Joseph Chamberlain, who
knew every move in that absorbing game. But there
was ample time. He was only twenty-four; it was still
1899; and that autumn Mr. Chamberlain's activities
gave him a better game to watch. For Paul Kruger sent
an ultimatum, and Great Britain was at war in South
Africa.

8

The trumpet sounded, and there was a pleasant stir
among the war correspondents. War in the last half of
the Nineteenth Century was waged to an agreeable
accompaniment of vivid prose purveyed by a succession of adventurous descriptive writers. The great war
correspondents, from Archibald Russell to Bennett
Burleigh, formed a hierarchy as nicely graded as the
soldiers; and younger men began to take their places
in the line, as enterprising officers aspired to military
careers in succession to the great names of Roberts,
Wolseley, Evelyn Wood, and now Kitchener. The old
hands were all there, the company *Dick Heldar* knew

when Kipling wrote *The Light That Failed*—the Ke-neu, the Great War Eagle, and Cassavetti, and the Nilghai, chiefest and bulkiest of war correspondents whose experiences dated from the birth of the needle-gun at Königgratz. But there were recruits. For the *Daily Mail* could not resist sending Steevens; and the *Morning Post* invited Winston Churchill to go out at a record-breaking salary.

This was a distinct improvement on his recent status. He accepted with alacrity, saw Joseph Chamberlain entrenched behind his immense cigar and opining sagely that Buller might arrive too late and find that White had settled the whole business with the sixteen thousand men already on the spot (for that was what the War Office had led him to believe), and then sailed by the same steamer which took out Sir Redvers and his staff. On arrival at Cape Town they found a military situation which endangered the last shreds of Winston Churchill's faith in official experts. Blind deference to the authorities had never been his forte. He much preferred to think out matters for himself (private reasoning had led him to refuse inoculation for enteric fever on the voyage out) and to go his own way. That, perhaps, was why he was in South Africa as a war correspondent rather than a subaltern.

But official forecasts and private skepticism left them equally unprepared to find that the enterprising Boers had invaded Natal and shepherded the British forces into Ladysmith, where they were now besieged. There was nothing to be done by a correspondent in pursuit of copy except to get as near the trouble as he could; and Winston Churchill found himself at Estcourt, where stray patrols rode almost into sight of Ladysmith and an armored train occasionally cruised precariously towards the Boer positions. One sad November day it was derailed by a well-placed obstruction on the track, and this catastrophe was neatly staged under a dropping fire from two guns, a pom-pom, and three hundred Boer rifles.

The correspondent of the *Morning Post,* who had been standing on a box in the rear truck to get a better view, alighted hurriedly, exchanging "the comparative peace and safety of a railway accident" for the firing-line. The firing, though, came mostly from the Boers; and Winston Churchill was prevailing on the injured engine-driver to return to his locomotive (which was still on the rails) and charge the wreckage in an effort to clear the line. For he was rarely capable of a spectator's rôle for long; and now he found himself in charge of a breakdown gang in No Man's Land under the clear light of South Africa. An hour and ten minutes passed in these agreeable exercises under fire. Then they piled forty wounded men into the engine and its tender, and steamed gingerly for home. By this time Churchill was directing operations on the locomotive. But after it had crawled to safety, he dropped off to rejoin the marooned infantry. They were nowhere to be found because, outnumbered and outgunned, they had surrendered.

Some Boers took two shots at him as he raced along

a railway cutting, and two more as he flattened himself against its side. He scrambled up the bank; a mounted burgher galloped by and called to him; and he groped for his familiar Mauser pistol. The range was short, and he could easily have dropped the rider. But he had left his pistol on the engine, which was just as well for Great Britain and South Africa, because the Boer horseman was Louis Botha. Both men survived, and their acquaintance was later of some service to both countries. For Churchill's warning brought Botha home to Pretoria on the eve of war in 1914, saving him from capture in a German ship, and placed South Africa in his sure grasp at a grave moment.

So the locomotive rumbled harmlessly towards Estcourt with Winston Churchill's pistol, while its owner, a dejected prisoner, traveled reluctantly in the opposite direction. He was slightly wounded in the hand. His identity was soon revealed; and the gleeful Boers added a lord's son to their bag of seventy prisoners from the armored train. Hostile French publicity, indeed, promoted him with its habitual magnificence to the rank of "Lord Churchill." But here he was, out of the game, a failure as a war correspondent, while Amery was free to send letters to *The Times* from Estcourt, and Steevens listened to the guns at Ladysmith. It had come on to pour with rain; his hat was gone; and an obliging Boer tossed him a British forage cap.

Winston Churchill in captivity resolved to leave it as soon as possible. It was humiliating; it was going to be intolerably dull; and the experience impressed him

*WANTED*—"Englishman, 25 years old; about 5 feet 8 inches tall, of indifferent build; walks with a little bend forward; pale appearance, red-brown hair, small mustache hardly perceptible; talks through nose, cannot pronounce 's' properly and does not know any Dutch." This is the text of the Boer poster describing Winston Churchill, war correspondent, who escaped from a prison camp, and returned with the British Army to the scene of his capture.

with a lifelong fellow-feeling for all incarcerated persons, which influenced him subsequently when he came to consider questions of prison reform as Home Secretary. His first project of escape was to hide underneath some litter on the floor of a shed in which they spent the first night of captivity, his next to walk boldly out of camp on the second night and make a dash for Ladysmith, and his third to drop off the train while passing through a tunnel on the way to Pretoria. Winston Churchill, it was evident, would prove a trying guest. But he arrived at that depressing destination and was soon deep in a delicious plan for an *émeute* of sixty British officers and two thousand men, who were to overwhelm their guards and seize the capital.

This was shortly superseded by a more commonplace design (his fifth), in which he was to escape with two brother officers and walk about three hundred miles with four slabs of chocolate, a few meat lozenges, a compass, and a map until they got to Portuguese East Africa. The demerits of the scheme were obvious. But there was nothing for it in face of the depressing vista of captivity, in which an endless round of cards, chess, cigarettes, and conversation with the same companions in the empty sunshine of Pretoria stretched out before him to infinity. Sometimes an argument with Boer visitors supplied a variation; and he was trying to resume his reading with relays of English books from the State Library. But Carlyle's *Frederick the Great* and even Mill *On Liberty* are a poor substitute for active life; and when he found himself confronting Lecky's

*History of England in the Eighteenth Century,* it was plainly time to go. Besides the Boer authorities persistently refused to entertain his plea that an unarmed journalist (he had been unarmed except for a few Mauser cartridges, when captured) should be released as a non-combatant.

In these circumstances there was obviously nothing for it but to release himself. Leaving a slightly ceremonious letter of farewell to the Ministry of War announcing his decision to escape and expressing a polite hope that they might meet again in Pretoria under different circumstances, he paid his mess bills, cashed a check for twenty pounds, appropriated a Dutch pastor's hat, and waited for the night.

Their first attempt was on a Monday; and as the afternoon dragged by, Professor Lecky never had a less attentive reader and his chess was never worse. But after dark a sentry stood precisely where their plan required no sentry to be standing, and the escape was off for that night. On the next evening he hid in a lavatory, chose a moment when two sentries' backs were turned, dodged out, scaled a garden wall, and found himself in a strange shrubbery. Presently a comrade's voice informed him under a protective screen of gibberish and dead languages that their guards suspected, and the rest of the party could not follow him. Now he had a choice of climbing back to prison or going on alone. He chose the latter, with a strong conviction that he would be recaptured and the added drawback that, while the chocolate was with him, map, compass, and meat lozenges were in a colleague's pocket on the wrong side of the wall.

He walked boldly down the garden, turned into the road, strolled past the sentry at the prison gates, and found himself at large in Pretoria on a fine evening. He came on a railway track; and as he walked along it in the dark, it struck him that three hundred miles is a long way to walk and that the hero of *Vice Versa* had escaped by rail. So he resolved to do the same, boarded a moving train, clambered from the couplings into a jolting truck, and found himself in the society of large numbers of sacks whose earlier existence had been passed exclusively with coal. He had been steering by the stars, and felt some doubt as to whether he was going in the right direction. But the train was going somewhere; it was warm among the sacks; and he slept happily.

It was still dark when he awoke and contrived to leave the moving train uninjured. Then he settled down for an uncomfortable day in hiding, hoping to resume his journey after dark. His sole companion was a large and hopeful vulture, whose interest in his condition was expressed in unpleasant noises of an anticipatory character. The traveler consumed a little of his chocolate, grew very thirsty, and prayed long and earnestly for help and guidance. His prayer was answered. For after dark he left his hiding place, drank at a stream, and after floundering through high grass and swamps towards a distant row of lights found himself in the small hours confessing his identity to a total stranger who providentially turned out to be an English colliery manager.

The worst was over now. With friends and food and drink he seemed to have a reasonable chance of traveling the next two hundred miles. That night they hid him in the mine. Before the cage dropped down, the engine-man—who came from Oldham—gripped his hand with the consoling whisper, "They'll all vote for you next time." He spent two days underground in the mine workings with ample food, refreshment, and cigars. He had books to read and candle-light to read them by, except when the rats ate the candles. In the world above the Boer authorities offered a modest reward of £25 for his recovery, alive or dead; and his recapture was freely rumored. But he was comfortably reading *Kidnapped* behind some packing-cases in an office at pit-head. For he had been promoted to this hiding-place, emerging for a walk at night and planning the next move. Three days later he stowed away between some bales of wool in a freight-train bound for the Portuguese frontier, and reached the security of neutral territory. As the train rumbled slowly towards Delagoa Bay, a ruffled head emerged from the tarpaulin of a truck, a happy voice was raised in riotous rejoicing, and a borrowed revolver fired several wholly unnecessary shots. For Winston Churchill had escaped.

This exploit made the young war correspondent a celebrated character. The war was going anything but well, and the public had endured a black succession of defeats. But Winston Churchill's escapade shone brightly on the somber background afforded by Stormberg, Magersfontein, and Colenso. His return was triumphal. At the port of embarkation a dozen English gentlemen with revolvers escorted him on board his steamer in case the Boers attempted to retrieve their missing treasure. But when he got to Durban, crowds and bands received him; and, hands on hips, he addressed a straw-hatted multitude outside the Town Hall. He was free and famous, and improved the occasion by a press telegram containing unpalatable truths about Boer fighting qualities. For his experience had taught him a salutary respect for the enemy. He had been pleasantly surprised to find them treating prisoners with kindness; his distaste for Boer politicians did not prevent him from describing the regime of his country's foes as "Tammany Hall . . . defended by the Ironsides"; and presently his tributes to a "dignified and honorable enemy" failed to rouse sympathetic echoes in his more indignant countrymen.

A war correspondent once again, he joined the fighting forces. If the Boers insisted upon treating him as a combatant, he might as well become one; and he resumed the Queen's commission as a lieutenant in the South African Light Horse. This corps of irregulars afforded opportunities of cavalry adventure in congenial, if slightly mixed, society and a large slouch hat with a becoming plume (which earned them the nick-

name of "the Cockyollybirds"); and beneath its shade
he conducted a brief experiment in growing a mustache, which never reached his father's lofty standard.
He was a Rough Rider now, while the other Rough
Rider across the Atlantic was already Vice-President of
the United States.

His duties took him to Spion Kop, where he saw
something of his seniors in circumstances which diminished his respect for seniority as a test of military value.
But he was happy, because he was going where he
liked and seeing all there was to see. His young brother
was slightly wounded just beside him, and sent down
to be his mother's first patient in her hospital ship
*Maine* at Durban, where Percy Scott gallantly named a
4.7 gun after Lady Randolph. Better times were coming soon, with Roberts deftly wheeling at the gates
of Kimberley; even Buller reached his objectives; and
presently Lieutenant Churchill was riding with the
first squadrons into Ladysmith. That night he dined
at headquarters and shared the very last of their supply
of beef with his emaciated hosts. Then he moved across
to see the fighting in the Orange Free State; but this
transfer was not facilitated by his published views in
favor of "a generous and forgiving policy" after the
war, his caustic comments on an Army chaplain's
ineptitude, or by the presence at headquarters of Lord
Kitchener, who had been among the less appreciative
readers of *The River War*. But his pass came at last,
and he was afforded further opportunities of watching
his contemporaries in action, being—

> . . . sugared about by the old men
> (Panicky, perishin' old men)
> That 'amper an' 'inder an' scold men.

For he was in Kipling's territory once again. But it was
a more chastened Kipling, respectful of his enemy and
vividly aware of the defects of those who—

> . . . used to belong in an Army once
> (Gawd! what a rum little Army once),
> Red little, dead little Army once!

Besides, he had seen war close at hand, "horrible war,
amazing medley of the glorious and the squalid, the
pitiful and the sublime, if modern men of light and
leading saw your face closer, simple folk would see it
hardly ever." (That was after one of Buller's unsuccessful passes at the fords of the Tugela.) He had done
a deal of thinking and some writing about "the patriotic virtues of the Boers," and he was more impressed
by Milner's level-headedness than by Jingo indignation with the beaten foe. For he was beaten now; and
Winston Churchill alarmed some readers of the *Morning Post* with demonstrations of the national inability
to hate their enemies. Kipling was mastered by the
same emotion, when he confessed his attitude:

> I do not love my Empire's foes,
>     Nor call 'em angels; still,
> What *is* the sense of 'atin' those
>     'Oom you are paid to kill?
> So, barrin' all that foreign lot
>     Which only joined for spite,
> Myself, I'd just as soon as not

> Respect the man I fight.
>     Ah, there, Piet? . . .
>     I've known a lot o' people ride a
>         dam' sight worse than Piet!

It was an extremely English mood; and Lieutenant Churchill was nothing if not English.

But though the enemy was beaten, there were still the pieces to pick up; and some of them were extremely lively. One day he was with the cavalry, when a cheerful leader of mounted irregulars offered him a "first-class show," which very nearly included a sight of the Hereafter. The landscape was familiar,

> . . . the African kopje,
>     The kopje that smiles in the heat,
>     The wholly unoccupied kopje,
>     The home of Cornelius and Piet.

It presently released the customary stream of well-aimed lead in their direction; and as they were dismounted, this was serious. When Churchill struggled to remount, his charger plunged and the saddle swung completely underneath the horse (just like the Prince Imperial's in Zululand). Then he galloped off, leaving his master stranded on the hillside, a lonely figure with a Mauser pistol. But not a stationary figure. He ran hard for safety without much prospect of attaining it, until a friendly horseman galloped by. Churchill hailed the rider, who checked and picked him up, mounting the war correspondent pillion behind him. So the two of them rode hard until they were out of range. But their common mount was badly hit; and his rescuer's sole comment upon being thanked for saving Winston Churchill's life was, "Ah, but it's the horse I'm thinking about."

Now he was campaigning cheerfully among his friends, accompanying Ian Hamilton on the great flanking march that brought them first (and Winston Churchill first of all) to Johannesburg, then to Pretoria, and finally sent him riding with a cheer and a lifted hat up to the very prison camp where he would still have been an inmate, if he had not escaped. The wheel had come full-circle. For he announced their liberation to his former fellow-prisoners. The war was dying down; and future operations seemed to hold little that would be worthy of his notice. A *diminuendo* of barbed wire and block-houses was somehow uninspiring. He was disinclined to be the chronicler of

A section, a pompom, an' six 'undred men

in perpetual pursuit of the unattainable De Wet; and after a small affair on the railway, in which he showed his customary tendency to board the locomotive and tell the driver what to do, he left for home to go into Parliament.

9

His homecoming in 1900 sustained the note of triumph. Oldham turned out en masse to greet him, as he drove through roaring streets in a procession of ten landaus; and when he told a crowded Theatre Royal about the Oldham man who helped to hide him in the coal-mine, a voice called, "His wife's in the gallery," and the triumph was complete. With a General Election in prospect this was not to be despised. For what other candidate had been captured by the Boers, consorted with an immense vulture, and lived to tell the tale? That autumn the Conservatives, acting with greater enterprise than had been evident in their conduct of military affairs, resolved upon the shrewd expedient of dissolving Parliament a year or so before its time in order to secure a firm renewal of their mandate.

In South Africa the British armies were still in the field; and it was indicated without false delicacy to the electorate at home that a vote given to the Opposition was a vote given to the Boers. The patriotic appeal was practically irresistible; and Joseph Chamberlain with eyeglass, orchid, and Imperial convictions presided over a party triumph. Sharp-featured and sharp-tongued, the Colonial Secretary who had thrown over Gladstone, balked Home Rule, changed sides in politics, and then defeated Kruger was a public idol. He even journeyed into Lancashire to speak for Winston Churchill; and with such assistance, supplemented by the saga of his escape, that fortunate young man succeeded in displacing Mr. Runciman by a small majority as junior member for Oldham, though even his new popularity failed to exceed the local influence of Mr. Emmott. But the seat was won.

It rained congratulations. Lord Salisbury telegraphed; Mr. Balfour ordered him to cancel an engagement and speak with him in Cheshire. He was already speaking when the young member walked on to the platform; the whole meeting rose and cheered; and then his leader introduced the victorious recruit. After that he was off to Birmingham at Mr. Chamberlain's request; and three Midland meetings, a special train, cheers everywhere, and the sunshine of his formidable leader's smile were a delirious initiation in political success.

But success alone is not self-supporting. Members of Parliament were unpaid in 1900, and Winston Churchill had to live. His books and journalism had brought in something; and he proposed to supplement it with a lecture tour. His pen was not so active, though he had made two small volumes out of his war correspondence from South Africa. But *London to Ladysmith via Pretoria* and *Ian Hamilton's March* were not to be expanded into a comprehensive work upon the war. For he preferred to earn a living with his lectures. In that distant age the lecture platform in Great Britain was neither undignified nor underpaid. Personages of real eminence took the chair (Lord Wolseley was his first chairman), while the magic lantern lent its modest aid. The staple of his lecture was, of course, the hairbreadth adventure of his escape; and he spoke to crowded halls all over England.

Then he crossed the Atlantic to repeat the process in the United States. His manager's exuberant publicity described the lecturer as "the hero of five wars, the author of six books, and the future Prime Minister of Great Britain." This was too much for Mr. Church-ill, and the announcement was withdrawn. But his tour succeeded. There was less sympathy, perhaps, with Britain's aims in the Boer War, and he sometimes en-countered opposition. There were interruptions at Chicago and empty seats at Baltimore, though Boston (where he had a lively celebration with his local syn-onym, the other Winston Churchill) was highly sym-pathetic. But he did not find much difficulty in getting on terms with American audiences. Was he not half American himself? Mark Twain was his first chairman in New York; but though the old man was firm with the speaker's British prejudices, he graciously signed copies of all his works for him. Then Canada renewed his course of undiluted triumph; and, safe at home once more, he completed the British lecture circuit.

These profitable exercises had precluded any earlier resumption of his political activities. Now, with his new-made capital safely banked, he was free to turn to poli-tics. The fifteenth Parliament of Queen Victoria would be meeting in the first weeks of 1901. But before it could assemble, an old lady faded out of life at Os-borne; and the new member for Oldham found him-self in the first Parliament of King Edward VII.

*CELEBRITY*—Winston Churchill's escape from the Boers was an exploit which "shone brightly against a black succession of defeats. When he got to Durban, crowds and bands received him. . . . His homecoming in 1900 sustained the note of triumph," and he was elected to Parliament.

*FUTURE WAR LORD*—Mr. Churchill with his Liberal Party leader, Asquith, in 1911. At the Admiralty he was apt to ask himself suddenly: "What happens if war with Germany begins today?"

## EDWARDIAN

"... *There won't be no war,*
*As long as we've a king like good King Edward.*"

OLD SONG.

## 1

THE Edwardian age was by no means a mere re-tarded echo of the Victorian. Its character was all its own, though (like the sovereign from whom it took its name) it was denied its full expression by the force of circumstances until rather late in life. Its patriotism, which had survived the challenge of events in Ireland and more recently in South Africa, was for that reason less instinctive and unquestioning than its predecessor's. It could recite the reasons for its British faith, because it had been forced to find out what they were; and a more reasoned loyalty found an expression that was more conscious in the same measure as the swelling note of Elgar's "Land of Hope and Glory" (composed for King Edward's Coronation) exceeded the artless airs of patriotic music in the reign of Queen Victoria. Was the note a little forced? Perhaps there was a growing sense that there were other countries in the world and that British voices must be raised a little, if they were to prevail. For it was an age of widening apprehension. Foreign rivalries had become unpleasantly apparent in the darker moments of the war in South Africa. It was evident that there would have to be adjustments and that the national equipment, both military and economic, might be called upon to face severer strains. This feeling brought a sense of urgency into political discussion by a public mind which was not unprepared to—

> . . . admit it fairly, as a business people should,
> We have had no end of a lesson: it will do us no end of good.

There were problems to be faced abroad, where England had been left without a friend, no less than in the shortcomings of the War Office, which had omitted to provide an army until the nation was at war, and in the structure of society at home. The old, unquestioning beliefs had vanished, and the public mind was ready for an era of self-examination and reform.

But the salutary process could not begin with the new reign in 1901, and the Edwardians were denied political maturity until 1906. The exceptional duration of his mother's life had relegated King Edward to a secondary rôle for the last twenty years; and another accident postponed effective action upon public questions for almost as long. When Mr. Gladstone chose the stony path of Home Rule as a way out of the mazes of the Irish Question, he changed the face of politics. The Liberals were split; the solid cohort of the Whigs departed with Lord Hartington; a great Radical was lost in Joseph Chamberlain; and these recruits, enlisted with Lord Salisbury upon the Irish issue, filled the Tory ranks.

Thus reinforced, the Tories won their victories upon the question of Home Rule; and the continuous unpopularity of that solution in Great Britain prolonged Conservative ascendancy beyond its time. For British voters, while their attention was increasingly engaged by other problems, were reluctant to entrust authority to the depleted remnant of the Liberals with their questionable Irish policy; and the fact that Unionists said what the British public wanted about Ireland enabled them to go on doing things that were far less popular on other matters. This false situation was prolonged into the new century by the ingenious expedient of the "Khaki Election" in 1900, which exhibited the Liberals once more as a divided and disloyal remnant.

Yet it was an illusion to suppose that the nation was staunchly Conservative in 1901. To all appearances it was content that its affairs should be ordered indefinitely by Lord Salisbury, a venerable leader whose arms were upheld on the mountain-top by Mr. Chamberlain and Mr. Balfour. But nobody supposed Lord Salisbury's gaze to be directed towards a Promised Land; and in 1901 the public mind had already begun to turn in such directions. For there were more questions than Mr. Balfour and his colleagues appeared to dream of, problems far beyond the urbane comprehension of Lord Lansdowne and Mr. St. John Brodrick.

Their sedate philosophy seemed curiously obsolete, with Bernard Shaw and Sidney Webb already middle-aged, the Fabian Society advancing to its third decade, and the Trades Union Congress authorizing Labor candidates for Parliament with Socialist opinions. The Edwardians were not afraid to question the whole

93

basis of society and economics; and in these circumstances it was plainly doubtful how long the Conservative ascendancy could last.

Winston Churchill took his seat in Parliament and waited for a subject upon which he could make his maiden speech. (By this time the other Rough Rider was Vice-President of the United States.) He did not have long to wait, because South Africa was obviously one of his subjects, and it was going to be raised in the debate on the Address. So he prepared a discourse, learned it off, and established himself in his father's seat. His predecessor in debate was a Welsh Radical a few years older than himself, who had been ten years in the House already and, courageous in his criticism of the war, had emulated Winston Churchill's escape from Pretoria in a Dutch pastor's hat by escaping from a hostile audience at Birmingham Town Hall in a policeman's helmet. The black-haired orator resumed his seat, and Mr. Churchill followed Mr. Lloyd George.

It was an unimpressive little speech, consisting largely of an answer to the points Sir Henry Campbell-Bannerman had made some days before, which Mr. Churchill was thus enabled to annihilate at leisure. For the beginner was not equal to the swift improvisations of debate, and careful preparation was his sole resource. He sat down breathing modest thanks to the House for its kindness and patience, "which have been extended to me, I well know, not on my own account, but because of a certain splendid memory which many hon. Members still preserve."

His father's memory was strong upon him; and at one instant he recalled his father's gift of making his own leaders jump by saying, "If I were a Boer fighting in the field—and if I were a Boer I hope I should be fighting in the field . . ." That was not the way to talk about the Boers; and Chamberlain turned sharply to his neighbor on the Front Bench with an unappreciative comment. Although he managed to be loyal to the Government, the new member's tone about the Boers was a shade unusual. For he told the House of his embarrassment at seeing British privates ordering about "respectable old Boer farmers—the Boer is a curious combination of the squire and the peasant, and under the rough coat of the farmer there are very often to be found the instincts of the squire." Even the Mahdi had once engaged his chivalry, and he had already written generously of the Boers. But was this quite the way for a young member to keep in step with his party?

The Liberal speaker who followed him in the debate noted the new departure with approval, though Chamberlain found something to commend and spoke affectionately of his father's memory "in the hope that we may see the father repeated in the son." The ordeal was over; and when someone introduced him to Lloyd George, the fervent Welshman told him that he was "standing against the light." The Tory novice answered that his new friend seemed to "take a singularly detached view of the British Empire." But as the years went by, Lloyd George drew closer to the British Empire and Winston Churchill saw the light.

His next appearance was a more successful intervention on a military matter. After all, the Army was his other subject (he had been reading a good deal of Clausewitz since he came back from the war), and he was heard with some attention. A few weeks later he addressed the House at length in a speech of which he thought well enough to send it to the *Morning Post* before delivery and to reprint it two years later in a small collection of his speeches dedicated to the electors of Oldham and entitled *Mr. Brodrick's Army*. That statesman, who had inherited the burden of the War Office, was elaborating schemes of military reform designed to fill the gap which had been indicated with such painful clarity by events in South Africa. But Winston Churchill's first criticism was less military than economic. For he alluded feelingly to the impropriety of spending the vast sum of thirty millions on the Army, referring to "a half-forgotten episode" in which a Chancellor of the Exchequer had once resigned because the Service estimates were not reduced. He even quoted his letter of resignation and claimed, "after an interval of fifteen years, to lift again the tattered flag I found lying on a stricken field."

For the Chancellor was Randolph Churchill, and his son resumed the fight. There was a touch of drama in his argument, in this resuscitation of Tory Democracy in the person of its founder's son; and the mockery was rich—"Has the English Channel dried up, and are we no longer an island? Is the revenue so easily raised that we do not know how to spend it? Are the Treasury

buildings pulled down, and all our financiers fled?"
He spoke of it as "a cause I have inherited, a cause
for which the late Lord Randolph Churchill made the
greatest sacrifice of any Minister of modern times."
Then he surveyed the problem of national defense,
asserting firmly that "the honor and security of the
British Empire do not depend, and can never depend,
upon the British Army. The Admiralty is the only
Office strong enough to insure the British Empire . . ."
(This was strange doctrine for a soldier; but Winston
Churchill had never been an ordinary soldier.) He
spoke scornfully of "the military hydrophobia with
which we are afflicted," indicated a deep horror of
European war, and defined his strategy—"With such a
Navy, we can hold any antagonist at arm's length and
feed ourselves in the meantime, until, if we find it necessary, we can turn every city in the country into an
arsenal, and the whole male population into an army."

The speech was a success; and something of the
future speaker begins to show in its allusion to "the
clanking military empires of the European continent"
and its announcement that "one great truth glows and
glares in our faces . . ." But full-dress assaults upon the
Secretary of State for War were scarcely in the line of
party orthodoxy; and Mr. Brodrick ensured a repetition of the offense by a sharp reply about his critic's
"hereditary desire to run Imperialism on the cheap."
This tempted Mr. Churchill to delight the Cambridge
University Carlton Club with a rejoinder to his leader
straying far from Service matters into the civilian field

of economics. He was diverging rapidly from the safe preserves of a young Conservative with military interests. True, he had helped Lord Hugh Cecil to form a little group (nicknamed the "Hughligans" or "Malcolmtents"), in which a Stanley, a Percy, a Cecil, and a Churchill joined with Mr. Ian Malcolm to dine once a week and indulge in mild Parliamentary escapades.

These were the recognized wild oats of young politicians, at which their leaders shrug indulgent shoulders and recall their own impulsive youth. But Winston Churchill drank at more perilous springs. His views upon the desecration of the Mahdi's tomb had sounded more like a Radical than a Tory subaltern; his attitude about the Boers was more acceptable to Liberals than to Conservatives (he once told a meeting that he "should like it all to end in a handshake"); and he was seeing a good deal of Lord Rosebery. He loved to hear that statesman talk about his father; for if he was Randolph Churchill's heir in politics, he must study his succession.

Where did Tory Democracy stand in 1902? It was not easy to locate it in the ranks of party orthodoxy behind Mr. Balfour, since the dead founder of the creed had written ruefully ten years before in an agonized confession of his failure:

So Arthur Balfour is really leader—and Tory Democracy, the genuine article, at an end! Well, I have had quite enough of it all. I have waited with great patience for the tide to turn, but it has not turned, and will not now turn

in time. In truth, I am now altogether *déconsidéré* . . .
All confirms me in my decision to have done with politics
and try to make a little money for the boys and for ourselves . . .

How could his son escape a feeling that, all questions
apart, Mr. Balfour sat where Randolph Churchill had
earned the right to sit? It was not easy for the Tory
Democrat to follow Mr. Balfour. Besides, his views
were scarcely those expected of Mr. Balfour's followers.
He was forming his opinions now, and they seemed to
find more comprehension among the leading Liberals.
Intellect and education always impressed him; and he
was drawn towards Asquith, Rosebery, and Grey. Here
was the fine flower of Oxford, of that wider education
which he had been denied by compulsory Greek. Nor
was his attraction confined to right-wing Liberals. For
John Morley fascinated him with immense erudition
and a generosity of view which had accorded with his
own about the Mahdi and the Boers. All this was more
attractive to an energetic mind than the arid grace of
Mr. Balfour and the fierce partisanship of Joseph
Chamberlain.

With these influences working on him Tory Democracy seemed unlikely to stay Tory long. Randolph
Churchill's party loyalty—"No power would make me
join the other side"—had led him to stay on, a discontented rebel, with the Conservatives. But with what
result? His son could see a wasted life and a slow
tragedy of empty years. Perhaps it was the lesson of
his father's failure that a man would be wise to follow

his opinions wherever they might lead—even into another party. For the present he was playing with vague notions of a new party in the State under Lord Rosebery's tutelage.

The hereditary banner of economy was unfurled, and the House heard him in the rôle of a stern, Gladstonian economist on the Budget of 1902, pointing with concern at an income tax of 1s. 3d. in the pound as "the extreme limit of practical peace-time taxation." But his arrows were reserved for Mr. Brodrick. The War Office was easy game. Besides, Mr. Brodrick had been disrespectful about his father, and reaped the uncomfortable reward in a succession of detailed and entertaining criticisms of his Army scheme. Mr. Churchill was derisive on the platform and in the House of Commons, mocking the phantom army corps of Mr. Brodrick's dream and his German taste in military headgear. The speaker's firm adherence to the Blue Water School was emphasized once more, and he surveyed the prospect of a European war with horror:

> Sir, let us make no mistake: if by wicked counsels we are drawn into war with a great European State, we shall fight that war—whatever our forethought—with breaking hearts and straitened means, with hunger in our streets and ruin in our market-places; success will be robbed of all its triumph; and when it is over—whatever the issue—we shall turn in poverty and grief, to find all our most formidable commercial rivals entrenched on all our old vantage-grounds.

He even toyed with the dream "that the cruel and

clanking struggle of armaments is drawing to a close, and that with the New Century has come a clearer and a calmer sky." For in 1903 it was not easy to foresee an issue in the world for which it would be worth endangering the rich fruits of Edwardian peace.

Still a Conservative, he gathered these admonitions into a small volume for his party's guidance. The preface warned them with Gladstonian austerity that their military policy "betrays immoral yearnings" and that the prevailing rate of taxation "really hurts." The reproof could hardly have been sterner, if its author had belonged to the Manchester School. He added that the policy would bring disaster on the party. They had been warned; and Winston Churchill persisted in the path of personal conviction. Where would it lead him? Liberals began to watch with interest, though not all of them with unmixed admiration. Old Sir William Harcourt wrote that "the want of judgment of the fellow is despairing, but there is a good deal of force in his oratory." (For Liberals had their own sectarian peculiarities, and association with Rosebery was not the path to Harcourt's heart.) The young member's inclination to take his own line made him interesting; and he was already prominent enough to figure, hands on hips, in a select group of Parliamentary celebrities for 1903. But the final touch came from another hand. For that summer Joseph Chamberlain revived Protection; and as Mr. Churchill's reflections led him to prefer Free Trade, the cup of his unorthodoxy as a Tory overflowed.

Winston Churchill's adherence to Free Trade did not involve a change of view. That fiscal principle, which had not been seriously challenged for the last fifty years, was the accepted doctrine of his country, approved by every economic textbook and believed with a fair show of reason to provide the basis of Victorian and Edwardian prosperity. From time to time a few eccentrics hinted tentatively at a contrary opinion; but caution required them to conceal their unhallowed taste for Protection, under the blameless alias of Fair Trade.

Lord Randolph in his salad days had swerved momentarily in that direction. But he retrieved the lapse after he had been Chancellor of the Exchequer, proclaiming publicly that cheap food was a political necessity and writing privately to warn enthusiasts against the electoral consequences of Protectionist campaigns. His son had indicated vaguely to the House of Commons in April, 1902, that the issue might be raised one day—"We shall find ourselves one day on an old battlefield. Around will be the broken weapons, the grass-grown trenches and neglected graves—reviving former memories—and party bitterness, such as this generation has not known." The prophecy was sound; but no indication of this fiscal Armageddon interrupted the prevailing harmony until Mr. Chamberlain's conversion to Protection (veiled discreetly with the modest name of Tariff Reform) at the ripe age of sixty-six.

Here was an issue which enabled Liberals to drop

their differences and gave them something more to talk
about than Ireland, licensing reform, and the reluctance of Dissenters to pay their education rate. A graver
problem faced Conservatives. For many felt themselves
unable to accept a swift conversion to the doctrine
which the country had repudiated half a century before. While Mr. Chamberlain had made his choice,
half the Cabinet preferred the opposing view and Mr.
Balfour seemed to hold them both. A fair proportion
of his followers aligned themselves behind the Duke
of Devonshire as Unionist Free Traders, including
Lord Hugh Cecil with his brother Robert and Winston Churchill. He was soon treading the familiar path
of Free Trade argument—cheap food, the vicious
power of protected industries, tariff wars, and the
whole range of fiscal controversy.

Somebody who met him late in 1903 found "a little,
square-headed fellow of no very striking appearance,
but of wit, intelligence, and originality. In mind and
manner he is a strange replica of his father, with all
his father's suddenness and assurance, and I should say
more than his father's ability. There is just the same
*gaminerie* and contempt of the conventional and the
same engaging plain spokenness and readiness to understand. As I listened to him recounting conversations he
had had with Chamberlain I seemed once more to be
listening to Randolph on the subject of Northcote and
Salisbury . . ." The party leaders had destroyed his
father; he was working on his father's *Life,* which
filled his mind with the old struggles; and now his

Free Trade heresy brought him into conflict with party leaders of his own.

His method was uncompromising. A published letter soon expressed his view that "Free Traders of all parties should form one line of battle against the common foe." This came dangerously near coalition with the Liberals; and when he gratified a Yorkshire audience with the doxology, "Thank God for the Liberal Party," Oldham Conservatives disowned their member. He still sat among the Tories in the House of Commons. But they made no effort to retain him. One evening in March, 1904, when he got up to speak, his party with Mr. Balfour at its head and something less than its customary courtesy left the Chamber. Years later Mr. Chamberlain told someone that Winston Churchill was "the cleverest of all the young men, and the mistake Arthur made was letting him go."

The Liberals of Northwest Manchester invited him to be their candidate; and he was soon following John Morley at a meeting in the Free Trade Hall with a loud aspiration for "a Government that will think a little more about the toiler at the bottom of the mine and a little less about the fluctuations of the share market in London . . . a Government and a policy which will think the condition of a slum in an English city is not less worthy of attention of statesmen and of Parliament than the jungle of Somaliland." The lesson of his father's life was that a man who did not follow his opinions into the party which believed in them was a tragic failure. Winston Churchill's views in 1904 were obviously Liberal; and a fortnight later he crossed the House to sit beside Lloyd George.

2

It was midsummer, 1904; and another chapter of his life was over. The first had ended when he left the Army, the second when he crossed the House of Commons and appeared among the Liberals. His views had undergone no sudden change, since his attitude about South Africa was already shared by his new associates, and Free Trade was a faith in which all of them had been brought up. But Liberals welcomed the new recruit with something of the warmth which true believers reserve for a distinguished convert. After all, he bore an honored name; he was in course of making one for himself; and a speech from Winston Churchill became a feature of the celebrations with which Liberals honored the Cobden Centenary and challenged Mr. Chamberlain's new-fangled heresy that year. As they campaigned gleefully about big and little loaves and the unhappy expedient of Chinese labor, with which the Government endeavored to relieve the situation in South Africa, Mr. Balfour's ingenuity was wasted in the tortuous devices of a losing fight. The long Conservative ascendancy was plainly ending, and it was quite evident that Liberals would find themselves in office before 1905 was out.

Winston Churchill was in the rising scale, a coming member of the coming party. He could still manage an indulgent backward glance at his former colleagues who managed to remain Conservatives without sacrifice of their Free Trade convictions, defending them from Mrs. Asquith's indignation with the plea that "the world is not made up of heroes and heroines—luckily or where would you and I find our backgrounds."

In the intervals of politics he was working at his father's *Life,* upon which he had been intermittently engaged since his return to England. A good deal of it was written at the House of Commons; and as his narrative proceeded, he questioned Randolph Churchill's contemporaries. (One of them, who called on the biographer at his rooms in Mount Street, was greatly struck with his resemblance to his father's "manners and ways, and the whole attitude of his mind." Mr. Churchill had just come in from polo, "a short, sturdy little man with a twinkle in his eye reminding me especially of the Randolph of twenty years ago.") He consulted Chamberlain, who asked him to stay, brought out old letters, and in a brief glance at the present told his guest that, feeling as he did, he was quite right to join the Liberals—"You must expect to have the same sort of abuse flung at you as I have endured. But if a man is sure of himself, it only sharpens him and makes him more effective."

The fastidious John Morley (recently emerged from the long task of Gladstone's *Life*) read his proofs, favoring him with lengthy comments and suggestions; and Lord Rosebery was his constant counsellor in the undertaking. Indeed, his counsel was a source of some embarrassment, since his interest in the subject impelled him to compose an appreciation of Randolph Churchill for inclusion in the book. A short piece of perfect prose and swift delineation, it was a noble gift. But authors hesitate excusably before inserting essays by other hands, however able, in their own compositions. Winston Churchill had designed his father's monument; and it seemed better that it should be completed by himself in his own way. Besides, Lord Rosebery's first paragraph alluded to his father as, "in a word, but a pregnant word at Eton, a Scug." His son was slightly shocked by this amiable epithet, demanded its omission, remained unconvinced by Rosebery's Etonian exegesis of the term, and left his sensitive collaborator under the impression that his contribution to the book had been rejected. Lord Rosebery, as Liberals were well aware, was easily discouraged; and Winston Churchill's book appeared without this brilliant addition, though it was published subsequently as a small volume, supplemented by warm and discriminating praise of the larger work.

This was completed before the end of 1905 and appeared early in the next year. *Lord Randolph Churchill* is, perhaps, the author's most completely satisfying book. His heart was in the subject; his prose was still unimpaired by platform eloquence; and it remains as one of the best political biographies in English. The scale was ample, since it was an age when biographers were held to have betrayed their trust unless their subject was conveyed from the cradle to the grave in two large volumes. John Morley had awarded three to Gladstone; few, if any, of his contemporaries had received less than two; and Winston Churchill satisfied his father's honor with the customary brace.

Eight hundred pages might seem a shade excessive for depicting a career with an effective duration of six years. But it was a rich and varied chronicle, in which its author staged "an authentic drama of the House of Commons." He picked his way skillfully across the cooling lava of recent politics. For Majuba, the Parnell Commission, and Home Rule were perilously near in 1905. The leading figures were all trenchantly portrayed—his own father in his gay impudence maturing swiftly into leadership and then tragically eclipsed; Gladstone, a "proud old man, feeling that the years were drawing to a close, yet remembering his triumphs and conscious of his power" reaching out for "the sledge-hammer of democracy"; Lord Salisbury, the long-suffering but not too long-suffering nobleman; Stafford Northcote, leading the party "in a condition when, as a doctor, lawyer or business man, he would have been unable properly to discharge his duties"; and W. H. Smith, "a stout-hearted bookseller whose perseverance as a Leader was making of his repeated failures a curious but undoubted success." The old men had the worst of it, because the moral of his tale was the defeat of brilliant youth by unimaginative age.

The Fourth Party was ultimately vanquished by the

"Goats"; and one day Winston Churchill would have to face "Goats" of his own. Not that he followed his own father blindly. For though the Liberal recruit was swift to indicate Lord Randolph's "latent Liberalism," he could see the tragic, if inevitable, error of his long adherence to the Tories. His son knew better. Winston Churchill had learned the lesson of his father's wasted life; and the literary monument which he erected to his memory satisfied his own piety and at the same time indicated plainly by what stars the author's course in politics was steered.

It was a fine performance, with more balance in its judgments than might have been expected of a devoted son. His copious material was admirably organized, and the writing was considerably less exuberant than its predecessors. To produce *The River War* at twenty-four was dangerously like an infant prodigy. But *Lord Randolph Churchill* was a mature production from a man of thirty-one. Even the literary ornaments, with which its chapter-headings were caparisoned, appeared to represent the fruits of his own reading (with the possible exceptions, a phrase from Tacitus, another from Claudian, and one in Greek) rather than the random raids on his *Familiar Quotations,* which had served to decorate *The Malakand Field Force* with impressive mottoes. But before the public could admire his new achievement, he appeared before them in a fresh rôle. For Mr. Balfour's Government, which had been an unconscionable time in dying, expired at last; Sir Henry Campbell-Bannerman kissed hands as Prime

Minister—the first Liberal Prime Minister for ten years; and Winston Churchill accepted office in the Liberal Government of 1905 as Under-Secretary for the Colonies.

3

He was just thirty-one, a member of the Government, and on the point of fighting Northwest Manchester in the General Election of 1906. This was something more than a routine election brought round in the normal course by the languid operation of the Septennial Act. For the Conservative ascendancy in Parliament, ingeniously prolonged by the "Khaki Election" of 1900 and Mr. Balfour's subsequent maneuvers, bore slight relation to the balance of opinion in the country; and a large proportion of the electorate was ready to reverse the scales. There were old scores to be settled. The Liberals had been excluded from the control of national affairs for twenty years apart from the brief interlude of Mr. Gladstone's last Government and a troubled sequel under Lord Rosebery. The prolongation of their exile by a war-time election had left bitter memories.

Liberals were never more united than in reviling Mr. Chamberlain; and when the fallen archangel of Radicalism, who had foiled Home Rule and started the Boer War, defied the cherished dogma of Free Trade, they had an issue which a business people was quite capable of understanding. Cheap food and cheap raw material were solid arguments. Besides, the Nonconformist conscience had been outraged by an education rate which sought to make them pay for religious instruction of which they disapproved. Even the field of national defense had been enlivened by Mr. Brodrick's absurdities. The Tories had outstayed their welcome; the pendulum was due to swing; and in 1906 it swung with a momentum which has rarely been excelled in English politics.

Winston Churchill was in the forefront of the battle. For election results in Manchester had a national significance. Was not Mr. Balfour himself fighting to retain Northeast Manchester, while Mr. Churchill contested the adjacent seat? His adversary was a London solicitor of limited intelligence named Joynson-Hicks. But the fight was stern; and Lady Randolph joined in the fray with all the ardor which had once set Victorian music-halls singing:

> Bless my soul, that Yankee lady,
> Whether day was bright or shady,
> Dashed about that district like an oriflamme of war.
> When the voters saw her bonnet
> With the bright pink roses on it,
> They followed as the soldiers did the helmet of Navarre.

Legend, indeed, irreverently said that her maternal feeling urged that, while the Tories offered them dear food, she offered them dear Winston. But the candidate had even more compelling arguments. There had been doubts at one time as to his ability to win the seat. Somebody had told his leader that Mr. Churchill might not be "quite the sort of man to capture the quiet non-party voter who went for Houldsworth because of his solidity and stolidity and eminent respectability." But all doubts vanished in 1906; the non-party voter went solidly for Free Trade; and when the count was over, the Conservatives had lost every seat in Manchester. The late Prime Minister was out, followed shortly by half his Cabinet; and Mr. Churchill was at supper with triumphant Liberals in the new glories of the Midland Hotel.

The Liberal recruit returned to London and his new official duties on the wave of Liberal success. In appointing him Under-Secretary for the Colonies (with an amiable chief who sat in the House of Lords) the Prime Minister entrusted Winston Churchill with a post of primary importance. This was no innocuous apprenticeship. For the Colonial Office administered South Africa; and its spokesman in the House of Commons was bound to play an active part in the solution of that thorny problem.

No question was nearer to the hearts of Liberals; and Mr. Churchill's views about the Boers had been almost more responsible than anything else for his enlistment in their ranks. He was soon informing them (not without military metaphor, to which he was always prone) that a solution would be sought on lines commanding Dutch assent as well as British wishes. In dealing with the Transvaal he was clear that there must be "no difference in this grant of responsible government between Boer and Briton in South Africa"; and in reconstituting the Orange Free State he was no less conciliatory to Conservatives than to Boers. Indeed, a discriminating fellow-member judged that his final appeal to the Conservatives upon the Transvaal constitution—"With all our majority we can only make it the gift of a party. You can make it the gift of England" —moved the House of Commons with the simplicity of real oratory. His departmental speeches in the House of Commons were studiously unprovocative, aimed at removing South African affairs from the arena of English party conflict and pointing generously towards "a tranquil, prosperous, consolidated Afrikander nation under the protecting ægis of the British Crown."

But other problems faced the world in 1906; and that autumn he was privileged to see one of them. Invited by the German Emperor to visit the *Kaisermanöver* in Silesia, he watched the faultless evolutions of horse and foot in solid masses and thought hard about the effects of musketry on the massed Dervishes at Omdurman and the lessons of South Africa upon fire-power and the use of cover. At intervals he was refreshed by Imperial banquets, Imperial eloquence, and even Imperial conversation. Kaiser Wilhelm talked to him about the Colonies and favored him with a staccato tribute to the neighborhood—"Fine country, isn't it? Well worth fighting for, and well fought over. These fields are ankle-deep in blood . . ." His host went on to allude lightly to Frederick the Great and to later victories over the French and then inquired solicitously whether they had shown the visitor "my new gun." It was duly demonstrated by reluctant gunners. For the All-Highest in his wisdom had evidently decided that the young Under-Secretary was worth impressing.

Restored to England, he applied himself once more to Colonial affairs and party politics. His recent experiences in Germany were traceable in a sober thanksgiving for the new *Entente* between Great Britain and France, "the two most genuinely Liberal nations in the whole world, locked together in a league of friendship under standards of dispassionate justice and international goodwill." But his attention was reserved for South Africa (where Lord Milner was gaily dismissed as "this disconsolate pro-consul") and for politics at home.

He scarified extremists as "political Flibbertigibbets . . . running up and down the land calling themselves the people of Great Britain, and the social democracy, and the masses of the nation"; and he was profoundly skeptical of their ability to "make the infinite complexities of scientific civilization and the multitudinous phenomena of great cities conform to a few barbarous formulas which any moderately intelligent parrot could repeat in a fortnight." The English mind is rarely sympathetic to the perfect symmetry of systems founded on pure logic. It finds the symmetry no less alarming than the logic; and Winston Churchill's attitude to Socialism was eminently English. But he had a salutary respect for the Trade Unions and, with 1906 behind him, insisted that the Liberal Party was the chosen instrument of progress—"The cause of the Liberal

Party is the cause of the left-out millions." (It was twenty-six years before Franklin Roosevelt made the same discovery about the Democratic Party and "the forgotten man.")

He was disinclined to be academic about individualism (his father in his later stages had developed an increasing taste for collectivist solutions); but he asserted firmly that "the existing organization of society is driven by one mainspring—competitive selection. It may be a very imperfect organization of society, but it is all we have got between us and barbarism . . ." That consciousness of proximity to the abyss always haunted him. The system must be made to work; if it should fail, he seemed to share Lord Tennyson's dire anticipations of "red ruin and the breaking up of laws." He was prepared to mitigate its rigors, to "draw a line below which we will not allow persons to live and labor," and to see Liberalism engaged in those beneficent activities. But it must not be too roughly handled, since it was the raft on which society floated precariously over unknown depths.

His work at the Colonial Office kept him busily employed through 1907; and in the spring he had a fascinating initiation in naval affairs, when he met Sir John Fisher staying in the same house at Biarritz and heard all about the dreadnoughts and the submarines and naval gunnery and Holy Writ and Nelson. They got on so well that King Edward found them "most amusing together. I call them 'the chatterers.'"

There was an Imperial Conference early in the year;

and he got on famously with the Boers. As General Botha, whom he had so nearly killed beside a wrecked armored train seven years before, passed Lady Randolph and her son at an official banquet, the Transvaal Prime Minister paused to tell her cheerfully that "he and I have been out in all weathers." It fell to Mr. Churchill to dismiss Protectionist appeals (upon which he had already "banged, barred, and bolted" the door) with the assertion that "the British Empire existed on the principles of a family and not on those of a syndicate"; and he was stonily opposed to taxing food and raw materials. But there was thunder below the horizon of politics, as the House of Lords persisted in rejecting Liberal attempts to legislate. Mr. Churchill termed their action "something very like an incitement to violence." For he was learning to be a Radical.

His cheerful readiness to turn his hand to anything led him to insist one evening that autumn, after dining with Charles Masterman, upon writing a good deal of his leading article for the *Daily News* and concluding with the cryptic question, "Where is the statesman to be found who is adequate to the times?" His sardonic guest divined the answer in Winston Churchill's mind and left him gaily insisting that this pronouncement was his last message to the nation, "if I'm eaten by some horrible tsetse fly in East Africa."

For he was off on a swift tour of Uganda, which took him from Mombasa to Khartoum. His record, which appeared in the *Strand Magazine* and was reissued in a volume entitled *My African Journey*, is not readily distinguishable from other records of travel by hands less eminent than Mr. Churchill's. Perhaps the grand manner is unsuited to the rendering of landscape. Nature is an elusive model and frequently escapes the touch appropriate to chronicling the fall of empires. But he told the story of his trip; and the record is notable for almost the first appearance of the word "safari" in popular acceptance and for a premonitory echo of a famous phrase, when the traveler reflects beside the exit of the Nile from Lake Victoria Nyanza that "nowhere else in the world could so enormous a mass of water be held up by so little masonry." When he returned by way of the Sudan, he was revisiting old scenes; but though Omdurman and the Atbara inspired him to mentions of Gordon and Wingate, there was none of Kitchener.

Soon after his return the King was talking to Mr. Asquith about him. It was March, 1908; the Prime Minister was failing; and if there had to be a change, Mr. Asquith would succeed Sir Henry Campbell-Bannerman. King Edward had heard talk of Mr. Churchill's ambitions for promotion to the Cabinet and spoke very highly of him, while Mr. Asquith testified to his good behavior on being passed over in favor of the less luminous abilities of Mr. Lewis Harcourt and Mr. Reginald McKenna. Within a month Campbell-Bannerman resigned, Asquith became Prime Minister, and Winston Churchill was promoted to the Cabinet. The Prime Minister mentioned the Admiralty. But his interests lay nearer home in 1908, although he had been heard to express a strong objection to the Local Government Board (declining "to be shut up in a soup-kitchen with Mrs. Sidney Webb"); and when the new appointments were announced, it was found that Mr. Churchill had become President of the Board of Trade.

4

It was April, 1908, when Mr. Asquith formed the Government upon whose membership his country has been living almost ever since. For the proportion of genuine ability was higher than anything that had been seen in public life since Mr. Gladstone's great administration forty years before. The Prime Minister with sober confidence in his own intellect was not afraid to have intelligent colleagues, and the result was formidable. Asquith, Grey, Haldane, Lloyd George, and Winston Churchill, with John Morley as their Elder Statesman, were a Cabinet of Prime Ministers, a team whose quality was written on the next thirty years of English politics.

Winston Churchill was just thirty-three when he took his seat among them, and he found it next to Morley's. But before he was fully qualified as a Cabinet Minister, he faced the fires of re-election. Northwest Manchester was restive now. Free Trade had been duly safeguarded in 1906; and, that overriding interest secure, Manchester showed signs of reverting to the Conservatives. For, apart from its progressive elements, the northern capital is settled in its ideas; and it was only the economic accident that Free Trade happened to be one of them which gave Liberals a temporary foothold on that slippery eminence.

But Mr. Churchill was growing Radical, with a strong tendency to private disquisitions on the poor (he had just discovered the unpleasant fact of poverty and was deeply moved by the discovery) and all he meant to do for them and his providential preservation for the purpose—"Why have I always been kept safe within a hair's breadth of death except to do something like this? I'm not going to live long . . ." He was still haunted by his father's early death. But he enjoyed it all immensely. Life, as a later critic wrote of him, melted in his mouth like butter. His immense gusto made him feel sometimes (as he told somebody one night that winter) "as if I could lift the whole world on my shoulders."

But gusto, aided (in John Morley's view) by injudicious electioneering, was insufficient to move Northwest Manchester in 1908. The Tory renegade drew devastating fire in a by-election aggravated by the first appearance of those advocates of women's suffrage who preferred sudden interjections to the tedium of reasoned argument. No less than three Pankhursts lived in Manchester, and the decorum of Mr. Churchill's meeting in the Free Trade Hall was sadly marred by unchivalrous ejection. It was a stormy contest, and the manly charms of Mr. Joynson-Hicks prevailed. But as the defeated minister passed through the gloomy Gothic portals of the Manchester Reform Club after the count, a telegram invited him to represent the unshaken Liberals of Dundee.

This time there must be no mistakes. Assailed by Labor and Conservatives (to say nothing of a Scottish feminist, whose leading argument was a large dinnerbell), Mr. Churchill pleaded with vigor. His attack on Socialism brought the whole audience, two thousand strong, out into the street after the meeting and following the candidate with cheers and songs all the way back to his hotel. He was prepared to face the full implications of being Liberal, including the Gladstonian aspiration "to reconcile Ireland to England on a basis of freedom and justice." So far as Socialism was concerned, he was for more collective action both by the State and by municipalities, especially in the case of monopoly services; but he rejected as "a monstrous and imbecile conception" the pursuit of collectivism as a universal principle. His platform style was lively. Gibbon had been quite discarded now, though he was still addicted to military metaphor; and when his peroration urged them to preserve "the true evolution of democracy . . . the golden thread of historical continuity," there was a faint echo of the Tory Democrat.

Dundee was duly won, and the new minister returned to London and his seat in Cabinet next to John Morley's. The old Liberal had a great liking for him and "his vitality, his indefatigable industry and attention to business, his remarkable gift of language and skill in argument, and his curious *flair* for all sorts of political cases as they arise, though even he now and then mistakes a frothy bubble for a great wave." He gave him a good deal of fatherly advice, imparted Liberal tradition, and urged austerely that politics involved something more than shrewd estimates of public reactions. The duties of the Board of Trade were a sound education in political realities; and while he learned his lesson and spoke in Parliament on the Mines (Eight Hours) Bill, he was initiated in the mysteries of Cabinet government round the big table at 10 Downing Street.

That autumn he received a greater initiation, when he married Miss Clementine Hozier at St. Margaret's, Westminster, one September day. The church was full; Victoria Street was full as well (although the Eucharistic Congress at Westminster Cathedral may have been partly responsible); and Lord Hugh Cecil, his leader in the days when he sat among the Tory "Hughligans," was best man. The bride was beautiful, the bridegroom's looks (in one guest's unkind verdict) "powerful if ugly"; both of them were pale; and the successful outcome was a completely happy marriage. Impulsive in other matters, he had waited until he was thirty-three to marry; and the last word was spoken by the bridegroom twenty-two years later, when he closed an installment of his autobiography with the smiling sentence ". . . until September, 1908, when I married and lived happily ever afterwards."

A happy marriage underlies most of the great careers in English politics. Lyric poets may thrive upon unhappiness; but public men do not. For the vicissitudes of politics demand a hostess, a steady helper, and a home where politics may be forgotten or contrived in peace. Mary Gladstone was the unshaken pillar of her husband's long career; Emily sustained her Palmerston, while he defied her country's enemies and sometimes its Queen, to say nothing of the Opposition and the newspapers; and Mrs. Churchill made him a home to which her fellow-subjects' debt is even greater than her husband's.

A few weeks later they had another newly-married couple in the Government to dine. Their host did most of the talking, with a tendency to range from Early Christians to Napoleon (he was reading a good deal about Napoleon just then), with occasional excursions into the "submerged tenth" and the necessity for an alliance between democracy and science. "Ferdinand Lassalle," remarked his guest. "Did he say that?" asked Mr. Churchill, "I've never read a line of him, but I always find these people come in having said things and spoiling my show." He was going north that night to make a speech in Scotland; and as the party left, one of the guests pointed at an Alp of luggage on the waiting cab. "All that," he inquired austerely, "for two nights?" "Clemmy," said Mr. Churchill meaningly. But his caravan reached Dundee; and he discoursed on Unemployment in a tone strongly reminiscent of Mr. Lloyd George, closing with a final vision of humanity "swinging bravely along the grand high road—and already behind the distant mountains is the promise of the sun."

*THE CHURCHILLS*—"Impulsive in other matters, he had waited until he was thirty-three to marry; and the last word was spoken by the bridegroom twenty-two years later, when he closed an installment of his autobiography with the smiling sentence '. . . until September, 1908, when I married and lived happily ever afterwards.'"

Lloyd George's influence was powerful upon Winston Churchill's course in politics. Sharply opposed at their first meeting in the House of Commons after his maiden speech, the two men were drawn irresistibly together. For Randolph Churchill's son had a good deal in common with the Welsh solicitor. Both of them had courage and vitality; both were self-educated; and neither was inclined to bow the head before orthodox opinion or established dignitaries. Their enduring friendship was a political event whose effects lasted for a generation. When he crossed the House, Mr. Churchill had taken his seat next to Lloyd George; and now they worked together in the Cabinet.

The way was led by the Welsh Radical, who had just been appointed Chancellor of the Exchequer and was eager to direct the Government towards an active social policy. Winston Churchill had to be persuaded (and occasionally taught) about such matters. Their proposals would cost money; and they were apt in consequence to press for economies in other fields. Naval expenditure was mounting, as the Admiralty kept pace with Kaiser Wilhelm's growing High Seas Fleet; and the two economists fought a hard battle on the Navy Estimates of 1909. For Lloyd George was not yet convinced of the German menace; and Winston Churchill, who still entertained a hope "that Sir Edward Grey will have crowned his work at the Foreign Office by establishing a better and kindlier feeling between the British and the German peoples," waved his father's banner of economy in energetic expositions to the

Cabinet. But they stopped short of resignation; Mr. Asquith exercised the arts of management; and the Admiralty got two more dreadnoughts than it had asked for.

The Cabinet heard a good deal of Mr. Churchill. One colleague remembered him "as long-winded as he was persistent," and another thought them "a very forbearing Cabinet to his chatter." But his contributions were not merely verbal. For his pen was no less ready than his tongue, and he was developing a tendency to circulate voluminous opinions in writing for his colleagues' guidance. Some of them remained unimpressed; but Mr. Churchill was a strong believer in the influence upon Mr. Asquith of "a carefully-marshaled argument, clearly printed, read by him at leisure," and attributed his subsequent promotions to the Prime Minister's favorable opinion of his frequent official writings. Mr. Birrell might be irked by the deficiencies in his literary education, and Sir Edward Grey once cried out in anguish that "Winston, very soon, will become incapable from sheer activity of mind, of being anything in a Cabinet but Prime Minister." It was an honorable accusation in such a company; and Mr. Lloyd George was differently affected by his irrepressible colleague. "Sometimes," he told a friend, "when I see Winston making these speeches I get a flash of jealousy and I have to say to myself, 'Don't be a fool. What's the use of getting jealous of Winston?'"

He spoke about their social policy and the mounting challenge of the House of Lords; he introduced a

Trade Boards Bill, established labor exchanges (after a preliminary study of the German system in operation in Alsace, interrupted by a brief inspection of the Franco-German battlefields of 1870), and initiated unemployment insurance. The Labor Department of the Board of Trade was rearranged to handle these novel instruments as well as to perform its normal function of adjusting trade disputes. For under Mr. Churchill his department began to perform the duties since allotted to the Ministry of Labor. These were mere beginnings; but they would cost money, no less than the Government's great venture in old age pensions; and as there was money to be found, there would have to be a budget.

It is not easy to recover from the gulf of time the anguish with which Edwardian taxpayers received a finance bill imposing income tax at rates graduated from 9d. to 1s. 2d., a modest Super-tax on incomes in excess of £3,000, death duties of ten per cent, an impost of twenty per cent on the unearned increment of land, and a halfpenny duty on undeveloped real estate. Their sorely-tried successors would view such burdens as the declaration of a dividend rather than the collection of a tax. But property was hard to please in 1909; and there were circles in which Mr. Lloyd George's budget was viewed as a cross between the social revolution and the Day of Judgment. Lord Rosebery emerged from his retirement to identify it with Socialism which, as his hearers learned, was "the end of all, the negation of faith, of family, of property, of monarchy, of Empire."

Even Mr. Churchill had his moments of weakness, when he muttered that they must be prepared for him to leave them, and charged the blameless Masterman with being "at the bottom of all this revolutionary talk."

But his spirits rallied, and he flung himself with ardor into the budget fight. Perhaps he was a shade distressed by some of Mr. Lloyd George's more spirited reflections upon the accidents of heredity. After all, he bore an ancient name himself. But he spoke assiduously in the House of Commons and the country through the troubled months of 1909, denounced the House of Lords, and praised the social policies on which the money would be spent. When a Budget League was formed for campaign purposes, he became its President; and his utterances on the subject were collected in a volume pregnantly entitled *The People's Rights,* in which the case was argued with appropriate bouquets for the peers, especially the "backwoods" peers, "all meditating on their estates on the great questions of Government, all studying 'Ruff's Guide' and other blue-books, all revolving the problems of Empire and of Epsom . . ." (Had not the other Rough Rider across the Atlantic denounced with equal ardor "malefactors of great wealth"? Such unkindness from a Churchill evoked corresponding warmth on the other side, and he became an object of indiscriminate abuse from those by whom he was regarded as a deserter of his class and party. The defense of property is an exciting cause, in which fine shades are frequently forgotten; and a rich commentary of defamation accumulated round Mr. Churchill's past, his military record, and nomenclature. He was a rewarding target, of which Conservatives made full and satisfying use; and their denunciations raised him proportionately in the regard of Liberals.

His spirit was unquenched; and an old acquaintance of Lord Randolph's, who saw something of him that year, found him "as unconventional as his father was, and as light in hand." He was full of views about the future and the past, and the defects of the Public Schools and his dislike of Kitchener. He praised Morley and Labouchere and admired Chamberlain "because he is unscrupulous and bold," and told them all about the butterflies that he had seen in Uganda. There was a long afternoon of easy talk; but though it was unguarded and he was prepared to adopt his host's unorthodox objections to secret diplomacy, he would not indulge his heresies upon Egyptian questions. For he was clear that Egypt must be held—"We shall continue to hold it whatever happens; nobody will ever give it up—I won't—except if we are driven out of it at the end of a war. It will all depend on whether we can hold command of the sea."

But they quite agreed about prison reform—"I am dead against the present system, and if I am ever at the Home Office I will make a clean sweep of it." His observant host found him *"aux plus petits soins* with his wife, taking all possible care of her" and responding with swift action to her fear of wasps. Another day they talked with equal freedom about India, and

127

Winston Churchill left Wilfrid Blunt under the impression that he shared his "ideas about the native question . . . and in general about the enslavement of the colored by the white races." But he termed himself an Imperialist, mainly interested in the poor of England—"I would give my life to see them placed on a right footing in regard to their lives and means of living. That is what I am paid for, and I would really give my life." So they sat talking politics and history in the autumn of 1909; and Mr. Churchill spoke with warm admiration of an Indian who had recently been executed for a political assassination, and of Lloyd George and Asquith, and with some distaste of Balfour. His talk flowed freely, though he did not tell them much about the German maneuvers, from which he had just returned. This time the operations bore more relation to reality, and the Kaiser was not so talkative, although he was facetious about the budget, and taxed the British Government with a plan for attacking Germany by way of Borkum.

That autumn politics rose to a *crescendo*, with the Lords challenging the budget, and Liberals threatening the Lords. There was to be a General Election in the first weeks of 1910, and Mr. Churchill's guests at lunch were entertained with his opinions (he was quite prepared to grant Home Rule and nationalize the railways) except for a domestic interlude when his baby was brought in with the coffee. She had once been the subject of a conversation on the Treasury Bench.

"Is she a pretty child?" asked Mr. Lloyd George.

Her father beamed. "The prettiest child ever seen," he replied.

"Like her mother, I suppose?" inquired Lloyd George politely.

"No," answered Winston Churchill solemnly, "she is exactly like me."

The General Election came and went; the Liberals maintained themselves in office; and Mr. Churchill hoped that he would be the new Home Secretary, although he might be willing to accept the Irish Office, if he could grant Home Rule. He had once told John Redmond that it was the ambition of his life to bring in a Home Rule Bill as Chief Secretary (had he not heard the Grand Old Man speak on the second reading of the Bill?) and the Irish leader was impressed with his sincerity. A guest who came to lunch in February, 1910, found host and hostess "on just the same honeymoon terms as ever"; and within a week Mr. Churchill was Home Secretary.

5

Just thirty-five, a Secretary of State, a happy husband and a father, Mr. Churchill occupied an enviable situation in the first months of 1910. Sharing with Lloyd George the leadership of the progressive Liberals, he seemed to be in line for even greater eminence. After all, Mr. Asquith could not live forever; and somebody would have to be Prime Minister. The ironic pencil of Max Beerbohm speculated on *The Succession,* staging an imaginary conversation on the

Terrace of the House of Commons, where a watchful pair stood fingering a coin:

MR. CHURCHILL: "Come, suppose we toss for it, Davey."
MR. LLOYD GEORGE: "Ah but, Winsie, would either of us as loser abide by the result?"

It was an unkind reflection. But the artist's divination was not wholly at fault, since the Dioscuri of the Radicals had their moments of jealousy, when Churchill told Lloyd George that "in spite of your trying to keep me out of the Budget I made a show after all," and Lloyd George crushed Churchill's hesitations about the House of Lords with a sharp reminder that a man cannot change his party twice. But these were passing clouds. High-powered organisms frequently emit a spark, and the twin dynamos of Mr. Asquith's Government generally hummed in tune with one another.

His democracy, perhaps, was of a milder quality than his Welsh colleague's. His interest in women's suffrage, in spite of Mrs. Churchill's enthusiasm, wilted slightly under the attentions of its militant supporters; and sometimes he was inclined to wish the time devoted to combating the House of Lords could be more usefully employed. "If we could only get it shunted," he remarked one day to his Under-Secretary at the Home Office, "think of all we could do—boy prisoners, Truck, feeble-minded." For he was immensely interested by his Home Office work. A permanent official recalled with glee how "once a week, or perhaps oftener, Mr. Churchill came down to the office bringing with him some adventurous and impossible projects: but after half an hour's discussion something was evolved which was still adventurous, but no longer impossible."

Almost his first act was to telegraph for Wilfrid Blunt's memorandum on prison reform. He had had a taste of prison at Pretoria himself; and it would be worth knowing what an over-zealous politician, who knew Irish prisons from the inside, had to say upon the subject. There was a new play of Mr. Galsworthy's at the Duke of York's Theatre which greatly interested the Home Secretary; and when Dennis Eadie stood in the half-darkness of his cell in the third act of *Justice* listening to the silence, Mr. Churchill was listening too.

His first statement upon prison policy gratified the reformers; and he persisted in ameliorations which had few influential advocates in 1910. There are not many votes to be won by prison reform. But Mr. Churchill pursued his task of visiting the prisons and introducing alleviations which struck some of his contemporaries as mildly amusing. The task brought its embarrassments as well, when General Booth called at the Home Office to express the views of the Salvation Army and accompanied his argument by loud prayer for the conversion of the Home Secretary. Ministers are not accustomed to kneeling visitors; but the occasion passed off with signs of mutual respect.

An added duty was his daily letter to the King reporting the proceedings of the House of Commons, and the sovereign enjoyed these spirited effusions. But soon they were addressed to a new monarch. For King Edward died that spring, and was succeeded by King George V. At the Home Office and in Parliament Mr. Churchill continued to perform his duties, varied by the habit of writing papers about other people's business (Sir Edward Grey was favored with a memorandum upon Egypt) and mitigated by a summer cruise which took him to the Greek islands and Constantinople. His friendships, like his father's, were not confined to his own party; and the guests included Mr. F. E. Smith, whose rich invective was one of the few remaining assets of the Conservatives.

He saw Rhodes; he saw the Dardanelles; he saw the Sultan; and when the trip was over, he motored down to a country-house in Sussex and told them all about it after lavishing a little of his spare mental energy on the congenial exercise (to which he was occasionally prone) of devising a highly individual costume. For the Home Secretary arrived "in a little close-fitting fur-collared jacket, tight leggings and gaiters, and a little round hat which, with his half-mischievous face, made him look, as Miss Lawrence said, 'the exact figure of Puck.'" But Puck was talkative, with views about prison reform and the German hold on Turkey and the relative improbability of a Turco-German invasion of Egypt and metaphysics and theology and the absurdity of the last autumn maneuvers on Salisbury Plain. The long attempt to settle the constitutional dispute about the House of Lords (with Mr. Churchill inclining towards a settlement) broke down at last.

There was another General Election that winter; and the world passed into 1911 with the Liberals in power and Mr. Churchill still at the Home Office.

The public mind, which normally withholds its admiration from such deserving objects as hard work in inconspicuous fields, is invariably captivated by the crude appeal of simple melodrama; and when it heard that Winston Churchill had been under fire in Whitechapel, that was about all the public cared to know about the Home Secretary. Borstal was all very well; but Sidney Street was something anyone could understand.

It all came about through his insatiable passion for seeing what was going on. It had lent savor to his reconnaissances before Omdurman; it had landed him in the armored train and a Boer prison camp; and when his telephone informed the Home Secretary that some foreign anarchists had been surrounded in an East End house and were shooting freely, the news was simply irresistible. (The Rough Rider of the White House would have succumbed inevitably to the same temptation.) He was shortly on the spot, watching siege operations by armed policemen and Scots Guards from the Tower and even suggesting, with a faint anticipation of the tank, a frontal attack upon the staircase behind a sheet of steel to be procured from a local foundry. The world was soon familiar with a press photograph of the top-hatted Home Secretary standing in the meager cover of a doorway with the fur collar of his coat turned up. Mr. Balfour observed unkindly that he understood "what the photographer was doing, but why the Home Secretary?" It was not easy to imagine any of his predecessors venturing himself in such surroundings.

But his presence had its uses, since he was able to prevent the London Fire Brigade from the heroic imbecility of extinguishing a fire that broke out on the besieged premises (because the regulations said that fires must be put out) regardless of the fact that the residents were shooting at all comers.

The incident enriched his saga with a slightly comic touch. It was felt to be magnificent, but not the Home Office. Yet possibly it left a deeper mark on Mr. Churchill. For the criminals who had killed several unarmed policemen in an earlier encounter, were a strange phenomenon in England. They possessed explosives, automatic pistols, and vague political affiliations; they originated in the Russian Empire, and treated London constables with the cold ruthlessness normally reserved for the Czar's police; and it is possible that Mr. Churchill's attitude towards the later phases of the Russian Revolution owed something to his experience in Sidney Street. Not that he took a tragic view of it in 1911. For when his Under-Secretary, who had been on the Continent with Lloyd George and Rufus Isaacs, returned to England and burst into his room with the irreverent inquiry, "What the hell have you been doing now, Winston?" the statesman's answer was disarming. "Now, Charlie," he replied, "don't be cross. It was such fun."

134

That summer, in the intervals of legislation about hours of work in shops and safety in coal mines, to say nothing of heated debates upon the Parliament Bill, he had more compelling interests. For in July, 1911, the Germans alarmed the world once more by sending a small warship uninvited to a port on the Atlantic coast of Morocco. This gesture was an open challenge to French claims in North Africa; and it was followed by an unpleasant silence, terminated unexpectedly by an impressive speech of warning from Lloyd George. Speaking at the Mansion House to an audience of City men, that statesman took his stand in clear opposition to a policy of peace at any price; and Mr. Churchill's view was just the same.

This was a surprise to those who expected left-wing Liberals to view their country's enemies with sympathy. "People think," as Lloyd George remarked that week, "that because I was a Pro-Boer, I am anti-war in general, and that I should faint at the mention of a cannon." He showed no tendency to do so then or later, and Winston Churchill was still less likely to be overcome by the smell of powder. His official life was complicated by a railway strike, which involved him in a fascinating whirl of military arrangements for the maintenance of essential services. For the European crisis was far graver than the country knew, and the Government could not afford the peace-time luxury of industrial paralysis on the eve of what might very well be war. Mr. Churchill plunged into troop movements with a vigor which slightly alarmed his Radical colleagues. His action was approved, but not the gusto with which he took it; and when the strike was settled, he seemed almost to regret the settlement. For he was prepared to save the State, and it was disappointing to miss the opportunity of saving it.

But the war danger still remained. The German threat at Agadir set the alarm bells ringing; and before they died away, two formidable Britons had been thoroughly alarmed. Indeed the chief result of Herr von Kiderlen-Wächter's unhappy inspiration about the voyage of the gunboat *Panther* was to impress Lloyd George and Winston Churchill with the German menace. The Home Secretary discovered suddenly that he was officially responsible for guarding certain naval stores of high explosive, startled a resentful admiral by calling on him to produce Marines, and finally prevailed on Haldane to send soldiers. Then he began to look into cognate questions about spies and, widening his range of interests, surveyed the military field at large. Lord Haldane, whose luminous intelligence had remade and largely re-equipped the Army since 1906, did not discourage his young colleague; and the soldiers were communicative. For the Chief of the General Staff had known Mr. Churchill as a subaltern on the Northwest Frontier, and Henry Wilson so far overcame his poor opinion of civilians as to expound the future from his large map of Belgium to "those ignorant men."

Mr. Churchill's competence upon such questions was recognized by his inclusion in a meeting of the

Committee of Imperial Defence summoned to consider the strategy of the impending war; and true to his belief in the effect of a lucid paper on Mr. Asquith, he had already favored the Prime Minister with a memorandum upon "Military Aspects of the Continental Problem." Although it struck General Wilson as "ridiculous and fantastic," and its proposal of a British concentration on the Loire (in anticipation of a French retreat) was out of harmony with War Office ideas, its predictions of German successes upon the twentieth day and Allied recovery upon the fortieth were almost precisely verified by events in 1914.

When the Committee met, the admirals showed some reluctance to participate in the War Office plan by ferrying the British Expeditionary Force to France immediately on the outbreak of war; and since Mr. McKenna, as First Lord of the Admiralty, endorsed their view, it was plain that somebody would have to take his place and prepare the Navy to play its part in Allied strategy.

Haldane, who had successfully completed the education of the Army, saw himself in the same instructive rôle at the Admiralty. The mild-mannered lawyer had a way with adult pupils in uniform. But Mr. Churchill was thinking hard about war problems, too. He was seeing a good deal of Henry Wilson; and Sir Edward Grey had the benefit of his advice on hot August days in London. It was his practice to fetch the Foreign Secretary from his room late in the afternoon and walk with him across St. James' Park for a swim at the Royal

Automobile Club. His mind was full of it when he got away for a few days to the quiet of a country-house; and as he sat looking out over the still countryside from a Somerset hill-top, Housman's lines kept running in his head:

> On the idle hill of summer,
>    Sleepy with the sound of streams,
> Far I hear the steady drummer
>    Drumming like a noise in dreams.
>
> Far and near and low and louder,
>    On the roads of earth go by,
> Dear to friends and food for powder,
>    Soldiers marching, all to die.

He was still favoring Grey with detailed advice upon the conduct of foreign policy, seeing more of Henry Wilson and even Kitchener; and when Asquith invited him to come to Scotland, he accepted with alacrity. The immediate crisis had blown over. But the German menace was now nakedly apparent; and when the Prime Minister asked him abruptly on the way home from golf whether he would like to go to the Admiralty, Mr. Churchill said, "Indeed I would." As they talked, they could see two battleships—two of his battleships—steaming slowly down the Firth of Forth. When they got back to Archerfield, he found a Bible in his room and, opening it at random with his head full of the formidable might of Germany and the work confronting him, read a page of Deuteronomy:

> Hear O Israel: Thou art to pass over Jordan this day, to go in to possess nations greater and mightier than thyself, cities great and fenced up to heaven.

British Combine (above) Pictures, Inc. (below)

*BEFORE THE LIGHTS WENT OUT IN EUROPE*—Mr. Churchill in uniform, center, watching maneuvers on Salisbury Plain (above) in 1910, and being greeted by the Kaiser at German Army field maneuvers.

2. A people great and tall, the children of the Anakims, whom thou knowest, and of whom thou hast heard say, Who can stand before the children of Anak!

3. Understand therefore this day, that the Lord thy God is he which goeth over before thee; as a consuming fire he shall destroy them, and he shall bring them down before thy face; so shalt thou drive them out, and destroy them quickly, as the Lord hath said unto thee . . .

When Lord Haldane arrived on the next day, prepared for his translation from the War Office to the Admiralty, his host informed him that Mr. Churchill "was immensely keen to go himself." Haldane reasoned with his young competitor and found him "very good," undertaking to work closely with the War Office, because Lord Randolph Churchill had always favored a single department for the fighting Services. But Haldane urged that though Winston Churchill's imaginative power and vitality were higher than his own, and there could be little doubt as to which of them was better suited to hold the post in time of war, the immediate problem was to satisfy the Navy and the public of the need for scientific preparation. This, he felt, could best be done by someone who had just performed the same office for the Army. He even suggested that he might take the Admiralty for a year, during which Mr. Churchill could hold the War Office, exchanging offices as soon as Haldane's naval work was done. For Haldane had his doubts of Mr. Churchill—"He is too apt to act first and think afterwards—though of his energy and courage one cannot speak too highly." But Mr.

Churchill remained unconverted, and Mr. Asquith was unmoved by these misgivings. It was essential, in his view, to have the First Lord in the House of Commons to confront the critics of the Admiralty. Besides, Haldane's appointment to the post might have seemed too conspicuous a triumph for the War Office to ensure smooth working with the sailors. So, after consultation at Balmoral with King George and Lord Knollys, he appointed Mr. Churchill to the Admiralty.

# WAR

*"When we've wound up the watch on the Rhine."*

OLD SONG

CONFRONTED with the unpleasant possibility of
war with Germany, Mr. Asquith's Government
had faced the facts. Grey's policy, consistent in its pursuit of peace, was no less consistent in its support of
France; and the Anglo-Russian Convention of 1907 had
startled a good many Liberals with its acceptance of
the Czar as an associate. But their activities were not
confined to the construction of a diplomatic front. For
Haldane had reorganized the Army, made a reality of
the General Staff, rearmed the artillery with a quick-
firing field-gun, replaced the traditional welter of Volunteers and Militia with the Territorials for home
defense, and created the Expeditionary Force, whose
employment on the Continent had even been discussed
in some detail with the French. The Navy was expanded
steadily; new types were introduced and the economists
in the Cabinet invariably overruled. The dreadnought
had transformed the naval situation; the fleet was concentrated in home waters; and while a sharp eye was
kept upon the rate of German naval construction, the
future was awaited with a fair degree of confidence. It
may be said, in retrospect, that Britain's war preparations in the years before 1914 will bear comparison for
vigilance, diplomatic wisdom, and military resource
with those preceding 1939. When developments at
Agadir sounded a further warning and it became ap-

parent that fresh activity was required at the Admiralty, there was no hesitation in transferring one of the most active members of the Cabinet to the post. For Asquith drove a brilliant team without a nervous sense of his own incapacity to drive it. Ability had not yet become a disqualification for high office; and if Mr. Churchill was a willing horse, that was an argument in 1911 for giving him a greater weight to pull.

He went to the Admiralty in October and was soon plunged in a new world of gun power, design, war plans, and naval appointments. A chart of the North Sea, on which the daily situation of the German Fleet was marked, appeared upon the wall behind his chair in emulation of Henry Wilson's map of Belgium at the War Office; and he was apt to ask suddenly, "What happens if war with Germany begins today?" For he was anxious to acquire (and to impart) "a sense of ever-present danger." Who could tell how long they had got to make the necessary preparations? Haldane soon found him "full of enthusiasm about the Admiralty and just as keen as I am on the War Staff." He took counsel with Fisher, opening a close correspondence in which that emphatic Nestor guided his "beloved Winston's" footsteps with oracular vehemence in an explosive blend of slang, theology, bad language, and quotations drawn from unlikely sources ranging from *The Christian Year* to the Cookery Book, and remained his pupil's "to a cinder" or "till Hell freezes" or "till charcoal sprouts."

But his lessons were all digested by the First Lord,

and shortly afterwards there was a new Board of Admiralty in Whitehall. Sea appointments were no less vital. He had already chosen Jellicoe, though he was "not yet sufficiently in command of the confidence of the Sea Service, to justify what would necessarily be a very startling promotion"; and his own Naval Secretary was a young Rear-Admiral named Beatty, who had once flung a badly-needed bottle of champagne from a Nile gunboat to a thirsty Lancer on the night before Omdurman and was now in rather a blind alley. But Mr. Churchill brought him out of it, took him to work with him at the Admiralty, and found that he could talk freely to a sailor who viewed naval warfare less as a marine mystery than as something readily comprehensible to an officer who rode to hounds, played polo, and had taken part in war on land. These qualities impressed the First Lord; and when the Battle-Cruiser Squadron subsequently needed a commander, Beatty was appointed to lead that sea cavalry.

The work was fascinating; and as it progressed, Mr. Churchill lost much of his old interest in the acerbities of party politics, although Conservative dislike of the deserter was undiminished and an excited Ulster member enlivened the proceedings of the House of Commons (already dignified by loud Opposition cries of "Traitor" addressed to ministers) by throwing a large book across the House at Mr. Churchill's head. But he was pressing the Prime Minister to bring Mr. Balfour back to the Committee of Imperial Defence and growing (as Lloyd George complained) more and more absorbed in boilers. His former ally, deep in the intricacies of National Health Insurance, was rather rueful on the point and deplored Mr. Churchill's inability to get full of a subject without overflowing. For the First Lord was apt to bear down on him with a preliminary, "Look here, David, I want to talk to you," and then (according to his victim) "he declaimed for the rest of the morning about his blasted ships."

The focus of his interests had changed. His eyes were strained across the North Sea now, and it was not surprising that Wilfrid Blunt found him sadly anti-German. "I could never learn their beastly language," he announced at lunch one day, "nor will I till the Emperor William comes over here with his army." His host attributed the change in his perspective to Sir Edward Grey—"Winston . . . will not hear of Grey as being other than a splendid specimen of an Englishman, the best of the type, and they are evidently close friends, indeed Grey is Winston's son's godfather." That was in 1912, when Mr. Churchill was expressing his belief that war with Germany could hardly be avoided, if France was not to be overwhelmed or forced into an anti-British combination. But did it really need Grey's persuasion to convince the First Lord of the Admiralty that Germany was Britain's enemy, when the whole work of his office pointed in the same direction? For whenever he met the heads of the War Office in the small co-ordinating committee, which they called the "High Level Bridge," or set problems to his sailors or played war games at the War College, it was inevitably Sylt and Borkum, Kiel, Heligoland, and Wilhelm-shaven that were in their minds and on their charts and in their calculations.

The naval question in those anxious years between Agadir and Sarajevo was, and could only be, the German question; and it was impossible for any man to rule the King's Navy without acquiring an eastward outlook. Its effect on his career was still uncertain. Manifestly he was no longer in the running for leadership of the left-wing Liberals. Lloyd George was now the undisputed master of that field in the first ardor of his efforts to induce reluctant dowagers to lick Insurance stamps, with a Land Campaign to follow; and progressive heads were sadly shaken over Mr. Churchill. But there was fascinating work to do; and wherever it might lead, he could say with satisfaction to somebody in 1912 that he had "never joined in any intrigue. Everything I have got I have worked for and have been more hated than anybody."

He was working at full pressure now; and he enjoyed it, spending all his spare time with the fleet, talking to all the officers he could, inspecting every naval establishment in home waters or the Mediterranean, transferring his office and almost his home to the Admiralty yacht, in which he knew the deep thrill of great naval spectacles—the loom of tripod masts out of the mist, the tilted guns, and then the flash and thunder of the salvoes—or cruised with the Prime Minister to meet Kitchener at Malta (after an interlude of Napoleonic sightseeing at Elba) and adjust the future balance of

British sea-power between the Mediterranean and the North Sea. If life melted in his mouth like butter, it had surely never tasted half as good as this. Now he could see everything for himself, find out "what everything looked like and where everything was, and how one thing fitted into another." That was his passion; and as the Navy was prepared to tell him, he served the Navy well. His sense of it was vivid—"Who could fail to work for such a service? Who could fail when the very darkness seemed loaded with the menace of approaching war?"

Not that he confined himself to war preparations. For he played his part in efforts to avert the war, inspiring with Lloyd George a private mission to Berlin in 1912, which led to Haldane's unsuccessful visit, and launching the proposal of a "naval holiday" in 1913 between the two competing Powers. But his best was not good enough for Kaiser Wilhelm; and Mr. Churchill was soon back at his war problems—the vast innovation of oil fuel, the development of submarines (which gallant veterans termed "Fisher's toys"), and the immense experiment of air warfare. That infant was his special charge, and its first steps were largely due to Mr. Churchill. So early as 1913 he was writing on the value of air observation for coast defense; and in the days when about forty naval pilots precariously operated an assemblage of miscellaneous machines, the First Lord (in Trinity House uniform) was a frequent visitor, swerved adventurously through the air above Southampton Water, and initiated ministerial colleagues and fellow-members of Parliament in the thrills of rudimentary aviation. He needed their support in the battle which he was waging to obtain provision for its needs, to initiate the Royal Naval Air Service, and defray the cost of its strange experiments in torpedoing from the air and launching aircraft from a ship's deck at Torquay. But the outlay was justified by the results, since the Naval review of 1914 saw nearly a hundred aircraft in being with the added pride of belonging to the only service in the world that launched torpedoes from the air or could carry anything as heavy as a machine-gun in its aircraft. Mr. Churchill was a helpful and enthusiastic parent of air warfare, even enriching its incipient vocabulary with the terms "seaplane" and "flight."

His large expenditure of public money on naval objects emphasized his separation from the left wing of his party, the Navy Estimates for 1914 occasioning acute divisions in the Cabinet adjusted by Asquith's genius for management and eliciting from Lloyd George an unkind allusion to Lord Randolph Churchill's resignation in the cause of economy. But the First Lord got his way and rewarded fellow-Liberals by a spirited participation in the Irish controversy. The impending passage of a Home Rule Bill alarmed Ulster into the first stages of armed resistance. Orange eloquence had been replaced by drill and even gun-running; and while the Army hesitated on the verge of intervening in a conflict awkward for so many British consciences, Admiralty dispositions showed signs of action. Ominous ship movements were announced (and promptly countermanded by the Prime Minister); and Mr. Churchill was vehement, strange commentary on his father's authorship of the historic aphorism, "Ulster will fight; Ulster will be right." But he made an appeal to reason on his own responsibility which Asquith subsequently approved, Balfour endorsed, and even Carson recognized as "not very far" from his own standpoint.

The sky darkened swiftly in another quarter one July afternoon, when Edward Grey read them a telegram in Cabinet announcing that the Austrians had sent an ultimatum to Belgrade demanding abject reparation for an Archduke's murder in Bosnia. That seemed to challenge Russia, as protector of the Slavs; and if Russia fought, Germany would support the Austrians, and then the French would have to fight as well. Mr. Churchill went back to the Admiralty and told them that it might be war. That night he dined next to an influential German and warned him that it would be foolish to assume that England would do nothing. On the next morning he surveyed the naval situation with the First Sea Lord. A happy chance (and the pursuit of economy) had replaced the usual naval maneuvers with a test mobilization of the fleet that summer; and two battle squadrons were still concentrated in the Channel. That piece of good fortune gave them a week-end before any further naval precautions need be taken; and Mr. Churchill spent a cheerful Sunday on the beach at Cromer with his children, punctuated by grave news from London which brought him back to town that evening.

He saw Grey and drafted an announcement that the fleet would be kept in readiness, for publication the next day. A week of anxious argument in Cabinet ensued, as the whole European entanglement developed. At the outset most of them were frankly hostile to the notion of a general conflict on the Austro-Serb dispute, although the watchful Morley thought that he detected dangerous symptoms in the course advocated "with his best demonic energy by Winston, with strenuous simplicity by Grey and *sourdement* by the Lord Chancellor." His young friend had already traveled a long way from his Liberal mentor; and on Monday night he warned naval Commanders-in-Chief that war was possible. On Tuesday he concerned himself with detailed arrangements in anticipation of events, including the position of the *Goeben* in the Adriatic.

He saw a good deal of Kitchener that week, and the judicial eye of Mr. Asquith discerned that "Winston who has a pictorial mind brimming with ideas is in tearing spirits at the prospects of a war, which to me shows a lack of imagination." But he concurred in the First Lord's order moving the fleet from the Channel to its war station in Scottish waters. On Wednesday the "warning telegram" went out to all ships by agreement with the Cabinet; and that night, when some of them dined together, one minister was "shocked at Haldane's war talk." The next day Mr. Churchill used his friendship with F. E. Smith as a channel of communication with the Opposition leaders, who assured the Government of their support; and on Saturday, at the receipt of news that Germany had declared war on Russia, the British Navy was mobilized on the First Lord's responsibility, with notice to the Prime Minister and in anticipation of approval by the Cabinet, which had refused an earlier demand by Mr. Churchill for its mobilization.

Morley's head was shaken sadly over "the splendid *condottiere* at the Admiralty," though he still looked at him "with paternal benignity" when he finally informed his colleagues that he could not stay with them in a war-time Government with a discouraging prospect of "everlasting wrestles with Winston."

The remaining steps were simple. Jellicoe was promoted to command of the Grand Fleet; and the fleet was ordered to sea. In Downing Street the last hesitations of an anxious group were ending. Morley and Burns resigned, while others changed their minds. The House of Commons heard Sir Edward Grey's plain statement of the issues, an ultimatum went to Germany, which had invaded Belgium because its military needs prevailed, as usual, over its pledged word; and as Mr. Churchill sat waiting for the answer, he had an odd sensation that it was like waiting for the count after an election. That evening he was introduced to some French admirals and told them, with becoming courtesy, to "use Malta as if it were Toulon."

It was a hot August night; and through the open windows of the Admiralty he could hear them singing

"God save the King" outside the palace. Then Big Ben boomed eleven; the British ultimatum had expired; the "war telegram" went out to all ships; and Mr. Churchill walked across to Downing Street to tell the Cabinet. A watcher on the stairs (who mistook the hour and may have been mistaken in much else) notes that he wore "a happy face." He might have, since he had done his duty.

2

When Great Britain went to war in August, 1914, Winston Churchill was still under forty and at the head of the great fighting Service upon which its outcome would depend. For Great Britain stood or fell with the Royal Navy. That was obvious to all his countrymen. Something was already known of his contribution to its strength, efficiency, and readiness; and the public hardly shared his elderly colleagues' misgivings on the subject of a minister who seemed to know what he was about. His cheerful readiness for action might alarm judicial minds; and the Prime Minister recorded quite indulgently that "Winston, who has got on all his war-paint, is longing for a sea-fight in the early hours of the morning to result in the sinking of the *Goeben*." But action is required in war-time. After all, he had specialized in naval matters, and the time to use his special knowledge had arrived.

His hour had come, since war relegated party politics, with all the bitterness of Home Rule and the attractions of Insurance and land reform, to a disregarded background. Morley had prophesied serenely that "if there is a war, Winston will beat Lloyd George hollow." That paladin was now reduced to inconspicuous performances in the field of national finance, while Mr. Churchill stepped forward into public view as the organizer of victory at sea with happy visions of sinking German warships and the White Ensign floating supreme upon the smoke of battle.

Opinion inclined to rank him next to Kitchener, whom the Prime Minister had called to the War Office on the outbreak of war. In spite of early differences between the Sirdar and the enterprising subaltern, who criticized his operations in the Sudan, they had come together in the anxious days before the war; and when the Field-Marshal joined the Cabinet, his seat (in strange succession to John Morley) was next to Mr. Churchill's. Unlike some of his colleagues, the First Lord of the Admiralty could understand what soldiers meant. He was an old friend of Sir John French, who was to command in France; he had made his peace with Kitchener, who reigned supreme at the War Office; and he was even tolerated by the fastidious Henry Wilson. For the First Lord's competence was not confined to purely naval matters. After all, he had once been a soldier himself, and the strategy of the next European war had been his chief concern since 1911.

His first contribution (apart from telegraphic orders on the subject of the *Goeben,* which had now reached the Mediterranean) was the bold Admiralty gesture which released the whole Expeditionary Force for ship-

ment to the Continent and undertook the dual burden
of their transportation and the defense of Great Britain from invasion. Both undertakings were brilliantly
fulfilled, although the minor enterprise in the Mediterranean was not running quite so smoothly, and Mr.
Asquith wrote with mild amusement that "Winston's
mouth waters for the *Goeben*, but so far she is still at
large." The army left for France; and as Mr. Churchill
took leave of Henry Wilson, the minister "began to
tell me he was sure I would 'lead to victory,' and then
he completely broke down and cried, so that he could
not finish the sentence. I never liked him so much."
For the First Lord was not unmoved by the stern
drama in which he played his busy part. He might enjoy his rôle; but he was perfectly aware of what it
meant.

As it unfolded, he was full of hopes of another Aus-
terlitz, until the Germans dislocated them with an irresistible advance through Belgium and a lunge at
Paris. Kitchener, immense and hoarse, appeared early
one morning in his bedroom door at the Admiralty
with the bad news; and its impact (muttered by Mr.
Churchill to the Chancellor in the interval of a Treasury conference with nervous bankers) revived Lloyd
George's fighting temper. If the French and the Expeditionary Force could not hold the Germans, they
would have to discover reinforcements somewhere
else; and Mr. Churchill's fertile imagination proposed
the shipment of Russian troops from Archangel to Os-

tend and even the recruitment of sympathetic Americans in Canada.

But the fighting on the Marne checked the German rush, while some of its momentum was diverted to resist the Russians in the east. (Small wonder that anxious watchers in London were profoundly grateful to the Czar's armies; and their gratitude was not easy to forget in later years, when Czar, officers, and army were all submerged in the gray tide of revolution.) The fighting in the west was stabilized along the Aisne; and Mr. Churchill paid his first visit to headquarters. He was a welcome visitor, and his friendship with Sir John French might enable him to be of service as an interpreter between the soldiers and the Cabinet. He always liked to see things for himself and watched the shelling near Soissons. But his real business was to discuss the transfer of the Expeditionary Force to a sector nearer the Belgian coast. They were in full agreement, though he was out of sympathy with the prevailing optimism of headquarters as to the duration of the war. For the visitor from London, fresh from Kitchener's long-sighted preparations, was out of harmony with Henry Wilson, who had been expecting until quite recently to be in the Rhineland "in four weeks" and was still under the impression that the war would be over before Kitchener could raise and train his armies. In this buoyant mood he naturally found Mr. Churchill's views "such nonsense . . . that I got to grips at once." A few weeks later the First Lord was back again on the same errand in an effort to reduce

the slowly widening breach between Lord Kitchener
and Sir John French and to secure the transfer of the
British forces to the Belgian coast, where they could
operate in combination with the fleet. For British operations are inevitably amphibious, and the Admiralty
must always play an active part in Britain's war direction.

Compared with the swift vicissitudes in France, the
naval war appeared to be deficient in definite results.
At the outset Lloyd George told somebody that "Winston, as First Lord of the Admiralty, reminds me of a
dog sitting on the Dogger Bank with his tail between
his legs, looking at the rat who has just poked his nose
out of the hole at the other side of the water." But this
expectant attitude somehow fell short of public hopes.
True, the German flag was steadily hunted from the
outer seas, and the Expeditionary Force had been safely
ferried over to the Continent. A systematic series of
descents upon the German colonies (which made the
Cabinet, in Mr. Asquith's words, seem "more like a
gang of Elizabethan buccaneers than a meek collection
of black-coated Liberal ministers") was unobtrusively
successful. But the *Goeben* slipped away to Turkey;
three British cruisers were torpedoed by a German submarine in the North Sea; and there was still no sign of a
successful action with the main body of the German
fleet.

The First Lord's anxieties embraced the seven seas,
the course of military operations in France, and a
branch of his own service which had established itself

at Dunkirk on the extreme left flank of the Allied armies and was engaged in harrying the enemy by methods of its own. This Continental base had been selected for the Royal Naval Air Service operating in the defense of England against air attack; and the security of its machines from roving groups of German cavalry at large in a peaceful countryside suggested the expedient of armed and armored cars. This innovation was promptly countered by the simple plan of digging trenches across roads by which the vehicles might travel; and by way of repartee the armored car began to develop means of crossing obstacles. Such is the improbable paternity of tanks, engendered on the Admiralty by Mr. Churchill and his favorite child, the Royal Naval Air Service, at Dunkirk.

But soon events directed his attention to the Belgian coast with graver consequences. The German surge through Belgium had hitherto left Antwerp with its fortifications, the Belgian army, and King Albert in comparative immunity. But in October it appeared that Antwerp was seriously threatened as the prelude of a German drive at the Channel ports, and information was received which seemed to indicate that the Belgians were not prepared to hold it. This unpleasant news reached Kitchener, who promptly sent for Churchill.

The First Lord was in a special train, which had already left London en route for Dover, on his way to inspect the outlying Admiralty establishment at Dunkirk. His train was stopped without explanations and brought back to London; and presently Mr. Churchill found himself in a midnight conference with Kitchener and Grey. He urged that Antwerp was far too valuable to be given up without a struggle, and they agreed to stiffen Belgian resistance with a telegram announcing that they would be sending some Marines and might be able to provide further reinforcements. The local situation was obscure, and it seemed just as well if somebody with military knowledge and sufficient status to confer with King Albert and his ministers could visit Antwerp. The choice was obvious. Lord Kitchener expressed, in Mr. Churchill's recollection, "a decided wish" that he should go. The Prime Minister was out of London and recorded tolerantly that, "with Grey's rather reluctant consent, the intrepid Winston set off."

The Belgian Government agreed to wait in Antwerp for him, and the next morning he was driving across Belgium from Dunkirk. On the road a Belgian soldier, who had once been employed in Parliament Street, recognized the unexpected visitor in semi-naval uniform. When he reached Antwerp, he managed to convince the Belgians that their withdrawal should be postponed for at least three days, though his command of foreign languages has always been determined rather than precise. (There is evidence that he once insisted on the importance of convincing neutrals that *"nous sommes gens qu'ils peuvent compter sur."*) He saw something of the fighting and was under fire once more; and as the situation developed, he began to feel that since his persuasions had prolonged the defense, he could hardly leave the city to be shelled and return in comfort to Whitehall. Besides, he was reluctant to desert the newly-raised battalions of the Royal Naval Division, which had been involved in this emergency before their training or equipment was complete. In these circumstances he offered to resign from the Admiralty (recommending Mr. Runciman as his successor) and take command of the British forces at Antwerp. Kitchener approved and was prepared to make him a Lieutenant-General; but other views prevailed, and Rawlinson was sent instead.

The German pressure was increased, and three days after Mr. Churchill's arrival all authorities at Antwerp concurred in the withdrawal of the Belgian army. He left that night for England. Yet his intervention had prolonged the resistance of Antwerp and dislocated the German time-table, though all that the public could see for the moment was a spectacular performance by the First Lord of the Admiralty ending in the fall of Antwerp. A thousand casualties suffered by the Royal Naval Division, to say nothing of about fifteen hundred of its men interned in Holland after retreating to Dutch territory, seemed an unhappy ending to the expedition. There was a vague feeling that Mr. Churchill's restlessness might be to blame, that he was too much inclined to go and see things for himself, that it was Sidney Street over again and with far less satisfactory results. But the most critical of English war historians has written that, "viewed in the perspective of history, this first and last effort in the West to make

use of Britain's amphibious power applied a brake to
the German advance down the coast which just stopped
their second attempt to gain a decision in the West. It
gained time for the arrival of the main British force,
transferred from the Aisne to the new left of the Allied
line, and if their heroic defense at Ypres, aided by the
French and Belgians along the Yser to the sea, was the
human barrier to the Germans, it succeeded by so narrow a margin that the Antwerp expedition must be ad-
judged the saving factor." Upon that reasoning it was a
just conclusion that Mr. Churchill's energy had saved
the Channel ports, although the public of October,
1914, could observe no more than a reverse at Antwerp
in which he had been picturesquely prominent.

Restored to London, he resumed his normal duties.
Shortly afterwards he recalled Fisher to the Admiralty
as his First Sea Lord; and the partnership of forty
with seventy-four operated on a peculiar time-table by
which the older man worked morning shifts starting
about 4 a.m., greeted his junior's awakening with a
daily letter, and declined through the afternoon, while
the younger partner (refreshed by an invariable rest
after lunch) worked far into the night. They formed,
in Fisher's phrase, "very nearly a perpetual clock." The
Admiralty lights were always burning; and as Mr.
Churchill habitually minuted his papers in red ink,
Fisher (whose official preference was for green) named
them "the port and starboard lights."

But they gleamed over an unpleasing prospect in
November, when von Spee destroyed a British cruiser

squadron off the coast of Chile. Mr. Churchill was prepared to detach a battle-cruiser from the Grand Fleet to avenge Cradock and eliminate the menace of the German cruisers from the trade-routes. Fisher went one better and sent two. Hurriedly refitted for foreign service, they made the long dash across the South Atlantic and were coaling in the Falkland Islands within five weeks of the first news of Coronel. The German squadron stumbled on this alarming outpost of British sea-power, and before night von Spee's command had ceased to exist. For the long arm of the Admiralty had reached out, and Cradock was avenged.

The battle of the Falkland Islands was a splendid tit-for-tat. But the decisive action nearer home was still delayed. German ships slipped out of harbor to drop shells in Scarborough and Hartlepool; and the public (to whom the German preference for unarmed targets was still a novelty) deplored the massacre of seaside residents and blamed the Admiralty, when swift vengeance failed to ensue. Mr. Churchill had once made a rousing speech intimating that if the German fleet did not come out, it would be "dug like a rat out of a hole." This rose to haunt him with each month that passed without a new Trafalgar. When victories were won, opinion praised the sailors; and when the main issue in the North Sea was still undecided, it began to ask if Mr. Churchill was to blame. Was he too enterprising?

The half-told tale of Antwerp was a shade disturbing to the public mind; there was an uneasy suspicion of civilian interference with operations; and the bright reputation with which he had begun the war was slightly overcast. One caller at the Admiralty, who found him at his desk in the first week of 1915, thought him looking "very pale and careworn. . . . As I walked out of the room he turned wearily to his desk to resume his work. He is one of the most industrious men I have known. He is like a wonderful piece of machinery with a fly wheel which occasionally makes unexpected movements." That was the disturbing thing about him. For most Englishmen dislike the unexpected, although its contributions to the conduct of a war are more likely to win battles than a sober pursuit of the obvious. Their preference was for war leaders with whom they knew exactly where they were, even though the enemy might know the same. That could not be said of Mr. Churchill, who deviated from their favorite type; and if his activities were not crowned with victory, they were unlikely to be merciful.

3

When the battle-cruiser *Goeben* vanished in the haze of an oncoming August night, it affected the whole course of human life from the White Sea to the Persian Gulf. As the ship's destination was Constantinople, Turkey's entry into the war upon the German side became a certainty; and her consequent defeat was followed by the disintegration of the Turkish Empire, the emancipation of the Arab states, and the Zionist experiment in Palestine. But before Turkey was defeated, her resistance interposed a fatal barrier between Russia and the western Allies, which deprived the Czar's armies of munitions. This rendered their military failure inevitable and brought in its train the political collapse of the Russian Empire. For the Revolution of 1917 was the child of defeat, which flowed in its turn from Allied inability to force the Dardanelles and bring supplies to Russia. The operations at the Dardanelles were an elementary requirement of the conflict; and their failure, among other consequences of the *Goeben's* cruise (so influential on the fortunes of Czar Nicholas II, Lenin, Trotsky, Dr. Weizmann, Colonel Lawrence, the Emir Feisal, and millions of their fellow-creatures) deflected Mr. Churchill's political career.

His attention had been engaged at an early stage by the possibility of operations in this region. When Turkey's hostile intervention was obviously imminent, he contemplated a combined offensive with the Greeks against Gallipoli, even envisaging the shipment of Russian troops from Archangel or the Far East. But Russia was now heavily engaged on other fronts, and the occasion passed. He was prodigal in his suggestions to Sir Edward Grey for enterprising diplomatic combinations in the Balkans with a view to the alignment of as many enemies as possible against the Turks. But they were largely unregarded or impracticable; and when Turkey went to war, the Allies had only their own forces to rely on. There was a brief naval bombardment of the coastal forts guarding the entrance to the Dardanelles in order to ascertain the range and power of their armament; and shortly afterwards Mr. Churchill proposed a more elaborate attack, with the alternative of operations against the coast of Palestine, in order to distract the Turks from an overland descent on Egypt. But there were no troops to spare for such enterprises in 1914, and the year went out upon a military deadlock in the West.

The Germans were precariously held in France along a line that stretched from Switzerland to the Belgian coast; and no one seemed to have a clear idea of what should happen next. There was not yet that general agreement, by which military thought was subsequently dominated, that nothing ought to happen or that, if it did, it could only happen on the Western Front. For Mr. Churchill was writing to the Prime Minister inquiring whether there were not "other alternatives than sending our armies to chew barbed wire in Flanders"; and brains were busy with the possibility of seizing German islands off the North Sea coast or even forcing an entrance into the Baltic by means of a descent on Schleswig-Holstein. That would enable them to join hands with the Russians, who were fighting hard along the Eastern Front in isolation from their Allies. But an operation in the direction of Constantinople would have the same result by opening the Russian Black Sea ports to British shipping carrying in Allied munitions and bringing out Russian wheat, besides dissipating the threat of an attack on Egypt by

165

the Turks. Unless the war was to be permitted to stagnate into an unimaginative stalemate in France, there was a good deal to be said for an operation at the Dardanelles; and it is not surprising that Mr. Churchill's active mind was powerfully attracted.

The project, which was at once effective and a trifle grandiose, made a strong appeal both to his sound military instinct and to his lively sense of the historic drama of the war. ("We are on the stage of history," as he once wrote to French.) The minarets of Stamboul were a considerable lure. Besides the field of naval strategy was growing unattractive now that the Germans had been driven from the outer seas and there was nothing to be done except to wait for a fleet action nearer home. He had his moods of impatience, when he informed the Prime Minister soon after Antwerp that he felt the call of active service and that he was hoping to exchange the Admiralty for a command in the field. Warming to the subject, he inquired with feeling whether these "glittering commands" were to be exclusively entrusted to "dug-out trash" and "military mediocrities who have led a sheltered life mouldering in military routine." The Prime Minister was treated to about fifteen minutes of his young colleague's eloquence, concluding with an unfavorable comparison of public life to martial glory, which left Mr. Asquith with a feeling that it was three-parts serious. For Mr. Churchill's element was action; and in Whitehall that was not always quite so easy as it looked.

As 1915 opened, he was pushing for a more imaginative conduct of the war, for the design of armored vehicles capable of crossing trenches upon caterpillar tractors or of crushing them by the use of linked steam-rollers, for the projection of smoke-screens (a shocking innovation), and for the first unpleasant dawn of chemical warfare. The First Lord was prepared to consider anything that seemed worth trying, undiscouraged by the experts (experts had their limitations, as he was well aware when he told a throat specialist, "I entirely disagree with your diagnosis") and irrespective of whether it fell strictly within the province of the Admiralty or not. Smoke-screens were, perhaps, legitimately naval business. But the development of armored vehicles, apart from their accidental birth at Dunkirk under naval auspices, was not. Yet Mr. Churchill persevered in experiments, in suggestions to the Prime Minister, and finally in the formation of the Land-ships Committee of the Admiralty, which actually made a tank. Its operations were financed, without reference to the Board of Admiralty, the War Office or the Treasury, upon the First Lord's personal authority; and by this grave departure from all departmental propriety the first of all the tanks was brought to birth. Technicians may dispute the paternity of its design. But, whoever thought of it, there cannot be the smallest doubt that without Mr. Churchill it would never have been made at all.

But tank attacks and all their later consequences were far away in January, 1915, with the Russians asking for a demonstration of some kind to relieve

167

Turkish pressure and Lord Fisher showing a strong tendency to resign unless the First Lord would consent to execute interned Germans in the event of civilian casualties being caused by air-raids. Mr. Churchill was unbending on the subject of reprisals, and nothing more was heard of Fisher's resignation. Life with that volcanic sage, whose chief interests were the invasion of Schleswig-Holstein and an immense construction program, was apt to be a trifle wearing. But he was more responsive than might have been expected to the Russian cry for help. Mr. Churchill had an instant talk to Kitchener, who surveyed the ground, regretted that there were no troops to spare, agreed that the best place to make a demonstration was the Dardanelles, and told the Russians something would be done. But Fisher's eager fancy was on fire with dreams of military landings on the Turkish coast; and a glowing plan was unfolded to the First Lord with a barrage of underlinings (slightly mitigated by the discouraged prelude that "we shall decide on a futile bombardment of the Dardanelles").

Fisher's revelation took the form of an Anglo-Indian descent on Alexandretta simultaneous with a Greek attack on Gallipoli and a Bulgarian thrust at Constantinople, while "Sturdee forces the Dardanelles at the same time with *Majestic* class and *Canopus* class! God bless him!" This set Mr. Churchill thinking. It was doubtful whether French and Kitchener would part with any troops, and Grey's scrupulous diplomacy seemed unlikely to enlist Balkan allies. But could old battleships be used to force the Dardanelles?

Fisher's last word (with triple underlinings) had been "Celerity"; and that day Mr. Churchill telegraphed to the naval commander off the Dardanelles inquiring whether he considered "the forcing of the Dardanelles by ships alone a practicable proposition." Fisher was still favorable to an operation of some sort at the Dardanelles, because "the naval advantages of getting possession of Constantinople and the getting of wheat from the Black Sea are so overwhelming"; and when the man on the spot replied that though the Straits could not be rushed, "they might be forced by extended operations with a large number of ships," it began to look very much as if something might be done.

Mr. Churchill was enthusiastic; two admirals in high position concurred; Lord Fisher had not dissented audibly; and the commander on the spot, who evidently favored the idea, was asked to produce a detailed plan. When this arrived, it called for the use of twelve battleships and three battle-cruisers. The Admiralty War Staff went one better, suggesting that the *Queen Elizabeth*, which had just been completed, might be added to the force for a short time and that her 15-inch guns would outrange the Turkish forts, performing the same office as the Skoda howitzers by which the Belgian forts at Liége were believed to have been destroyed. The remaining battleships might be legitimately risked in closer combat with the coast defenses, as they were all pre-dreadnoughts, unfit for the line of battle in the North Sea and due to go to the ship-breaker's yard in the near future. An operation on these lines was urged by Mr. Churchill on the War Council. Lord Kitchener approved; Lord Fisher and Sir Arthur Wilson made no comment; and the War Council accepted the proposal. The subsequent arrangements were made without eliciting an indication of dissent from any quarter.

Ten days later Beatty and his battle-cruisers met the Germans off the Dogger Bank, sank one, damaged two, and chased them home to Germany. Preparations for the naval attack on the Dardanelles proceeded. But Fisher's first enthusiasm had begun to wane. The margin of naval superiority in the North Sea was causing him anxiety, and it dawned upon him that the Dardanelles competed dangerously with his cherished operation in the Baltic. In this mood of growing doubt he grew unhelpful, pressed for a reduction in the British naval force to be employed, and even indicated that the plan was one in which he did not concur. But by this time the French and Russian Governments had been informed of the proposed operation; and it came up for further consideration by the War Council.

When Fisher indicated that he proposed to intimate his disapproval by staying away, he was not excused; and in a preliminary discussion with the Prime Minister and Mr. Churchill, in which Lord Fisher's objections (as recalled by Mr. Asquith) were "not based upon the technical or strategic demerits of a Dardanelles operation, but upon the fact that he preferred another and totally different objective in the Baltic," he seemed to acquiesce. But at the meeting, in which Kitchener, Balfour, and Grey expressed complete approval, Fisher tried to leave the room in order to resign. Kitchener persuaded him to take his seat again, since he was in a minority of one. That afternoon he went over all the ground again with Mr. Churchill. The First Lord was persuasive; and he brought all his guns to bear on Fisher, who finally gave in. But Fisher was no weakling and, as he subsequently said, "when I finally decided to go in, I went the whole hog, *totus porcus.*"

The next stage was to make assurance doubly sure by obtaining military support for the naval effort in the Mediterranean. This was not designed in the first instance for a land assault on the Gallipoli Peninsula, but as a token of British resolution for the encouragement of Greece and Serbia; and there was no certainty whether the force would be employed at the Dardanelles or at Salonika. (Mr. Lloyd George, who was developing opinions of his own about the war, had a weakness for Salonika.) Mr. Churchill went to France once more and persuaded Sir John French to waive his claim to two divisions that would be coming out to France in March. Relieved of this liability, Kitchener consented to release the 29th Division for the East. Fisher was eager for its prompt employment at the Dardanelles, and Mr. Churchill hoped for a successful operation which would bring over Greece and Bulgaria to the Allied side.

The first impact of the naval bombardment of the forts in February was powerful. The diplomatic consequences were excellent; and by the first days of March the commanding officer anticipated that a fortnight would suffice to penetrate the Straits. But the military force that might have turned a raid into an occupation was not there, since Russia, resenting the indignity of letting Greeks into Byzantium, disdained their offer of assistance, and Kitchener had changed his mind. The situation, serious in France, was even graver on the Russian front; and his uncertainties were comprehensible. But three weeks later he changed his mind again, this time in favor of the enterprise; and Sir Ian Hamilton was summoned to the War Office, addressed by his alarming chief with "flashing spectacles," and sent out on the path of conquest with a handbook on the Turkish army as it had been some years before, a pre-war report on the Dardanelles, and a highly questionable map. Prompt action was not facilitated by the embarkation of the 29th Division in such magnificent haphazard that it was necessary to divert the transports to Egypt and sort their contents into the right order.

But was prompt action by the Army really needed? Could the Navy do all that was required by itself? At the Admiralty hopes were high, and Fisher even offered to go out and take command himself. One afternoon in March the ships tried their strength against the Narrows, and the experiment was costly. Three battleships were sunk (though with relatively small loss of life) and three damaged; Ian Hamilton watched the little ships huddled round the mined, lop-sided battleships and wrote in his diary that "Winston in his hurry to push me out has shown a more soldierly grip than those who said there was no hurry." The First Lord was waiting for the news in the comparative relaxation of a trip to the French trenches on the Belgian coast. When it came, he waited for the next attempt. But when would that be made? The admirals were nearly all against him now. The notion of a purely naval operation at the Dardanelles was abandoned after one unsatisfactory experiment. Now the Army would co-operate in its own time; and that, it seemed, would not arrive until some time in April. Till then the enemy was free to improve the defenses of the Peninsula. The interval (attributable to the pace at which the troops had been sent out) was fatal to success; but the First Lord was not to blame.

As the time approached, Lord Fisher viewed the Dardanelles with an increasing chill—"You are just simply eaten up with the Dardanelles and cannot think of anything else! Damn the Dardanelles! They will be our grave!" He accepted his own responsibility for the enterprise; but he was not prepared to increase the stakes. Fisher could still write, "I think it's going to be a success, but I want to lose the oldest ships and to be chary of our invaluable officers and men for use in the decisive theatre." The first military landing on the

Peninsula, with all the wasted gallantry of the beaches and the *River Clyde,* was a disappointment. They gained a foothold; but it was evidently going to be a long business. Could they stay the course? The sailors were not feeling quite so enterprising now; Fisher was gravely apprehensive; and when another ship was sunk, he insisted upon bringing home the *Queen Elizabeth* in view of the risk from German submarines. The First Lord concurred. But Fisher, dreading the increasing drain of naval reinforcements for the Dardanelles, decided to part company; and one May morning Mr. Churchill received a chilly intimation of his resignation, embellished with an aphorism attributed to Dr. Jowett.

The old admiral was almost mutinous, completely disappeared (probably to Westminster Abbey, which was his favorite retreat), was run to earth with a peremptory order from the Prime Minister in the King's name, and partially returned to duty. An anguished correspondence with Mr. Churchill ensued, in which their divergences were restated. Their parting, as Fisher wrote later, was "pathetic." For he retained his faith that "Mr. Churchill's audacity, courage, and imagination specially fitted him to be a War Minister." Twelve months later he was still asseverating that the First Lord was "a War Man." But the qualities which he admired in Mr. Churchill had directed his attention to the Dardanelles, and that commitment was now unforgivable.

Fisher's resignation was maintained, and Mr.

Churchill was faced with the problem of finding a successor. To his surprise and pleasure Sir Arthur Wilson, a stern veteran who shared Fisher's eminence with something less than Fisher's unaccountability, consented to accept the post; and on Monday morning the First Lord was ready with the news of Fisher's resignation and the appointment of Sir Arthur Wilson. He had been seeing a great deal of Mr. Balfour. Somebody had even hinted to the Prime Minister (and Mr. Lloyd George thought there might be something in the story and said as much, when Mr. Asquith asked him) that Mr. Churchill, whom the pace of Grey's diplomacy had failed to satisfy, was maneuvering to replace him at the Foreign Office by the more supple qualities of Mr. Balfour; and when the First Lord told him about Fisher, Mr. Balfour undertook to break it to the Conservatives. But the news was there before him. For Fisher had sent a broad hint, unsigned but in his unique handwriting, to Mr. Bonar Law. The Leader of the Opposition was disturbed and called at the Treasury to see Mr. Lloyd George. The Chancellor confirmed the facts; and Mr. Bonar Law insisted that if Fisher was resigning, Mr. Churchill would have to go.

The Conservatives, who were growing quite reconciled to Mr. Lloyd George, had not yet forgiven Mr. Churchill. Besides, a public controversy on the subject of Lord Fisher's resignation might be extremely dangerous; and if that could not be avoided, they would hardly escape another on the equally explosive theme of alleged deficiencies in the supply of shells, a subject upon which an enterprising military journalist was just beginning to campaign against the Government with serious effect. The best solution seemed to be the sacrifice of Mr. Churchill and the formation of a Coalition Government. Armed with this indication of the Tory view, Mr. Lloyd George went across to Mr. Asquith, who agreed with surprising promptitude. His own thoughts, indeed, had been moving in the same direction.

Public controversy would have most undesirable effects upon the delicate negotiations just then in progress with Italy, whose collective statesmanship was now concentrating on the nice problem of determining which side was likelier to win the war. So it was agreed to form a Coalition Government; and when Mr. Churchill called at Downing Street with the good news of his reconstituted Board of Admiralty, he was told by the Prime Minister that he would have to go himself.

The blow was unexpected; but Mr. Churchill had not many friends in May, 1915. The Conservatives had never forgiven his apostasy; his qualities did not commend themselves to the drab acrimony of Mr. Bonar Law; he was not on the best of terms with Mr. Lloyd George (they had been in sharp disagreement at a recent meeting of the Munitions Committee); and Mr. Asquith was always apt to underrate the qualities of anyone whose education did not conform to his own pattern. Mr. Churchill (owing, partly, to the untimely insistence of the University upon compulsory Greek) was not a Balliol product; and the Prime Minister seemed to regard him with affectionate amusement. "The adventurous Winston," he had written, "is just off to Dunkirk"; "the intrepid Winston," he recorded of his trip to Antwerp, "set off at midnight." He had a modified respect for his junior's equipment—"Our two rhetoricians, Lloyd George and Winston, as it happens, have good brains of different types. But they can only think talking: just as some people can only think writing. Only the salt of the earth can think inside, and the bulk of mankind cannot think at all."

Mr. Asquith surveyed his colleagues from the altitude of an indulgent headmaster; but Mr. Churchill did not seem to be his most promising pupil—"It is a pity that Winston has not a better sense of proportion. I am really fond of him, but I regard his future with many misgivings. I do not think he will ever get to the top in English politics." Besides, if Mr. Churchill's thoughts had really been allowed to stray in the direction of replacing Grey with Balfour, the Prime Minister's most cherished prejudice was threatened. It was hard, of course; but if the Conservatives had really made it a condition, he would have to go.

So he was gently asked whether he would prefer another office in the Government or a command in France. Mr. Lloyd George, who happened to come in just then, suggested that he might do great work at the Colonial Office. But nothing came of it. For the Conservatives were not prepared to acquiesce in anything except a minor post for Mr. Churchill. It was all extremely painful for the Prime Minister, because the newcomers positively insisted on his breaking the circle of his own intimates and sacrificing Haldane too. It might be true that Haldane had remade the British Army; but somebody had just remembered that he made a pro-German speech some years before the war. So the cause of national unity demanded the elimination of Lord Haldane, who had made the Army, and of Winston Churchill, who had mobilized the Navy. These patriotic requests were proffered on behalf of the Conservatives by Mr. Bonar Law, who was completely untried in public service, and by Lord Lansdowne, whose administration of a chaotic War Office had complicated the early stages of the South African War. But as the King's government must now be carried on with Conservative assistance, Mr. Asquith made the sacrifice in his least Roman attitude.

Lloyd George still tried to do his best for Mr. Churchill, proposing him for the India Office or even the Viceroyalty itself. But India was felt to be a little difficult, and his Miltonic fall down the long scale of offices continued.

> From morn
> To noon he fell, from noon to dewy eve,
> A summer's day, and with the setting sun
> Dropt from the zenith, like a falling star.

Nine months before at the outbreak of war he had presided over a great fighting Service; and now, while Mr. Lloyd George rose from the Treasury to become Minister of Munitions, Mr. Churchill sank to the depressing dignity of Chancellor of the Duchy of Lancaster. It was a strange reversal of Morley's prophecy that if there was a war, he would "beat Lloyd George hollow."

At the very end he seemed to see it coming. While he was still at the Admiralty, he told a visitor, "They may get rid of me. If they do, I cannot help it. I shall have done my best. My regiment is awaiting me." That thought was always with him. But it was no real consolation. When the blow had fallen, he announced that he was "finished . . . finished in respect of all I care for—the waging of war; the defeat of the Germans. I have had a high place offered me—a position which has been occupied by many distinguished men, and which carries with it a high salary. But that all goes for nothing. This"—he was still in his room at the Admiralty— "is what I live for." He had his consolations, though. Sir Arthur Wilson, who had consented to succeed Fisher, declined to serve under any other First Lord; and on the dark day after his dismissal Kitchener paid him a visit. The Field-Marshal told him all the latest news; and as he turned to go, the big man said to him, "Well, there is one thing at any rate they cannot take from you. The Fleet was ready."

4

The next stage was a depressing postscript. Though he still kept his seat next to Kitchener's in Cabinet and served with eight colleagues on the Dardanelles Committee, Mr. Churchill had fallen from high office. There was no appeal from the decision, and the public were left to draw their own conclusions from the re-arrangement by which the First Lord of the Admiralty was transferred to the less arduous duties of the Duchy of Lancaster. It had been insisted on by Conservative mediocrities, by the same depressing element which had suppressed his father; and he accepted his dismissal —"I shall give the Government my support. I shall make a few speeches and then I shall go to the Front. I could not continue to hold a sinecure office at such a time." That was his first reaction to the catastrophe.

But he made no speeches; and presently he was at his old occupation of writing memoranda for circulation to his colleagues. His administration of the Navy was vindicated at some length, and he surveyed the military situation at fairly frequent intervals. But these compositions were a poor substitute for real business. He had been accustomed for the last ten years to hard departmental and Parliamentary work; and he passed a wretched summer, mitigated by the discovery of a novel pastime.

One Sunday morning at a country-house he saw a relative sketching in the garden. Here was a pursuit that was quite new to him. If she could do it, so could he; and though nobody had ever taught him, he was quite prepared to try. (That receptive attitude formed his approach to almost all his galaxy of minor accomplishments, including fiction and, at a later stage of his career, bricklaying.) The children had some paints, which he annexed; and the results encouraged him to purchase the next day an immense equipment of artist's material and apparatus. All that now remained was to paint a picture. Nobody had told him how that could be done; so he started rather tentatively, until Lady Lavery led his first assault upon a canvas. Her husband added further counsel; nor did Orpen and Sickert withhold their guidance at a later stage. He liked to work in oils; he liked bright colors; he enjoyed a set of novel problems (of which he sometimes seemed to think in military terms); and, above all, he had discovered an absorbing occupation for his involuntary leisure.

That summer the bitterness of his own failure was aggravated by a nightmare situation in which he had full knowledge of events without power to control them. The unhappy consequences of his fall were feared at the Dardanelles, where Sir Ian Hamilton confided to his diary that it "would be an awful blow to us out here; would be a sign that Providence had some grudge against the Dardanelles. Private feelings do not count in war, but alas, how grievous this set-back to one who has it in him to revive the part of Pitt, had he but Pitt's place."

The lively Hamilton had always liked him. More intelligent than it was altogether soldierly to be, he was unafraid of intelligence in others and had assessed Mr. Churchill's exploit at Antwerp more highly than some of his contemporaries—"Very likely the next great war will have begun before we realize that the three days' delay in the fall of Antwerp saved Calais. . . . Any comfort our people may enjoy from being out of cannon shot of the Germans—they owe it to the imagination, bluff and persuasiveness of Winston Churchill and to this gallant Naval Division now destined to be starved to death." He foresaw a dismal prospect at the Dardanelles with the Admiralty's interest in the enterprise chilled by a new First Lord and the Prime Minister left without "his mainspring." In London Mr. Churchill was writing memoranda helplessly; but decision had been replaced by deliberation, as Mr. Asquith drove his team of incompatibles a little gingerly. Events rolled slowly forward. When the next assault upon the Turks was made, it failed at Suvla Bay; and when the Dardanelles Committee was reconstituted without Mr. Churchill in November, it was time for him to go. He could do no more to help the project, since evacuation was already in the air. Nobody appeared to pay much attention to his views about the conduct of the war; and as he could take no effective part in it in London, he resigned in order to see what there was for him to do in France.

His resignation afforded an opportunity for a full statement in the House of Commons before entering upon "an alternative form of service to which no exception can be taken, and with which I am perfectly content." He confined himself to four episodes of his war-time career—the victory and destruction of von Spee, the loss of three cruisers in the North Sea, Antwerp, and the Dardanelles. The statement filled twenty-two columns of Hansard, of which sixteen concerned the Dardanelles.

The speaker's narrative was free from eloquence and singularly moderate in tone. There was drama in the situation, since he was about to go abroad on active service, and the speech might be his last. But he made no effort to exploit it, apart from the slight flourish of entrusting his interests and papers to F. E. Smith and the effective understatement, "I do not expect to address hon. Members again for some time." Mr. Asquith bowed him out with a lapidary tribute to "a wise counsellor, a brilliant colleague, and a faithful friend" and sent him on his new career with "the universal good will, hopes, and confident expectations of the House and of all his colleagues." After all, the name of Churchill was not unknown on British battlefields.

5

One November day in 1915 Major Churchill, of the Oxfordshire Yeomanry, walked off the leave-boat at Boulogne. His regiment was in rest billets in the neighborhood, and he was on his way to join them. Someone who had met him dining with Lord Northcliffe the night before found him "in great form and tearing spirits . . . abandoning what he calls his 'well-paid inactivity' "; and on leaving England he had written to General Seely of the "relief to let all that slide off one's mind." But a summons to headquarters took him to St. Omer, and the next morning Sir John

French asked him what he would like to do. Whatever he was told, said Major Churchill. The Commander-in-Chief asked if he would command a brigade, and the ex-minister accepted on condition that he was first given some practical experience of trench warfare. He chose the Guards Division as the scene of his instruction, lunched with Lord Cavan at La Gorgue, and was entrusted to his new commanding officer.

The 2nd Grenadier Guards were plodding through the drizzle of a late November afternoon towards the line, and Major Churchill rode with the colonel and his adjutant between the stricken trees and shattered farmhouses of Artois. For about half an hour nobody said anything. Then the colonel observed without geniality, "I think I ought to tell you that we were not at all consulted in the matter of your coming to join us." This welcome was supplemented, after a further interval of silence, by the adjutant's announcement that circumstances had compelled them to reduce Major Churchill's kit to his shaving gear and a spare pair of socks.

They arrived at their depressing destination, composed in equal parts of sandbags and fragments of a farmhouse, refreshed themselves with tea interrupted by the arrival of a dead Grenadier for burial, and prepared to retire for the night. Major Churchill, offered the alternatives of a flooded dugout and a crowded signal office, chose the company of Morse and four signallers and was not left in the slightest doubt that he was in the Army now.

This conscientious effort to put him in his place ended in a slightly warmer feeling. For as he plodded with the colonel on his nightly rounds, that warrior occasionally went so far as to invite the major to ask any questions that might occur to him, adding that it was his duty to furnish all information and that he was quite willing to do so. Emboldened by this geniality, the major subsequently asked to be transferred from battalion headquarters to the trenches (where something warmer than tea was obtainable); and his education proceeded to the normal accompaniments of trench life. One chilly afternoon a military dignitary summoned him to a rendezvous, kept him waiting for about an hour at an unhealthy cross-roads, and then sent word that there had been some mistake about the car. The rendezvous was off; and Major Churchill was extremely annoyed, though his annoyance subsequently vanished on discovering that his dugout had been blown up by a shell five minutes after his departure.

After this initiation he was promoted to command the 6th Royal Scots Fusiliers (with a youthful major named Archibald Sinclair) near Ploegsteert, of which his deep distaste for foreign names welcomed the British variant of "Plugstreet." He had expected a Brigade, and French had actually named his new command. But before this elevation French was recalled (they spent an unhappy day together in the driving rain, as French drove round his armies for the last time); and Haig withdrew his predecessor's offer. An old friend, who met Churchill just after this unpleasant news, had never seen him so disappointed. For it seemed to close the way to a military career; and he was left with nothing but a regimental interlude in France. But he made the best of it, spending a great deal of time in the front line and mitigating these severities with an unusual costume of which a French helmet and a good deal of fur supplied the main ingredients, while he was honored by distinguished visitors including the majestic Curzon and the sprightlier Smith.

His headquarters were palpably unsafe; and tradition cherishes his repartee to a cautious general, who pointed out that it was "a very dangerous place." "Yes, Sir," said Colonel Churchill with respect, "but, after all, this is a very dangerous war."

His larger interests were not forgotten. For he had already composed a memorandum for the guidance of G.H.Q. and the Committee of Imperial Defence on "Variants of the Offensive." This dealt authoritatively with the use of armored shields for reducing casualties (an expedient that had appealed to him ever since Sidney Street) and attack by tanks and "above all *surprise.*" That base expedient, however, was disdained by the military mind, which much preferred the simpler (if more costly) method of infantry attacks at points widely advertised by long preliminary bombardment.

In March, 1916, Colonel Churchill returned to the House of Commons to speak on the Navy Estimates. His tone was blandly critical of his successor and of the passivity which seemed to have descended upon naval

*BEHIND THE FRONT*—"His notion of a holiday was to fly to France and spend two days with the armies in the field. . . . A fair proportion of his departmental work was done in France." Mr. Churchill on October 28, 1918, watching troops of the 47th Division march past.

strategy, and his closing passage suggested with some
magnanimity the recall of "the power, the insight, and
energy of Lord Fisher." It produced no result, though
gossip said that he had sat up half the night before
discussing it with Mr. Garvin of the *Observer*. For he
valued his press contacts, and he was soon discussing a
new speech with *The Times*' military correspondent.
His battalion had been amalgamated now, although he
still retained his military rank. But that summer he
was more in the House of Commons (Carson, who
acted as Leader of an informal Opposition, had suggested his return), speaking on the need of an Air
Ministry and on Army questions. He had begun to
write for newspapers and magazines; and he obliged
Mr. Balfour by drafting a communiqué upon the Battle of Jutland in order to alleviate the consequences of
the Admiralty's first announcement, which left everybody under the impression that a decisive victory had
been a grave reverse.

He was reverting to civilian life. The summer of
1916 with the Irish rising and misadventure in Mesopotamia, scarcely relieved by the aimless slaughter of
the Somme and the developing disloyalties of Mr.
Asquith's Coalition Government, was not a cheerful
scene. Mr. Churchill surveyed it from his place in
Parliament, from a variety of country-houses (where
his painting made impressive progress) and from the
London dinner-tables where Colonel Repington of
*The Times* listened to the well-informed and lectured
to the well-connected. In August his opinions on the

futility of Haig's offensive were circulated to the Cabinet with a cautious foreword by F. E. Smith; and in October he spent four days giving evidence before the Dardanelles Commission.

As the scene darkened after Kitchener's tragic removal, the Conservatives became more restive, and Mr. Lloyd George was more deeply impressed with the imperfections of nearly all his Liberal colleagues. The crash came in December, 1916; and when he formed the second Coalition Government, Mr. Lloyd George was doubtful whether the Conservatives would let him find a place for Mr. Churchill. They dined together, and Mr. Churchill's hopes were high. But afterwards Max Aitken dropped a hint that there was nothing for him; and he left angrily, a disappointed exile once again. Later on Mr. Lloyd George commissioned somebody to "see Winston and explain why he had been left out, and tell him that he (L. G.) would endeavor to find some position for him, such as Chairman of the Air Board, when the Report of the Dardanelles Commission had been published."

The mission was discharged, and Mr. Churchill's answer was: "I don't reproach him. His conscience will tell him what he should do. Give him that message and tell him that I cannot allow what you have said to fetter my freedom of action. I will take any position which will enable me to serve my country. My only purpose is to help to defeat the Hun, and I will subordinate my own feelings so that I may be able to render some assistance."

John Morley's prophecy about his two young colleagues was now completely falsified. For Lloyd George had thoroughly outdistanced Winston Churchill. But though he was Prime Minister, he was not entirely his own master; and he could hardly find a post for Mr. Churchill in face of Lord Northcliffe and the Conservatives. There was some excuse for his omission so long as the Dardanelles affair was still *sub judice*. But the Commission published its report in March, 1917, and Mr. Churchill dealt with it at length in the House of Commons. There was still no offer, though he spoke with great effect in a secret session, urging abstention from precipitate offensives before the weight of the United States could make itself felt in Europe. After this speech Lloyd George assured him privately that he meant to bring him back to office and let him see important papers; and when Mr. Churchill went to Paris shortly afterwards, the watchful Henry Wilson guessed that he was "evidently in high favor with Lloyd George."

But the months went by. The Conservatives were still implacable; Mr. Bonar Law was as mistrustful as before; and one agitated minister warned Lloyd George against "a dangerously ambitious man," who might (in another nervous colleague's judgment) be "a potential danger in opposition" and "an active danger in our midst." But the intrepid Welshman, who knew him better than the Conservatives, took the risk (but not too much). For he discreetly chose a moment when Lord Northcliffe was in America, and offered Mr.

Churchill a choice between the Air Ministry and the Ministry of Munitions. He chose the latter.

6

When Mr. Churchill went to the Ministry of Munitions in July, 1917, that organism had passed its first alarming period of growth. Under its founder, Mr. Lloyd George, it had engulfed the armaments industries; large numbers of the business community, enlisted in its swelling ranks, alarmed the Civil Service with the splendid haphazard of business methods; and its administrative center occupied a generous proportion of the hotel accommodation of the Metropolis. But his successors, Mr. Montagu and Dr. Addison, had curbed (or gratified) its territorial ambitions; and it was now a fairly normal part of the national machinery, devoted to the steady satisfaction of the Allies' need for war material.

Mr. Churchill's advent caused an unpleasant flutter among the Conservatives. A hostile deputation of his party in the House of Commons waited on Mr. Bonar Law; the National Union of Conservative Associations passed an indignant resolution; and the stage-hands of a West End theater, where *Romance* was embodied in Miss Doris Keane, were so deeply outraged as to lose their pristine faith in Mr. Lloyd George who must, they felt, be no more than a mere politician, if he could do such things. But Mr. Bonar Law repressed his own misgivings and returned a fitting answer to the angry deputation; and when he faced re-election on his new appointment, Dundee returned Mr. Churchill by a handsome majority.

After all, his elevation was not quite so lofty as his critics might have feared. True, he was a minister once more. But ministers were not so influential as they had been in Mr. Asquith's time. For they were under the War Cabinet, of which Mr. Churchill was not a member; and (as he wrote a little ruefully in later years) "not allowed to make the plans, I was set to make the weapons." He discharged his duty faithfully. One caller found him working hard in an old gray frock-coat and delighted to be back in harness, if only as a dutiful subordinate. It was all very different from his old official life. For he saw little of his colleagues now, and worked all day long at the Ministry of Munitions. But he had quite enough to do; and that prevented him from worrying about the war.

At first he was a little bothered by the genial disorder of a war-time Ministry, in which each one of fifty branches appeared to enjoy the privilege of equal and simultaneous access to their minister; and this slight excess of freedom was shortly remedied by the institution of a more centralized Munitions Council on the model of the Board of Admiralty. Within a month of his appointment he was casting envious eyes upon the Navy's steel consumption, proposing an intelligent reorganization of purchases in the United States, arguing about artillery requirements for the campaign of 1918, and demanding clear decisions on the problem of man-power, from whose complexities at the Ministry of National Service Mr. Neville Chamberlain had just withdrawn disconsolately to the calmer air of Birmingham. Then he was off to France on a short visit to Haig at G.H.Q. and French ministers in Paris. The empty restaurant at Calais station reminded him of former visits in the first weeks of the war, when the railway sidings were all full of Belgian engines in flight from the invasion; and they went up to Wytschaete for a look round under fire.

Haig's austerity was unfriendly to much talk at dinner. But next day Mr. Churchill paid a pleasant visit to his brother, who was with the Anzacs near Poperinghe. He was recognized and cheered by some North-country troops on the march, which pleased him; but the news from Russia, where the civic virtue of Kerensky seemed to be prevailing over the limp Bonapartism of General Korniloff, was most depressing. They drove across Picardy, and the white crosses in the graveyards reminded him of snowdrops. Before the tour was over, he had seen Foch and Loucheur and Painlevé, the new Prime Minister, and recovered something of the old feel of great affairs.

Restored to London, he was dutifully asking the War Cabinet, "What is the War Plan? When is it to reach its climax? Have we the possibility of winning in 1918, and if so, how are we going to do it?" Such questions lay beyond the competence of Mr. Churchill now. But he could still write memoranda for the War Cabinet, though his immediate concerns confined him to

such matters as steel requirements and the possibility
of using girders from unfinished buildings or the rail-
ings of Hyde Park and the novel problem of air-raid
shelters. The Prime Minister consulted him on larger
matters, though; and when the unpleasant news of
Caporetto came, he sent for Mr. Churchill. His visits
to the Continent became more frequent. He often flew
to France; and on one flight, when the engine failed
above the Channel, he began to wonder how long he
would be able to keep afloat and noticed that "a curious
calm" came over him. Someone asked him afterwards
whether he had felt afraid of dying. "No," he replied,
"I love life, but I don't fear death." After all, he had
been fairly near it in his time.

Now he was busier, although he was not yet admitted
to the control of great affairs; and his progress moved
a committee of Conservative M.P.'s to pass a resolution prohibiting the Prime Minister from taking Mr.
Churchill into the War Cabinet. But he multiplied his
surveys of the war "ostensibly" (as he confessed) "from
the Munitions standpoint"; and he was often in refreshing contact with reality behind the line in France.
In the dawn of a March morning in 1918 he listened
to the opening diapason of the German guns, as they
launched into the final onslaught by which Luden-
dorff proposed to end the war; and three days later,
when the German tide appeared to be submerging
everything in front of it, Lloyd George asked him in
the little garden at 10 Downing Street why there was
any prospect of Haig's armies, if they could not hold

their long-prepared positions, holding any others further back. He did his best to reassure the Prime Minister, and they arranged to dine together. Events, it seemed, were now almost grave enough for Mr. Churchill to be readmitted to supreme counsels; and they spent an anxious evening with the Chief of the Imperial General Staff, who was on his way to France. The harassed soldier, hard to please where politicians were concerned, found Lloyd George "on the whole . . . buoyant," Bonar Law "almost depressing," and Churchill "a real gun in a crisis."

The military situation was quite grave enough; for the Allied line, yielding to German pressure, had developed an unpleasant bulge. There were even indications that Pétain was ordering the French armies to fall back southwards in defense of Paris, leaving the British to make their own way north, as best they could, towards the English Channel. This was a strange conception of Allied strategy. But Pétain had been telling Clemenceau that the Germans would defeat the British and then turn upon the French and defeat them too. That was how Pétain, who impressed Haig as being "very much upset, almost unbalanced and most anxious," reacted to a crisis. But his old Prime Minister was more soldierly. For Clemenceau complained to the President of Pétain's pessimism, and promptly countered it by moving Foch one step nearer to supreme command. (But what would come to France, if she were ever in grave peril and there were no Foch

or Clemenceau at hand to furnish the resolve that
Pétain lacked?)

On the night of these decisions Mr. Churchill was at
Downing Street, and he breakfasted with Mr. Lloyd
George next day. For now he was living at the very
center of affairs. He had been sleeping at the Ministry
since the German break-through; and the Prime Minister sent for him to Downing Street early one morning. Lloyd George was still in bed; the bed was a sea
of papers; and its occupant wished Churchill to go out
and see the French. Before his train left Charing Cross,
he had a word with Henry Wilson. Then he crossed the
Channel in a destroyer, looked in at G.H.Q., drove on
through pouring rain to Paris, and went to bed after
midnight in an empty Ritz.

On the morrow he did Munitions business in Paris.
But early the next morning Clemenceau was greeting
"Mr. Wilson Churchill" in his best English, and promising to go everywhere and see everything with him. At
Beauvais Foch lectured them upon the slowly bright-
ening prospects of the battle with a wall-map, a large
pencil, and his inimitable pantomime; and when his
exposition was victoriously concluded, Clemenceau advanced upon him with an ecstatic cry of *"Alors, Gén-
éral, il faut que je vous embrasse."* (The will of France
in 1918 was incarnate behind the large mustaches of
that ill-assorted pair.) Their next call was at Rawlinson's headquarters, where the prevalent emotion found
more restrained expression; but it all ended in com-

plete agreement between Clemenceau and Haig about the arrival of French reinforcements.

Then the indomitable old man insisted upon going off to see some fighting on the British front. Shells whined overhead; the rifle fire was quite close; and somewhere just in front they could see a fragmentary line of British troops—the precarious front line itself. Old Clemenceau talked to some weary British officers and attended to a wounded horse. Then anxious staff officers persuaded Mr. Churchill to recall him. He had enjoyed himself immensely. *"Quel moment délicieux,"* he murmured to his guest; and when Mr. Churchill told him that he really ought not to spend too much time under fire, the old man replied, *"C'est mon grand plaisir."* (That was the school at which Mr. Churchill learned deportment for Prime Ministers in time of war.)

He was still in France, when Mr. Lloyd George arrived for the decisive conference at Beauvais on the unified command. Indeed, Mr. Churchill had telegraphed for him to come; and he drove nearly to G.H.Q. with the Prime Minister and the Chief of the Imperial General Staff. But he left them before the meeting which appointed Foch and opened a broad road to final victory. Now he was nearer the controls. His memoranda to the War Cabinet abandoned departmental points appropriate to Munitions and dealt frankly with the larger aspects of the war; and he was often with the British and French armies in that eventful summer, when the German bar began to bend.

His advice was freely offered to the Government on strategy, on the prompt shipment of American troops, on every aspect of Anglo-American co-operation (after the war he was awarded the United States' Distinguished Service Medal, presented by General Pershing), on shipping and man-power problems. His notion of a holiday was now to fly to France and spend two days with armies in the field, and he was seeing a good deal of Haig. A fair proportion of his departmental work was done in France, where he was suitably installed in a *château;* and he was in Paris, when the news of Bulgaria's collapse arrived. But he was back in London at his window in the Hotel Metropole, staring up the street towards Trafalgar Square, on the November morning when the clock pointed to eleven, and the war was over, and the bells began to ring. Then his wife came down to the office, and they drove across to see the Prime Minister with happy people clambering all over the car.

## POST-WAR

*"Thank the Lord, the war is over."*

THE CHOCOLATE SOLDIER.

# 1

THE war had been a great and, in many ways, a chastening experience for Mr. Churchill. He had gone into it at thirty-nine, a coming man. Indeed in 1914 it was not too much to say that Mr. Churchill, in charge of the most vital element in the nation's defenses, had arrived. His name ranked behind, but only just behind, those of such martial celebrities as Kitchener and French and, perhaps, in front of the relatively unknown sailors, Jellicoe and Beatty. It was not easy to discern what other politician could expect to run him close, if the war followed anything like a normal course. But wars are rarely normal; and when the Armistice arrived, his figure scarcely cast a shadow on the public scene. He had known the bitterness of failure and the first interruption of his smooth ascent towards the very top of public life.

True, he was still a minister. But ministers in 1918 were little more than background for Mr. Lloyd George. The Prime Minister was first, and the rest nowhere. For the public mind, gratefully aware of his immense personal achievement, was not greatly interested in his colleagues. Indeed, few of them were conspicuously interesting. Mr. Bonar Law lacked color quite as much as Mr. Balfour, and Lord Curzon seemed to lack novelty; Lord Milner's appeal had always been confined to specialists; and Sir Eric Geddes stimulated little more than idle speculation as to how long it would be before he returned to railway management, his brother Auckland to the medical lecture room, Sir Albert Stanley to the Underground, and even Mr. H. A. L. Fisher to his academic groves.

Somewhere in that variegated procession Mr. Churchill paced in the subordinate, and now largely meaningless, rôle of Minister of Munitions. His presence in the Government had a faint air of sufferance about it. Unsupported by anything in the nature of a popular demand or a group of personal adherents, he was largely dependent on his long-standing friendship with the Prime Minister. For the Conservatives, with a few individual exceptions, were still unsympathetic to Mr. Churchill, and the affections of Coalition Liberals were strictly confined to Mr. Lloyd George. This precarious position was in strange contrast with his brilliant prospects in 1914. But the war had run its course. The wheel had turned, and its swift revolution relegated Mr. Churchill to a secondary part. He would soon be forty-four. His Ministry had ceased to signify; and his future, like that of nearly all his colleagues, depended on Mr. Lloyd George.

Influential on the course of his career, the war was not without its influence on Mr. Churchill's views. Few men's esteem for popular opinion is increased by being seriously misjudged. Besides, his war-time contacts which had largely been confined to the soldiers and sailors served to some extent to throw him back upon his past. He had inevitably parted company with

*European*

*ARMISTICE*—Mr. Churchill, second from left, with Cabinet ministers at the Cenotaph on an Armistice Day celebration. "When the Armistice arrived, his figure scarcely cast a shadow on the public scene. He had known the bitterness of failure and the first interruption of his smooth ascent towards the very top of public life."

the main body of Liberals, who still adhered to Mr. Asquith in a sort of Opposition. But he had not drawn much nearer the Conservatives; and Labor seemed unlikely to find him a recruit. For a Minister of Munitions in time of war scarcely sees Labor at its best. The conflicting urgencies of war supply and wage demands converge upon his office; and he finds himself compelled by harsh military exigencies to follow courses which are apt to suspend his own sympathy with social causes, and to impair his popularity in those quarters where they are still cherished.

A series of munition strikes in July, 1918, by which the aircraft production program was seriously jeopardized, entailed firm action by the Minister. Coventry was gravely warned of the alternatives of war work or military service; Trade Unionists with personal experience of enemy activities at sea (supplemented, with a pleasing irony, by Suffragists who were now in the pink of patriotism) descended on the district to add their persuasions; and the strike collapsed. But though it had a happy ending, such experiences tend to leave an unhappy residue of mutual misgivings. For the Ministry of Munitions was inevitably a point of friction, equally prejudicial to Labor's view of Mr. Churchill and to Mr. Churchill's estimate of Labor; and it could hardly fail to influence his future course.

That depended at the moment on Mr. Lloyd George. The two men sat talking after dinner in the Cabinet room on the November evening when London ran wild because the war was over. In Trafalgar Square well-meaning revelers were burning German field-guns at the foot of Nelson's monument, and waves of cheerful sound drifted into the quiet room in Downing Street. They spoke about the Germans, about their enormous effort and the necessity of their participation in the new international society. There was a haunting notion that starvation and defeat might send them down the same dismal road which Russia had already traveled to social disintegration and political collapse; and Mr. Churchill was in favor of the prompt despatch of a dozen food-ships to Hamburg. The Prime Minister seemed to think something of the scheme. But it vanished on the rising mood in which the British public celebrated victory after four years of war by the General Election of 1918.

Four years of war, embellished by the German innovations of poison gas, bombing open towns, and the promiscuous murder of seafaring civilians by submarine, had banished chivalry and left British voters in a temper of vindictive justice. When the joint appeal of Mr. Lloyd George and Mr. Bonar Law invited them to confirm the Government in power, they responded handsomely, but without the slightest tendency to recommend the prisoner to mercy. Mr. Churchill had submitted his election address for the Prime Minister's approval one night at Walton Heath. But when he reached Dundee, he found his eloquence keeping pace as best it could with public indignation on a mounting tide of reparations and indemnities. He had felt (and expressed to his colleagues) some private misgivings on the picturesque expedient of prosecuting Kaiser Wilhelm. But the electors of Dundee insisted; and Mr. Churchill returned to Westminster with the commitments common to all supporters of the Coalition.

He had already reversed the engines at the Ministry of Munitions. Industrial demobilization was in full swing; and it would shortly be succeeded by the detailed problems of disposing of the nation's vast military surpluses. But Mr. Churchill's energies were required elsewhere. The Prime Minister invited him to choose between the Admiralty and the War Office; either appointment would carry with it the Air Ministry, which it was not proposed to maintain in being as a separate department. He took a night for consideration, and chose the Admiralty. But in the interval an increase of Army demobilization difficulties led Mr. Lloyd George to feel the need of an enterprising Secretary of State for War and he pressed Mr. Churchill to reverse his choice. No other course was possible; and while the Navy passed under the peaceful rule of Mr. Walter Long, Mr. Churchill went to the War Office in the third week of 1919.

2

Now he was Secretary of State for War, with a promise from Mr. Lloyd George that Cabinet ministers would soon be restored to their old importance. For Mr. Churchill throve in Cabinet, in free discussion, in the frequent circulation of well-turned memoranda to his colleagues; and he was less at home in the war-time system which confined ministers to the depressing solitude of their own departmental business in dutiful obedience to the War Cabinet.

Not that War Office business lacked interest in 1919. There was an Army of close on four million men, impatient to be demobilized upon a labor market whose ability to absorb them was highly doubtful. Too much haste might glut the market, already overcrowded by its immense intake from the demobilization of the munitions industries, and thus precipitate civilian unemployment; while too little speed in demobilization could very easily produce the equally unpleasing alternative of military unrest, of a rising sense of injustice among men detained under discipline long after its apparent need had vanished in victory, of insubordination and even mutiny. Either prospect was unpleasing and not without alarming features for public men who had just been enabled to observe the devastating consequences of a collapse of discipline in Russia.

True, Britain was not Russia; there was nothing comparable in the mild grievances of British politics to the accumulated discontents that formed the irresistible motive-power of the Russian Revolution. But the spectacle of a society in liquidation, of swift and satisfying vengeance, of the bleak beginnings of a new community constructed upon unfamiliar premises was more than disconcerting, when it was accompanied with vociferous intimations that the same agreeable process would shortly be repeated, with the necessary local variations, in other countries.

While the Russian drama of 1917 was still so very near and Communism lived in an uncomfortable phase of preaching world-revolution, it was not surprising that the thought of Russia was often in men's minds, and that their judgment was occasionally distorted by false analogies.

These apprehensions hung about him, as Mr. Churchill went to the War Office in January, 1919. There was some disapproval of the appointment; and Henry Wilson, who had reached the eminence of Chief of the Imperial General Staff by combining an unwavering distaste for politicians with a faithful reproduction of their methods, wrote "Whew!" in his diary. For it was one thing to applaud Mr. Churchill's energy from a respectful distance; but it might be quite another to have a departmental chief who knew his mind, and would not necessarily prove wholly amenable to Wilson's blandishments. Besides, the soldier disapproved of the arrangement by which his Secretary of State absorbed the functions of Air Minister, and asked a trifle cavalierly at their first meeting where the Admiralty came in. But the major problem of demobilization faced them, complicated by the further need of finding men for the remaining duties in the British Army on the Rhine, in Ireland, and in various outlying theaters of diminishing activity.

Sporadic disorder, the unauthorized arrival in Whitehall of stray parties of excited soldiers in borrowed army lorries, and a slight tendency to use impressive Russian names for simple British institutions alarmed the official mind with visions of Soldiers' Councils in the act of fraternizing with workmen and peasants. It had its graver aspect, though; and Mr. Churchill was prompt with the production of a scheme for the creation of a post-war army. The mercurial Wilson approved his efforts; and they went off to Paris, where Lloyd George was already deep in the Peace Conference, in order to obtain the final sanction.

On the way home he talked as freely as he always had. Russia was a good deal in his mind. Was it not his official duty to preserve Britain from the uncomfortable fate of Russia? Besides, his sympathies were strongly affected by the course of Russian events. The bare anonymity of pure collectivism made no appeal to Mr. Churchill. A picturesque society had vanished in distressing circumstances, which left some observers indisposed to calculate the folly and brutality by which it had invited its own destruction; and its successors seemed determined to repeat the same drastic reconstruction wherever they could find a hearing. For Communism in the age of Trotsky was in a missionary mood, to which the transformation of Russia meant no more than a first installment of the world-revolution. Few English fancies turned in such directions in 1919, and Mr. Churchill's was not among the few.

It was not easy for his chivalry to overlook the deep debt incurred by the Allies to the Czar's armies in the first years of the war or to forget that officers, by whom the German pressure in the West had often been relieved in the course of 1914 and 1915, were now unhappy victims of the revolution or in the field opposing it as White partisans. That circumstance inevitably inclined his mind against it. Nor could it be denied that the collapse of Russia had been a direct consequence of failure at the Dardanelles. If only they had forced the Straits, a steady stream of munitions must have ensured the fighting-power of the Russian armies, and defeat might never have become the breeding-ground of revolution. Now the harsh decision of the Dardanelles could never be reversed; but it was tempting to undo, if that were possible, one of its most devastating consequences.

That was his approach to Russian problems. But Mr. Churchill had no share of responsibility for the origins of military intervention by the Allies in Russia, which dated from 1918. At that time such questions of high policy lay far beyond the competence of a Minister of Munitions; and when superior authorities decided to arrest the flow of German influence in time of war across the prostrate spaces of a disintegrating Russia, it was not his affair. Yet it had been quite reasonable to protect the vast accumulations of military stores at the White Sea ports and oil in Transcaucasia, and even to attempt the reconstruction of an Eastern Front in place of the Czar's vanished armies, by the despatch of Allied forces to Siberia and the support of such Russian forces as were still willing to fight on.

When the war ended, it was decided in spheres loftier than those occupied by Mr. Churchill to persist in these commitments; and on reaching the War Office, he inherited far-flung responsibilities on several fronts in Russia with an uncomfortable certainty of diminishing resources. He was already writing to Lloyd George that he was unhappy about Russia; and as he drove to Amiens after their Paris conference on Army matters, he was talking about the possibility of action by British, French, and American volunteers. Acutely conscious that the splendid war-time period of common effort by a united nation was over now, he was anxious to retain the collective energies of ex-service men for public purposes.

His Liberal objectives—higher wages, cheaper housing—still attracted him; and he spoke gratefully of the lessons that he had learned in war-time. His speaking had, he thought, improved; and he descanted on the new duty of a statesman to look cheerful. He was sometimes the reverse himself, when his mind was busy; but he explained that it would not do, that it was the smiling age, that whereas statesmen had once looked solemn, nowadays the smile was all the fashion—the Lloyd George smile, the Woodrow Wilson smile . . . He was happier, he said, than he had ever been, with strong affection for Lloyd George and a sad backward glance at Asquith. For his immense gusto never left him, so long as there was work for him to do. As they passed the ranked crosses of a war cemetery, "Poor fellows," he remarked, "I wish they had lived to see the end of the war."

But the war was over now, and he was hard at work in the Secretary of State's big room. A caller at the War

Office found him "in good form, very energetic and cheerful." The pressing problems of demobilization and recruiting were yielding to firm treatment. But Russian policy was still distressingly ambiguous. In those early weeks of 1919 the habitable world was governed from the ornate rooms in Paris, where the collective wisdom of Lloyd George, Clemenceau, and Woodrow Wilson presided over the uneasy birth of a new dispensation. But its masters seemed in some uncertainty whether to admit Soviet Russia to the family of nations, or to continue their sporadic encouragement of those Russian elements which were still in arms against it.

Mr. Churchill had fewer doubts; and as British military aid in the form of technical advice and surplus army stores formed a large ingredient in any policy involving the continuation of the Civil War, it was essential for the War Office to know precisely where it stood. He had been pressing the Prime Minister, whose natural instinct was to leave Russian questions to be settled by the Russian people and to come to terms, if possible, with its nominees. But this was not quite so simple as it looked; and in February, Lloyd George agreed that Winston Churchill should seek a decision at the judgment-seat in Paris.

When they reached the Quai d'Orsay in the gloom of a winter afternoon, a full session on the future League of Nations was in progress (with Mrs. Woodrow Wilson in attendance); and the martial intelligence of Sir Henry Wilson was shocked by "nauseating nonsense about peace, etc." The President of the United States was due to leave that evening for Cherbourg on his way back to Washington for an attempt to deal with his critics in the Senate. For America showed a distracted world the way back to the delightful, if destructive, pursuit of peace-time politics. But he found time for a short meeting before dinner, in which somebody asked a question about the Dutch, and Mr. Churchill raised the Russian dilemma.

The President, who had already got up to go, listened politely to his argument and delivered an ambiguous oracle leaning on the back of Clemenceau's chair. Then he left to catch his train. Next day the subject was resumed under the chairmanship of Clemenceau's formidable skull-cap and gloves; and the Supreme Council proceeded without undue haste towards something in the nature of a decision. Lloyd George, who was inclined to be skeptical about his colleague's Russian anxieties, was not encouraging. But a degree of precision had been achieved; and the War Office proceeded with a comprehensive program of extricating British troops from Archangel and Transcaucasia, while Admiral Koltchak and General Denikin were to be supported in the Civil War with military stores and instructional staffs.

Spring turned to summer; and as the peace treaty took shape in Paris, Mr. Churchill's departmental round went on at the War Office. His faithful secretary concealed his healthy taste for polo among the sober round of his official appointments under the discreet alias (borrowed from the stately vocabulary of the French army) of "Collective Equitation." Few ministers play polo at forty-four. But Mr. Churchill retained his vigor.

That autumn he was even anxious to go out to Russia and see things for himself. It had always been his way. But Lloyd George dissuaded him, and he continued to preside at long range over the slow dissolution of the Russian situation. Before another winter came to the White Sea, the war-weary British conscripts of the Archangel garrison were extricated under cover of a newly-raised contingent of British troops, who protected their evacuation and finally withdrew themselves after a vigorous diversion. Koltchak subsided gradually through the unhappy year, and Denikin's generous supply of British stores was insufficient to resist the rising tide of Bolshevism. General Yudenitch hung on the edge of Petrograd with a delusive air of victory; but he got no further than Gatchina. The British left Siberia; the French left Odessa; and as resistance ebbed, Soviet authority spread steadily behind the Red armies. For a half-hearted negative could not withstand a fixed and single purpose; and if Allied intervention in the Civil War had failed, it failed because it was never seriously tried.

Although the enterprise had been conducted with French, American, Italian, and Japanese assistance and, so far as Britain was concerned, with full Cabinet approval, the public mind at home identified the unsuccessful (and, as many felt, superfluous) experiment

with Mr. Churchill. For the British part in the operations obviously fell within the sphere of War Office
responsibility; and he made no effort to conceal his
sympathies. True, he insisted on the primary necessity
for Russian to be "saved, as I pray she may be saved,
by Russians." But he was in no uncertainty as to what
she must be saved from and by which Russians. That
followed naturally from his prepossessions on the subject.

But the consequences for Mr. Churchill did not end
with the last flicker of resistance to the Soviet. For his
uncompromising attitude renewed the old uneasy impression that he was more active than he should be.
There was a feeling among the growing number of his
Liberal and Labor critics that he had been in favor of a
wanton prolongation of the war, that his restlessness
would have denied his countrymen the deep repose for
which they longed in 1919. His popularity could only
suffer from such impressions except in circles which
welcomed anti-Bolshevik activities *à tout prix;* and
the effect on his political alignment might be serious.
For Coalition Liberals, eager to emphasize the few remaining traces of their Liberalism, hastened to repudi-
ate reactionary courses; and Conservatives, collaborat-
ing in the Coalition with their progressive opposites,
were growing out of the more obstinate phases of Con-
servatism.

A crusade in Russia was inacceptable to either group;
and though the limitations of Allied policy had precluded anything faintly resembling a crusade and Mr.

Churchill's enterprise had been almost confined in practice to an ineffective series of evacuations, the popular belief that he would have preferred something more vigorous was disturbing to the public mind.

His War Office duties were all performed as thoroughly as his departmental work was always done. He favored an extensive project for amalgamating the War Office, Admiralty, and Air Ministry under a single Minister of Defence—with few doubts as to the most suitable incumbent and a friendly notion of Lord Hugh Cecil and Captain Guest for two of his Under-Secretaries. But the Prime Minister seemed unconvinced; and Mr. Churchill waited twenty years to become Minister of Defence until he was Prime Minister himself. That summer he toured the Rhineland to inspect the Army of Occupation; and 1919 went out upon the slowly darkening scene in Russia and an unpleasant drift towards civil war in Ireland. It was plain that 1920 was going to be generally uncomfortable, and Mr. Churchill watched without enthusiasm developments which he was comparatively powerless to influence. The dwindling Army was administered with care, and he made an effort to reconstitute the Territorials. But the War Office, with no problems left worth mentioning, had ceased to be a focal point in 1920; and early the next year he was transferred to the Colonial Office with the somewhat livelier responsibilities in the form of Palestine and Mesopotamia.

3

When Mr. Churchill became Colonial Secretary in January, 1921, his main preoccupations lay in the Middle East. He had already made acquaintance with the military aspect of its problems at the War Office, although he assured a high official that he had a virgin mind (eliciting the slightly menacing response that his visitor was there to ravish it); and he took steps to simplify the administration of the area by unified control centered in the Colonial Office. For Arab questions had been scarcely manageable under an eccentric system by which the Foreign Office had administered Palestine and Trans-Jordania, while the India Office controlled Irak. These troubled regions were now transferred to a new Middle East Department of the Colonial Office; and the Secretary of State, resolved upon heroic expedients, enlisted Colonel Lawrence in his administrative team.

This intractable eccentric, whose war service in Arabia had revealed an unmanageable blend of egoism and ability, was the most singular of Mr. Churchill's conquests. For he ran satisfactorily in departmental harness, attended to his business, and collaborated in the production of a general settlement which satisfied his own exacting sense of justice. The divergent claims of Arab sentiment, war-time promises, British interests, and Zionist appeals were not easily reconciled; but, in Lawrence's opinion, Mr. Churchill "in a few weeks made straight all the tangle, finding solutions fulfilling

(I think) our promises in letter and spirit (where humanly possible) without sacrificing any interest of our Empire or any interest of the peoples concerned." Better still, his presentation copy of *The Seven Pillars* testified that Mr. Churchill "made a happy ending to this show."

Following his usual inclination, the Secretary of State had studied matters on the spot. In the spring he presided at a conference in Cairo, which had excellent results so far as the Middle East was concerned and gave him a splendid opportunity to paint the Pyramids. But its immediate effect on his political career was less beneficial. For while Mr. Churchill was away in Egypt, Mr. Bonar Law resigned and the Prime Minister was left to find a new second-in-command.

There was some expectation that Mr. Churchill would become Chancellor of the Exchequer. But promotion rarely comes to absentees; and he was left at the Colonial Office, while the appointment of Sir Robert Horne to the Treasury preserved the Coalition's party equipoise. His Middle Eastern settlement, by which King Feisal was established in Irak and the situation in Palestine was stabilized by the White Paper, gave some promise of enduring peace; and Lawrence sang his *Nunc dimittis*. Mr. Churchill offered him a career in Colonial administration. But the elusive stylist answered that the job was done, and that it would last, and that all his minister would see of him was a small cloud of dust on the horizon. It had been an unusual partnership.

Stranger associations waited for him that year, as the Irish tragedy veered towards settlement. He was a member of the Cabinet committee which negotiated endlessly in Downing Street with Griffith and Collins; and as the interminable rigmarole proceeded, Mr. Churchill's initial aversion from his country's enemies was changed to something like regard, so far as Michael Collins was concerned. After all, the Government (as he once told the Irishman) had put a price upon his head two hundred times as large as the Boer estimate of his own value. For Dublin Castle's offer of £5,000 for Collins compared favorably with the more modest £25 reward for the recapture of Winston Churchill.

When the treaty had been signed, he became officially responsible for its administration; and his departmental life in 1922 was filled with its uneasy aftermath. Walking warily between Sinn Fein and Ulster, he trod the burning lava of boundary questions and Southern Loyalists and troop movements and the Royal Irish Constabulary. Sir James Craig and Michael Collins met in his room at the Colonial Office; and he persisted in the effort to close the Irish Question once and for all. (Had it not been one of his early ambitions to bring in a Home Rule Bill?) But statesmen who handle Irish problems move in an over-heated world where suspicions of impartiality are invariably fatal and are apt to lose their friends on both sides; and Mr. Churchill's Irish activities did something to increase his political isolation. Collins had sent him a farewell message— "Tell Winston we could never have done anything without him." But soon Collins was dead, and Ireland was once again a depressing battlefield of Irishmen in conflict. Yet Mr. Churchill had done more than a little to withdraw Britain from the unhappy contest and to stabilize the Irish Free State.

Ireland, though, was not his sole anxiety. Russia was bad enough; but Turkey was a more immediate menace. It was no easy matter to reconcile Mustapha Kemal's noble dream of a resurgent Turkey with M. Venizelos' no less noble dream of an equally, if not more, resurgent Greece. Mr. Lloyd George was consistently pro-Greek, and his policy prevailed over Mr. Churchill's frequent and well-argued misgivings.

A Greek defeat in the heart of Anatolia was followed by a disheartened retreat towards the sea; and in September, 1922, swift Turkish victory reversed the peace treaty, swept the Greeks out of Asia, and bore down upon the Allied Army of Occupation in the neutral zone of Constantinople and the Dardanelles. It was an extremely unpleasant situation; and Mr. Churchill had continually questioned the policy from which it sprang. But situations must be faced, and he was no less reluctant than most of his colleagues to yield to Turkish force what might be conceded to Turkish argument.

The British position at the Straits was quite defensible, and the Cabinet resolved to defend it. On their instructions the Colonial Secretary drafted an inquiry to the Dominions, inviting their association with the British action and offers to send Dominion troops to defend the Dardanelles. He also obliged his colleagues by composing a reasoned statement of the case for publication in the press, which unfortunately reached the Dominions in advance of the official inquiry and consequently caused some embarrassment. At Chanak the French and Italian contingents were withdrawn by an obscure maneuver of French diplomacy, leaving the British to confront the rising flood of Turks. There was no reason to suppose that an attack could not be dealt with effectively; and in London Mr. Churchill was busy co-ordinating the operations of the three Services. But after an uncomfortable interval the scare subsided. There was no attack; an armistice was signed; and silence settled once again on the quiet cemeteries at the Dardanelles.

Although there had been no explosion, this imbroglio was followed by grave consequences in domestic politics. The Tory elements of the Coalition had been feeling unsettled for some time. Preserved in 1918 and afterwards by their association with Mr. Lloyd George, many Conservatives were disconcerted by the unduly progressive policies to which he had subsequently committed them in Ireland and elsewhere. Besides, his personal ascendancy was wearing thin; and the silent masses of the Tory rank and file were ripe for a reversion to party independence. Mr. Bonar Law, who had returned to politics, favored a break-away; and the prospects of a continued Coalition were obscure.

Its Liberal components, whose future as a personal

following of Mr. Lloyd George was problematic, favored a prolongation of the combine; and Mr. Churchill advocated the formation of a National Party. His view was shared by Lord Birkenhead, and the more intelligent of his Conservative colleagues were reluctant to desert Mr. Lloyd George.

This delicate position was not improved by the Chanak crisis, which left a strong impression that the country had been brought to the brink of war on issues in which it was not conspicuously interested. So far as Mr. Churchill was concerned, the unhappy chance which had located the storm-center at the Dardanelles revived old memories injurious to his career. The telegrams to the Dominions passed through his office; his pen had drafted the press statement on the subject. That was all the public knew. Was Mr. Churchill eager to renew old struggles between Turk and Anzac on the bare hill-sides of Gallipoli, where the wire of seven years ago still rusted? Nothing could be further from the facts; but the appearances were damaging.

The disintegration of the Government was accelerated by the Turkish crisis. Through the autumn of 1922 Mr. Churchill was busily engaged in keeping it together; and Balfour, Austen Chamberlain, Curzon, and Birkenhead seemed willing to collaborate. But Curzon fell away during the crisis at Chanak; and in October the Conservatives, in conclave at the Carlton Club, destroyed the Coalition. The dim figure of Mr. Bonar Law had re-emerged to lead them; and the silence of their discontented rank and file was aptly epitomized in Mr. Stanley Baldwin, whose contributions in Cabinet had been mainly confined to the steady music of his pipe. (That was Mr. Lloyd George's chief recollection of his latest President of the Board of Trade.)

The Prime Minister and his more enterprising colleagues were challenged by this sober figure in the decisive meeting at the Carlton Club; the avenging march of the mediocrities was irresistible; and the Coalition ceased to exist. Its violent decease was followed by a confused and (so far as Mr. Churchill was concerned) highly unsatisfactory General Election. Immediately before it he went down with appendicitis; and while he languished in a London nursing-home, Dundee was fought by Mrs. Churchill and his friends.

The atmosphere was unpropitious. For the flowing tide was with the critics of the Government; events in Russia and at the Dardanelles had been unfavorable to Mr. Churchill's popularity; and his supporters' meetings were uniformly stormy. Two days before the poll he arrived in the constituency. It was only three weeks since his operation, and with an unhealed wound of serious dimensions he attempted to address the electors of Dundee from an invalid chair. Angry faces, shaken fists, and systematic interruption greeted him; and he lost the seat by a large majority. So the Coalition had collapsed; and Mr. Churchill was out of office and, for the first time since 1900, out of Parliament as well.

4

The early months of 1923 saw him a convalescent, who seemed a long way from recovering his health and still further from restoration to his place in public life. The South of France afforded him a milder climate than Dundee, and brighter colors (he always liked bright colors) to put on canvas. As he climbed slowly back to health, he professed without conviction to be getting used to "sitting in arm-chairs in front of the fire and going to sleep." But he filled his leisure with a vigorous return to authorship. For the first volume of his *World Crisis* was nearly finished.

Few men were better qualified to write a comprehensive survey of the war years. Mr. Churchill had been a member of the Cabinet which faced the coming of the war; his position at the Admiralty placed him at the very center of Britain's war preparations; and he had played a leading part in war direction for the first ten months. The first installment, which took the story to the end of 1914, was a stately exercise in the grand manner. Sometimes, perhaps, the author was a shade too eloquent for the requirements of the written word, and there was a suspicion of a pause for cheers at the end of some of its resounding paragraphs. For it was twenty years since he had tried to write a book; and in the interval he had become an orator. Sometimes his keen appreciation of the drama of events led him to over-dramatize a little. The sober operations of Sir Edward Grey were scarcely recognizable in his excited whisper:

> A sentence in a despatch, an observation by an ambassador, a cryptic phrase in a Parliament seemed sufficient to adjust from day to day the balance of the prodigious structure. Words counted, and even whispers. A nod could be made to tell.

But when the situation called for a touch of drama, his method was impeccable; and nothing could be better than his treatment of von Spee's horrified discovery of Sturdee's battle-cruisers at the Falkland Islands:

> A few minutes later a terrible apparition broke upon German eyes. Rising from behind the promontory, sharply visible in the clear air, were a pair of tripod masts. One glance was enough. They meant certain death. The day was beautifully fine, and from the tops the horizon extended thirty or forty miles in every direction. There was no hope for victory. There was no chance of escape. A month before, another Admiral and his sailors had suffered a similar experience.

Fortified with a wealth of official documents, *The World Crisis* was an iridescent blend of history and personal reminiscence, of which Balfour wrote sardonically that he was "immersed in Winston's brilliant Autobiography, disguised as a history of the universe."

But history was a poor substitute for action; and in 1923 his prospects of a return to active politics seemed highly doubtful. Indeed, it was not altogether clear on what side he belonged. Progressive persons were inclined to view him as an emblem of unconcealed reaction. Mr. H. G. Wells, indefatigable midwife of the future, diagnosed him without affection, since Mr. Churchill's attitude to the latest manifestations of progress in Russia was a sad disappointment:

> He believes quite naively that he belongs to a peculiarly gifted and privileged class of beings to whom the lives and affairs of common men are given over, the raw material of brilliant careers. His imagination is obsessed by dreams of exploits and a career. It is an imagination closely akin to the d'Annunzio type. In England, d'Annunzio would have been a Churchill; in Italy, Churchill would have been a d'Annunzio. He is a great student and collector of the literature of Napoleon I, that master adventurer. Before all things he desires a dramatic world with villains—and one hero . . .

This was hardly just. But it was typical of a contemporary tendency to caricature Mr. Churchill in cast-off Napoleonic uniforms, of which Mr. Wells produced a full-length version in his *Men Like Gods*. The idyllic peace of one of those prophetic blends of nudism and University Extension, by which the author's fancy was attracted, was sharply interrupted by the arrival of an entertaining travesty of Mr. Churchill, accompanied by his faithful (and no less unsympathetically delineated) private secretary. The externals are brilliantly portrayed, if without undue tenderness:

> He put back his coat-tails, rested his hands on his hips, thrust his head forward, regarded his audience for a moment with an expression half cunning, half defiant, muttered something inaudible and began.

His opening was not prepossessing. There was some slight impediment in his speech, the little brother of a lisp, against which his voice beat gutturally. His first few sentences had an effect of being jerked out by unsteady efforts . . .

As the speech went on, his listeners "forgot that slight impediment and the thickness of the voice that said these things"; and a fair reproduction of Mr. Churchill's platform eloquence conveys a ruthless panegyric of "the bracing and ennobling threat and the purging and terrifying experience of war." Equipped with such opinions, his caricature inevitably abhorred the ordered sanctity of summer underwear and pure research, of which the slightly anæmic future seemed to consist, and planned a highly anti-social conquest of the world with a head full of martial dreams. This might not be how Mr. Churchill really felt. But if he could be made to look like that (and his Russian projects, combined with the unfortunate coincidence of a recurrence of the Dardanelles, contributed to the effect), it was doubtful whether he would be able to return to the progressive side of politics.

Where, then, did he belong? The kaleidoscope of party politics was strangely disarranged in 1923. Reading from Left to Right, it ranged from Labor, which professed its faith in Socialism, by way of Mr. Asquith's Independent Liberals, who were receptive of all forms of progress excepting any advocated by Mr. Lloyd George, to Mr. Lloyd George's slightly ambiguous Coalition Liberals and the solid mass of the Conservatives. As Mr. Churchill was a little apt to view Socialism as halfway to Moscow, he was plainly excluded from communion with Labor; and a pillar of the Coalition Government was obviously ineligible for reunion with Mr. Asquith.

He was, in actual fact, a Coalition Liberal. But was he likely to remain so? His leading interest appeared to be the preservation of his country from a revolution, though he diverted Mr. Asquith, who was seated next to him at a royal wedding, with a progressive housing policy—"Build the house round the wife and mother: let her always have water on the boil: make her the central factor, the dominating condition, of the situation . . ." (He was building one himself just then at Westerham on the magnificent proceeds of *The World Crisis.*)

Close friendship and long association united him to Mr. Lloyd George; but there was manifestly some divergence in their views. For Mr. Churchill's antirevolutionary bias inclined him towards association with Conservatives, and Mr. Lloyd George had escaped from the Coalition with evident relief. He had never shared Mr. Churchill's misgivings about Russia, and Mr. Churchill had not succumbed to the Gladstonian glamour of the Greeks. Differing to some extent on foreign policy, their views were no less incompatible at home. It had been one thing for them to campaign together on social causes in the relative stability of Edwardian society. But it was quite another matter to toy lightly with established institutions in an epoch which had witnessed the disintegration of entire communities; and if Mr. Lloyd George was blind to the increasing gravity of the situation, that could only mean that Mr. Churchill was unlikely to remain a Liberal for long.

But he was hardly a Conservative in 1923. Conservative at heart by virtue of his general antipathy to world-revolution and to anything that might lead in that direction, he was by no means Conservative in party allegiance. For the party was controlled by the same stolid elements which had consistently obstructed his career, to say nothing of his father's. Its mediocrities had barred Lord Randolph's way; his son had been dismissed from the Admiralty in 1915 at the behest of mediocrity, conveyed by Mr. Bonar Law; embattled mediocrities had steadily opposed his subsequent advancement; and the meeting at the Carlton Club which killed the Coalition, was a crowning triumph of party mediocrity. Its favorites were now installed in office under the dim leadership of Mr. Bonar Law, with Mr. Baldwin at his elbow. Ability had been discarded as a test of public men in favor of a more passive quality ambiguously defined as "character." For ability might lead to enterprise, enterprise to action; and who knew what might happen then?

True, he had friends among the Conservatives. But Birkenhead and Austen Chamberlain were almost equally suspect of intellectual activity; and Tory mediocrity kept them in quarantine after their dangerous association with Mr. Lloyd George, while office was reserved for the more stationary (if more sterling) intellects of Stanley Baldwin, Edward Wood, Neville Chamberlain, and Joynson-Hicks. It was the apotheosis of the second-rate. A company of this caliber was unlikely to welcome Mr. Churchill as a returning prodigal, and he retained a formal allegiance to the Coalition Liberals.

He was clear about his destination, though. For he informed a London audience that spring that Liberals and Conservatives ought to collaborate in order to avert the graver menace of government by Socialists. Later in the year he published a second volume of his *World Crisis*. Dealing with events in 1915, it tended to revive old controversies on the subject of the Dardanelles with the unhappy consequence that Mr. Churchill appeared to be a politician with a past rather than with a future. Indeed, his future was slightly complicated by Mr. Baldwin's impulsive action in dissolving Parliament late in 1923 on the issue of Protection.

If Mr. Churchill was plainly headed for the Conservatives, it was hardly possible for him to take the plunge upon their sudden challenge to Free Trade. For that was the very issue upon which he left them twenty years before. Besides, he was not a Protectionist. But in his choice of a constituency he emphasized the fact that his major interest was in the defeat of Socialism. For he refused the offer among others, of a relatively promising seat in Manchester and went off to oppose a Socialist at West Leicester. Fighting as a Coalition Liberal, he recited the familiar litany of Free Trade argument; but he turned his main attention to the refutation of Labor doctrines. These were largely supplemented from his audiences by retrospective and often disorderly denunciations of the Dardanelles, and he was beaten once again.

As 1924 opened upon the installation of a Labor Government with Liberal support, things were growing serious for Mr. Churchill. He would soon be fifty; he had suffered two defeats without apparent prospect of retrieving them; and he was in some danger of becoming perilously isolated. That was hardly to his taste. Life as an anti-Socialist Stylite on a lonely pillar in the political Thebaid would lead nowhere. But it seemed to be his melancholy portion in 1924. For his isolation from the Liberals was inevitable in view of their unhappy lapse in putting Socialists in office, from which he dissented publicly; and the Conservatives were hardly showing signs of roasting fatted calves against the hour of his return.

But he was unlikely to remain in solitude for long. He has written shrewdly on the uses of the wilderness to prophets. Such lonely intervals afford valuable opportunities of uninterrupted thought; but the resulting prophecies require a sounding-board for their effective delivery. That, in the case of politicians, is supplied by affiliation to a party; and if Mr. Churchill seemed to have none at the moment, he would probably procure one before very long. For it would never do to linger on as a disgruntled Liberal. That was how his father had wasted the last years of his political career; and Winston Churchill had already learned the lesson of Lord Randolph's tragedy.

Twenty years before he had followed his opinions boldly into the Liberal party. Now they seemed to lead back to the Conservatives. If the French Revolution had transformed Burke's party affiliations without impropriety, there seemed no reason why the Russian Revolution should not do the same for Mr. Churchill's. The Conservatives were more receptive now. For the adversity of Opposition had reconciled them to Mr. Churchill's old associates in the Coalition Government. His Tory friends were out of quarantine, and now there were sympathetic eyes among Conservatives to watch his evolution.

A further opportunity to indicate the course to which his compass pointed came early in 1924. Soon after the General Election a vacancy occurred in the Abbey Division of Westminster, and Mr. Churchill stood as an Independent Anti-Socialist. Though an official Conservative was in the field, his candidature was supported by a considerable body of influential Conservatives, including Lord Balfour, Lord Birkenhead, Austen Chamberlain, and Lord Rothermere's publicity no less than his heir.

The contest was enlivened by a galaxy of fashionable, sporting, and theatrical participants; and the finish was extremely close. Indeed, at one time Mr. Churchill was thought to be in by a hundred votes. He was out by forty, though. But this time defeat brought him appreciably nearer to success. For Conservatives acclaimed him as a fighting advocate, and he reciprocated by a public offer of co-operation and a modified acceptance of applied Protection. His ship was nearing port; and that autumn, when he contested Epping at the General Election, he fought as a Constitutionalist (a vague denomination carrying the somewhat sweeping implication that King, Lords, and Commons were in equal danger from his blameless Liberal and Labor rivals). There was no rival Conservative, and he was duly elected to the House of Commons once again.

But the General Election of 1924 brought Mr. Churchill more than re-election. For when Mr. Baldwin formed his new Government, the ban on average intelligence was raised. True, Sir William Joynson-Hicks became Home Secretary and Mr. Neville Chamberlain reverted to the Ministry of Health. But Austen Chamberlain went to the Foreign Office, Lord Birkenhead to the India Office, and Winston Churchill (by the most surprising promotion of them all) to the Treasury. So the prodigal was home indeed.

5

A Conservative once more, Mr. Churchill faced the world towards the end of 1924 as Chancellor of the Exchequer in Mr. Baldwin's second Government. He put on his father's robes of office, which Lady Randolph had preserved for nearly thirty years (although she was not there to see him in them now); and as he put them on, there was a feeling that his full career had been neatly rounded off. He would be fifty in a week or so, and he had sat in almost every ministerial seat in Whitehall and its neighborhood—Board of Trade, Home Office, Admiralty, War Office, Munitions, Colonial Office, and now the Treasury.

In view of his unusual party record it seemed unlikely that he would ever scale the final slope and find himself Prime Minister. For elevation to that height implies election to the party leadership; and under normal circumstances few parties acquiesce in being led by a returning prodigal, especially when a fair proportion of their members have their doubts as to whether the guest of honor is really a good party man. Indeed, there was not much in Mr. Churchill's record to suggest that he possessed that sober quality. But there he was, safely installed in Mr. Baldwin's Cabinet; and when he next contested Epping, he fought (and held) the seat as a plain Conservative without further subtleties on the subject of his political allegiance.

Few Chancellors of the Exchequer are quite as memorable as they seem. For most budgets cast a longer shadow on the year which they affect than on the course of history, since their consequences are (with rare exceptions) less durable than those of other acts of policy and legislation. Budget history is almost as perishable as the annals of the stage with which, indeed, it has something in common. For there is a wealth of traditional effects—the deep, preliminary secrecy; the smiling progress to the House of Commons; the antique despatch box; and then the lengthy exposition, opening with an endless survey and approaching with coy reluctance the only passages that anybody wants to hear.

Mr. Churchill played the part with gusto, even adding a new line to the familiar business with concealed refreshments in the course of his first budget speech ("It is imperative that I should fortify the revenue, and this I shall now . . .").

His financial operations failed to command the approval of Mr. J. M. Keynes, who devoted a spirited pamphlet to *The Economic Consequences of Mr. Churchill;* and the asperity of Mr. Philip Snowden's criticisms in the House of Commons produced an annual fixture which assumed an almost sporting character by virtue of both combatants' ability to give and receive punishment. But that was Mr. Churchill's function on the Treasury Bench, over whose other occupants he towered (as Lord Oxford wrote with genial condescension), "a Chimborazo or Everest among the sand-hills of the Baldwin Cabinet."

Not that these more modest eminences were uniformly at their ease in his shadow. For one thing, it was not cast exclusively upon Treasury business. That came, to any serious extent, but once a year; but Mr. Churchill came more often. For it had always been his way to favor his Cabinet colleagues with memoranda upon affairs in general wholly irrespective of their strict relevance to his own ministerial duties.

After all, if Cabinets enjoyed the burden of collective responsibility, there was no valid reason why their

BRICKLAYER—Mr. Churchill at his country home, Chartwell, with Albert Einstein. The brick wall in the background might have been built with his own hands, for he is an expert bricklayer. At one time the Bricklayers Union admitted him to membership, but later called in his card because they objected to accepting a Tory politician as a member.

members should not make copious and well-reasoned contributions on the subject of their common problems. Besides, he had practical experience of almost every department. This method, which had served him well enough with Mr. Asquith and Sir Edward Grey, was less favorably received in the era of Mr. Baldwin and Sir William Joynson-Hicks; and the Prime Minister complained with feeling that "a Cabinet meeting when Winston was present did not have the opportunity of considering its proper agenda, for the reason that invariably it had first to deal with some extremely clever memorandum submitted by him on the work of some department other than his own."

Cleverness was not, on Mr. Baldwin's lips, a term of praise; and nothing could be more unsettling than a colleague who persisted in thinking for himself in all directions. The Prime Minister transmitted these misgivings to his heir; and when Mr. Chamberlain succeeded in due course to Mr. Baldwin's grim inheritance, they helped materially to exclude Mr. Churchill from his Government.

But though his less enterprising colleagues watched him with some anxiety, they availed themselves of Mr. Churchill's versatility in the cold spring of 1926, when an interminable dispute about the mines turned swiftly to the General Strike. The Trade Unions' attempt to paralyze the community into acquiescence in their view of a just settlement was unsuccessful largely because it tried a pre-war weapon on a post-war public.

An essential element in the maintenance of confidence was the continued dissemination of news. Broadcasting had not yet become a universal medium, and the newspapers had practically vanished. In these circumstances there was a good deal to be said for improving an official journal; and who was a more likely editor than Mr. Churchill? True, he had done nothing of the kind before. But his colleagues entertained a touching faith in his journalistic experience, and presently he found himself in charge of the presses of the *Morning Post* with editorial control of a new daily paper named the *British Gazette*. It managed to get printed and distributed; its circulation soared; and the editor enjoyed himself immensely.

Years afterwards he spoke of his delight in the spectacle of "a great newspaper office, with its machines crashing and grinding away, for it reminds me of the combination of a first-class battleship and a first-class general election"; and here he was in May, 1926, with his own editorial command to exercise in the heartening stamp and thunder of his own presses. It was a great experience; and it did good service in the controversy which called it into being, although it failed to satisfy those of its readers who took a more detached view of the issues raised by the General Strike.

After this strenuous excursion into journalism he took a holiday abroad and saw the Pyramids, the Parthenon, and Mussolini. Two of the three attracted his observant brush; but Mussolini's portrait waited for his pen and a darker hour of his country's fortunes. His duties at the Treasury interested him, although

236

they were not so absorbing as to exclude the exercise of other accomplishments. For the two final volumes of his *World Crisis,* which finished off the story of the war, would be appearing soon; and Lord Oxford, busy on a more austere composition, commented unkindly on "a curious compound of fine writing and boisterous clap-trap," though his sonorous periods entranced Mr. Garvin and won slightly patronizing praise from Arnold Bennett.

Nor were letters the sole occupation of his leisure. For in his eternal willingness to try something new he made a bold experiment in home bricklaying, from which he derived a good deal of pleasure and Trade Unionists, when he gravely joined the Amalgamated Union of Building Trade Workers as an adult apprentice, some alarm. The years slipped by; and Mr. Churchill introduced his budgets (there were five of them in all), debated hard with Mr. Snowden, and made a start on a supplementary volume of *The World Crisis* to be called *The Aftermath* and take his narrative to the fall of the Coalition in 1922. But all things must end; and Mr. Baldwin's Government ended in the General Election of 1929, which brought Labor back to office and sent Mr. Churchill painting the Canadian Rockies. He had been duly returned as a Conservative for Epping. But the Conservatives were out; and was it certain that when they came back again, they would take Mr. Churchill with them?

## JEREMIAD

*"Slowly comes a hungry people, as a lion
    creeping nigher
Glares at one that nods and winks behind a
    slowly-dying fire."*

LOCKSLEY HALL.

# 1

THE times were out of joint. That was quite evident, though it was far from certain whether Mr. Churchill would have any opportunity to set them right. But if one thing was clear in 1930, it was that the age and Winston Churchill were out of harmony with one another. His qualities and outlook had been in tune with the first twenty years of the century. He was at home in the era of Joseph Chamberlain and Asquith and Lloyd George, moving freely among the certainties of a time when most people knew what they believed as plainly as what England stood for. But it was succeeded by an age of doubt. Weak-kneed skepticism found its expression in half-hearted policies and uncertain ethics; and as the Twenties followed the ambiguous gleam of Mr. Aldous Huxley to an accompaniment by Mr. Noel Coward, great affairs were left to Mr. Stanley Baldwin in discouraging rotation with Mr. Ramsay MacDonald.

What place was there for Mr. Churchill's positive beliefs in such a scene as this? Its defects were outlined in the somber diagnosis with which he concluded his Romanes Lecture in 1930:

These eventful years through which we are passing are not less serious for us than the years of the Great War. They belong to the same period. The grand and victorious summits which the British Empire won in that war are being lost, have indeed largely been lost in the years which

241

followed the peace. We see our race doubtful of its mission and no longer confident about its principles, infirm of purpose, drifting to and fro with the tides and currents of a deeply-disturbed ocean. The compass has been damaged. The charts are out of date. The crew have to take it in turns to be Captain; and every captain before every movement of the helm has to take a ballot not only of the crew but of an ever-increasing number of passengers. Yet within this vessel there abide all the might and fame of the British race and all the treasures of all the peoples in one-fifth of the habitable globe.

With those beliefs and that healthy appetite for action it was hardly possible for Mr. Churchill to feel at home among the half-measures of the Twenties. For he belonged to an earlier age with more exacting standards and a far higher scale of values, in which Mr. Baldwin's ambiguities and Mr. MacDonald's incoherence would never have been tolerated in important rôles. But the stature of politicians was diminished now; and as he viewed the field of current politics, he might almost have borrowed Landor's survey—"A few public men of small ability are introduced, to show better the proportions of the great; as a painter would situate a beggar under a triumphal arch, or a camel against a pyramid." But there was one important difference. For if Mr. Lloyd George still survived as a neglected Arc de Triomphe and Mr. Churchill as a forgotten pyramid, the effective control of public business was left almost exclusively to the humbler figures in the foreground.

Unsympathetic to the broad tendencies of the time

in which he found himself, Mr. Churchill was hardly more in harmony with its domestic detail. For his impenitent felicity in married life was sadly out of date. He had been married over twenty years; and a supremely happy home showed no signs of modish ennui. This obstinate normality was as unfashionable as his political beliefs on fundamental questions. For Mr. Churchill was quite as far from *The Vortex* as from Mr. MacDonald's muddled idealism or Mr. Baldwin's organized inertia. These were the elements which lent their characteristic flavor to the Twenties; and nothing could be more evident than that it was not Mr. Churchill's decade.

But if he found the Twenties hardly to his taste, signs began to multiply that the Thirties were unlikely to be more congenial. For there was a Labor Government in office; the Liberals seemed to abet it; and even the Conservatives, under Mr. Baldwin's mild direction, were less unhelpful than Mr. Churchill could have wished. He looked on with somber disapproval. But what could he do? The times were out of joint, and he could scarcely mend them single-handed. Unpleasant developments confronted him on every hand; and as he watched the darkening scene it almost seemed that Mr. Churchill, at the early age of fifty-five, was growing old.

2

The first object of his discontent was India, where Lord Irwin with a favoring breeze from Mr. MacDonald and without audible discouragement by Mr. Baldwin navigated the ship of state on lines that were profoundly distasteful to Mr. Churchill. The critic had not the slightest inclination towards the maintenance of authority by armed force. That was plain from his stern comments on General Dyer's proceedings at Amritsar ten years earlier—"Frightfulness is not a remedy known to the British pharmacopœia . . . this is not the British way of doing business." But he viewed Lord Irwin's policy as an ungraceful and unnecessary abdication.

Acutely conscious of the deep significance of India to Britain's world position, he echoed the sentiments expressed forty years before by Lord Randolph Churchill as Secretary of State for India and refused to contemplate "casting away that most truly bright and precious jewel in the crown of the King, which more than all our other Dominions and Dependencies constitutes the glory and strength of the British Empire." (Had not his father termed it "that most truly bright and precious gem in the crown of the Queen, the possession of which, more than that of all your Colonial dominions, has raised in power, in resource, in wealth and in authority this small island home of ours far above the level of the majority of nations and of States"?)

Starting from these lucid premises, he was not attracted by the more nebulous ideals which appeared to constitute the elusive lodestar of official policy. Yielding to none in expressions of his esteem for "the well-meaning and high-minded Viceroy," he was not captivated by what he termed "his misguided benevolence"; and when Mr. Baldwin seemed to lend his countenance to these unfortunate proceedings, Mr. Churchill could only speak his mind on the subject as an independent member—"I do not speak for the official Opposition nor for my right hon. friend the Leader of the Opposition. I speak solely as a Member of Parliament, of some service in this House, who holds views upon this matter which ought not to go unrepresented in this discussion."

That was in January, 1931. By the next month he had withdrawn from the inner counsels of the party by resigning from Mr. Baldwin's Business Committee. It was the practice of parties in opposition to entrust the direction of their policy to a "shadow Cabinet," largely composed of the last administration and broadly foreshadowing the next; and by his resignation Mr. Churchill frankly sacrificed his further chance of holding office under Mr. Baldwin. Indeed, he stated plainly his own inability "to serve in any Administration about whose Indian policy I was not reassured."

This sacrifice purchased his right "to marshal British opinion against a course of action which would bring in my judgment the greatest evils upon the people of India, upon the people of Great Britain, and upon the structure of the British Empire itself"; and he was unremitting in the task. But though he remained a Conservative, his stand on Indian affairs brought him into plain conflict with strict party orthodoxy and embarked him in lively controversy with its official guardians. Had not Lord Randolph Churchill once done battle with the bearded "Goats" of orthodox timidity? Now Mr. Baldwin and Sir Samuel Hoare sat in the seats of Mr. W. H. Smith and Sir Stafford Northcote, while conviction and heredity both sent Mr. Churchill up against the clean-shaven "Goats" of his own day.

The controversy was exacting. But its practical significance closed for the moment with the passage of the Government of India Bill against his unrelenting protests. Yet one consequence remained. For he had opened his campaign with a blunt announcement that "nothing will turn me from it, and I have cheerfully and gladly put out of my mind all idea of public office." He could not expect it now from Mr. Baldwin, and still less from Mr. MacDonald, when his strange gyrations brought him to power with Mr. Baldwin at his elbow and a large Conservative majority in the latter part of 1931. So Mr. Churchill had retraced his footsteps towards the wilderness again. He was still a Conservative, too good a Conservative, perhaps, for party managers and the strange hybrid of the National Government. For it was not easy to imagine him as the successful colleague of Mr. Snowden and Mr. J. H. Thomas or as a dutiful subordinate of Mr. Ramsay MacDonald, whose elusive qualities he had already attributed with felicitous irreverence to "The Boneless Wonder." But he remained Conservative, hanging on the party's flank and equally prepared to charge its enemies or to correct its leaders' line of march.

## 3

On these terms Mr. Churchill's politics failed to provide a whole-time occupation; and as idleness was not his *forte,* his pen was busier than ever, with the addition of an American lecture tour enlivened by his unsuccessful encounter with a New York taxi on a corner of Fifth Avenue. Between 1930 and 1939 he published nine substantial volumes, excluding a selection of his recent speeches edited by his son Randolph. Of this impressive total two were collections of reprinted journalism and miscellaneous pieces; but the rest were books. It was a formidable output, which suffered slightly from his fluency and from the ability to organize large works, which he had acquired in the composition of *The World Crisis.*

The earliest addition to his bibliography, with which he occupied his leisure in 1930, was in many ways the most satisfying. For *My Early Life: a Roving Commission* is a genial account of the first phases of his long career, narrated without affectation and in a less majestic tone than readers were inclined to fear from him. Opening with infancy, it carried him through his military adventures into politics and closed with the auspicious day when "I married and lived happily ever afterwards."

This was followed in the next year by a final volume

of his *World Crisis* dealing with *The Eastern Front*. The earlier installments, founded on the personal experience of a British minister, had concentrated upon those theaters of war in which British fleets or armies were directly engaged. But no one was more acutely aware than Mr. Churchill that the war, no less than its most devastating consequence, had consisted largely of events in Russia; and this supplementary volume redressed the balance of his narrative. He always wrote well about war, and his ability to dramatize the dramatic was finely illustrated by a tragic picture of the Russian commander on the northern front after the elimination of Samsonoff at Tannenberg and Rennenkampf at the Masurian Lakes:

> There he sat at the same desk in the same room with the same ceremony and decorum around him, a failure, a byword in history, a cause of his country's undoing— all because he had sent telegrams from time to time as was his duty, and events had belied these telegrams. There were the maps, there were the telegrams, there was the quiet room, there was the horrible disaster. And this was the glamour of a high Command—almost the highest—in modern war! This was what was supposed to equal the opportunities of the great Commanders of history. What a swindle, what a mockery! They at least rode their horses in the battle smoke and shared the perils of the soldiers they actually led. But here all around were only the maps and the jiggling flags, the counterfoils of telegrams, all read by the enemy, and incoming disconnected tidings of ruin, and glum staff officers slouching in with more.

Then, after the agreeable miscellany of his *Thoughts and Adventures,* he approached a major enterprise.

The vindication of the great Duke of Marlborough was a hereditary duty for which the Blenheim papers had long been reserved. Lord Balfour and Lord Rosebery urged it on Mr. Churchill with that unselfish ardor with which large undertakings are frequently proposed to authors by persons who have no intention of doing anything of the kind themselves. Its appeal was obvious; and when the disheartening continuance of Baldwin-MacDonald Government appeared to promise him a further term of leisure, he approached his task in a mood of devotion to an ancestor who was a perfect husband, a great soldier, and a good Englishman.

The results were formidable, since the completed work surprised its author, who had proposed to write two or, at most three volumes, by involving him in a fourth. It ran, indeed, to more than two thousand pages. This excess of length was largely due to his righteous determination "to examine every criticism or charge which the voluminous literature upon this period contains, even where they are plainly tinctured with prejudice or malice, even where they rest on no more than slanderous or ignorant gossip." A reasoned vindication is bound to move more slowly than a simple narrative. Besides, the author frankly set himself to present the immense panorama of his hero's times as well as to narrate his life, and even to include a high proportion of his letters. The design is grandiose, the scale a little larger than life-size; and if the effect occasionally recalls those acres of triumphal canvas in which French official memories delight to dwell upon French military success, it is not, perhaps, unsuitable that Marlborough's monument in prose should bear more than a faint resemblance to the Salle des Victoires at Versailles, of which it is the British counterpart.

But at the center of his glowing tapestry the author skillfully displays the rather chilly charms of his common-sense hero. Sometimes his story suffers from the fatal lullaby of a majestic style; and the reality of events is occasionally veiled behind the easy cadences of historians' English. But there is a wealth of slow, Gibbonian fun; and his old-fashioned awareness of the reader's presence is an engaging mannerism.

Perhaps the author who dictates his book is in some danger of producing nothing more than a very long speech; but it is an admirable speech, a highly spirited performance occasionally enlivened by interminable arguments with Lord Macaulay in the wings. Given Mr. Churchill's point of view about the Duke, it was inevitable that there should be something in the nature of a running fight with Macaulay, who is sometimes treated as unceremoniously as though he were a member of the Labor Government. But he contrives to avenge himself by leaving on his adversary unmistakable traces of his style. Mr. Churchill can always be relied upon to make controversy entertaining; and it is comforting to the irreverent to watch him mauling the omniscient Acton, "the great mute student."

These, however, are mere side-shows; and in spite of its excessive length the whole performance is inspiring, a broad survey of great events that might have ended

*RULE BRITANNIA*—Mr. Churchill, with the salt of the sea in his blood, is completely at home on the wet deck of this destroyer as he makes one of his many trips inspecting naval defenses.

in the noblest of all war aims—"peace rising out of an otherwise endless warfare, and order emerging from chaos, with England the glorious deliverer at the summit"—evoking "a spectacle, so moving for the times in which we live, of a league of twenty-six signatory states successfully resisting and finally overcoming a mighty coherent military despotism."

The last installment of his *magnum opus* was published in September, 1938, when Marlborough and victory seemed very far away from Mr. Chamberlain and Munich; and Mr. Churchill's further writings had a more immediate character. He had already published an informing group of personal sketches in his *Great Contemporaries,* of which a friendly critic wrote that "Mr. Churchill gleams back at us from twenty-five looking-glasses, formidable, affectionate and lovable." This was not altogether just, since less assertive personalities than his have encountered the same difficulty in excluding their own figures from their reminiscences of other people. His picture gallery is full of interest. But his retrospective studies were concluded now. For the present grew absorbing once again, and through 1936 and the succeeding years Mr. Churchill wrote a fortnightly newspaper commentary on current events, which was reprinted in *Step by Step.* History was coming nearer; and as he studied its approach from his watch-tower the note of warning crept into his voice.

4

There had been a stir of 1931, when Mr. Ramsay MacDonald, suddenly aware of the economic consequences of his own Government's proceedings, decided to change sides. He promptly formed a National Government with the unusual, if rewarding, gesture of the commander of a besieged garrison placing himself at the head of the besiegers. Its composition was quite national enough to include himself, a few respected colleagues and a small entourage, the Conservatives en masse, and Liberals of both persuasions—those who had remained faithful to the memory of Mr. Asquith, and a more flexible variety upon whom a continued diet of locusts and wild honey, which was all the wilderness afforded to Sir John Simon, Mr. Runciman and Mr. Hore-Belisha, had begun to pall. But there was no place for Mr. Lloyd George or Mr. Winston Churchill. True they had more practical experience of Coalitions than most public men as well as a far more distinguished record of public service. But their abilities were felt to be superfluous in the galaxy of talent assembled round Mr. Ramsay MacDonald and Mr. Stanley Baldwin.

In reality, especially after a General Election which brought sweeping victory to the Conservatives, it was a Conservative administration with a few trimmings drawn from other quarters. For its support rested on Mr. Baldwin's big battalions. Though he claimed no more than the second place, Mr. Baldwin was the real

master of the Government; and in that quarter Mr.
Churchill had already cut himself off from any hopes of
office by his uncompromising attitude on India. So, in
default of a more active part, he assumed the unsatisfy-
ing rôle of an Elder Statesman with a watching brief.

His principal preoccupations were in the larger field
of foreign policy, where European statesmanship struggled inconclusively with Disarmament and Germany
was still a problem rather than a menace. For Adolf
Hitler was no more than an unpleasant possibility,
though Mr. Churchill indicated at midsummer, 1932,
that he was already "the moving impulse behind the
German Government and may be more than that very
soon."

His main anxiety at this stage was that "Britain is
weaker; and Britain's hour of weakness is Europe's
hour of danger." But he was prepared to use the interval before further disarmament reduced the European margin of safety in "the removal of the just
grievances of the vanquished. . . . To bring about anything like equality of armaments if it were in our power
to do so, which it happily is not, while those grievances
remain unredressed, would be almost to appoint the
day for another European war—to fix it as if it were a
prize-fight. It would be far safer to reopen questions
like those of the Danzig Corridor and Transylvania,
with all their delicacy and difficulty, in cold blood and
in a calm atmosphere and while the victor nations
still have ample superiority, than to wait and drift on,
inch by inch and stage by stage, until once again

vast combinations, equally matched, confront each other face to face." Wisdom after the event is always easy; but that was Mr. Churchill's wisdom in November, 1932. Two months later Hitler was Chancellor, and the opportunity began to fade.

As the roll of Nazi drums grew louder and the wheels of Germany's rearmament hummed to a faster tempo, Mr. Churchill began to think less in terms of solving Europe's problems than of Britain's safety. He could still "thank God for the French Army," while Mr. MacDonald soared into the incomprehensible in pursuit of "the broad, just, fundamental, eternal thing" and Mr. Baldwin wrung helpless hands over the prospect of a war that would inevitably end civilization.

No isolationist, Mr. Churchill preached "a certain degree of sober detachment from the European scene," so far as Britain's individual policy was concerned, and urged the collective use of the League of Nations, "not for the purpose of fiercely quarreling and haggling about the details of disarmament, but in an attempt to address Germany collectively, so that there may be some redress of the grievances of the German nation and that that may be effected before this peril of rearmament reaches a point which may endanger the peace of the world."

That was his advice in 1933; and when it was not acted on, the speaker turned vehemently and repeatedly to the grim alternative of strengthening Britain's defenses. The new menace of air attack impressed him deeply—"This cursed, hellish invention and development of war from the air has revolutionized our position. We are not the same kind of country we used to be when we were an island, only twenty-five years ago . . ." and he pressed for "an Air Force at least as strong as that of any Power that can get at us." His warnings grew more insistent through 1934, eliciting from Mr. Baldwin a hypothetical undertaking that the Government "will see to it that in air strength and air power this country shall no longer be in a position inferior to any country within striking distance of our shores."

Looking still further into the practical requirements of an unpleasant future, Mr. Churchill pleaded for a combined Ministry of Defence to co-ordinate the needs of the three Services and even overcame his former prejudices so far as to welcome Soviet Russia to the League of Nations. But his clearest call was for "a large vote of credit to double our Air Force . . . and a larger vote of credit as soon as possible to redouble the Air Force."

Obsessed with the exposed position of the country and "our enormous Metropolis here, the greatest target in the world," he asked pointed questions about the furtive growth of German air power and stated that it was already overhauling Britain's and would pass it in the course of 1936. While Mr. Baldwin eloquently located the British frontier on the Rhine, Mr. Churchill looked with concern at what was actually happening on the further bank and called up uncomfortable visions of incendiary raids on London and its docks. His lurid prophecies were founded upon categorical assertions

255

as to Germany's present and potential air power—"Beware. Germany is a country fertile in military surprises"—which Mr. Baldwin met with comfortable contradictions.

The pace quickened in 1935, as the curtain gradually rose on the alarming spectacle of Germany's rearmament. Mr. Churchill's statistics grew more menacing; and the Government, unpleasantly enlightened by Sir John Simon's unilateral conversations with Hitler in Berlin, began to retreat uneasily from its denials. The prophet of woe had the melancholy satisfaction of announcing that "for many months, perhaps for several years, most critical for the peace of Europe, we are inexorably condemned to be in a position of frightful weakness . . . condemned to protracted, indefinite and agonizing inferiority." But he did not confine himself to lamentations. For he recommended swift rearmament and a policy of collective action under the League of Nations—"Such a policy does not close the door upon a revision of the Treaties, but it procures a sense of stability, and an adequate gathering together of all reasonable Powers for self-defence, before any inquiry of that character can be entered upon. In this august association for collective security we must build up defence forces of all kinds and combine our action with that of friendly Powers, so that we may be allowed to live in quiet ourselves and retrieve the woeful miscalculations of which we are at present the dupes, and of which, unless we take warning in time, we may some day be the victims."

It was too late now to apply his earlier formula: "Redress of the grievances of the vanquished should precede the disarmament of the victors." For the vanquished had already taken the law into their own hands and rearmed themselves. But there might still be time for other folk to arm; and when the Anglo-German naval agreement legitimized the *fait accompli* of a German Navy, which the peace treaty had prohibited, he greeted it contemptuously as "a side deal with Germany which we thought to be in our interest and not contrary to other interests in Europe," and called insistently for the rebuilding of the British fleet.

He was equally concerned with the large issues of policy and with the vital detail of anti-aircraft research, with which he and Professor Lindemann pursued Mr. Baldwin to the Continental spa where his taste for the English countryside was annually refreshed. But the outlook from his watch-tower was not enlivening, as 1935 went out upon the spectacle of Italy joining the company of international law-breakers with fair prospects of success, and Mr. Baldwin (now Prime Minister in name as well as in fact) maneuvering uneasily to reconcile his election pledges to support the League of Nations with a strong tendency to desert it, and Sir Samuel Hoare in temporary partnership with Pierre Laval to settle the Abyssinian problem by the simple expedient of eliminating Abyssinia.

Events moved rapidly towards a climax in 1936. For the Germans re-occupied, garrisoned, and fortified the Rhineland in violation of the peace treaties and their own voluntary signature (duly confirmed by Hitler) at Locarno; the Italians successfully defied the League of Nations in Abyssinia; a group of Spanish officers seized power and engaged in a protracted civil war with German and Italian support in the Peninsula, whose situation on the flank of Britain's seaways to the East and West has always rendered an independent Spain a British interest of the first order; and the Belgians evinced unpleasant symptoms of a desire to act independently of France and England.

It was a distasteful harvest of the haphazard sowings of the easy, Baldwin years; and it began to look as though Mr. Churchill had been right after all. He was still haunted by the vision of "the great wheels revolving and the great hammers descending day and night in Germany," and urged a real policy of collective security—"I am looking for peace. I am looking for a way to stop war." His notion was to proceed by a swift gathering of the world's law-abiding forces and a guarantee to Germany of her own frontiers followed by a frank negotiation upon her rearmament and all her grievances. "But do not let us be a rabble flying from forces we dare not resist. Let us negotiate from strength and not from weakness; from unity and not from division and isolation; let us seek to do justice because we have power."

It was a reasonable program, the "Grand Alliance of all the nations who wish for peace against the Potential Aggressor, whoever he may be." But his suggestion of 1936 was not acted on before the spring of 1939; and he was reduced to pressing for a reasonably organized aircraft industry, a Ministry of Munitions Supply (with some attention to the problem—how remote it seemed in 1936—of air-borne invasion), and a private deputation to the Prime Minister at which he endeavored to disturb Mr. Baldwin's composure by a statement, which took an hour to read, on the deficiencies of the Royal Air Force.

He was rueful about Abyssinia and inclined to be a little hopeless about Spain—"The obvious interest of France and Britain is a liberal Spain restoring under a stable and tolerant Government freedom and prosperity to all its people. That we can scarcely hope will come in our time." But he had hopes of Russia "as a Soviet Socialist state strongly armed to maintain its national independence, and absolutely divorced from any idea of spreading its doctrines abroad otherwise than by example." In this more favorable guise he felt that "she may play a part in preserving the general peace." That was the main objective; and he could not avoid a feeling that its prospects in 1937 and 1938 had been gravely compromised by the airy negligence of 1934 and 1935—"the years," as one unhappy minister termed them, "that the locust hath eaten."

He had no doubts of Mr. Baldwin's supreme responsibility, "decided only to be undecided, resolved to be irresolute, adamant for drift, solid for fluidity, all-powerful to be impotent"; and when he stigmatized it in the House of Commons one November day, the Prime Minister replied with the startling confession that if he had gone so far as to announce the need for rearmament at any earlier stage, he could not have won the General Election of 1935—"Supposing I had gone to the country and said that Germany was rearming and that we must rearm, does anybody think that this pacific democracy would have rallied to that cry at that moment? I cannot think of anything that would have made the loss of the election from my point of view more certain."

Already a diminished figure, whose public reputation had been seriously damaged by the dubious maneuvers of the Abyssinian affair, Mr. Baldwin was left almost in eclipse by this astonishing admission of elaborate duplicity upon the gravest question of the day; and as he dwindled, his unwearied critic gained proportionately in popular and Parliamentary esteem. Was Mr. Churchill coming into his own at last? It looked very like it in November, 1936.

5

The position of the two statesmen was reversed by the events of five days in December, 1936. For on the morning of December 3 Mr. Churchill was the successful critic of a discredited Prime Minister. But by the afternoon of December 7 he was the unwelcome advocate of a lost cause, and Mr. Baldwin's intermittent star was lord of the ascendant once again. His comfortable genius for letting things alone had been disastrously applied to the European situation and to the urgent problem of Britain's rearmament; and its consequences were equally unhappy in the case of his sovereign's domestic future. For there, also, Mr. Baldwin did nothing in particular and hoped devoutly for the best. As Mr. Churchill wrote regretfully a few weeks later, "it was not in October, but in August or earlier, that the first serious advice should have been tendered to King Edward VIII." But the Prime Minister was a great believer in time's healing power, and he made no move until there was no move that he could make by which events might be deflected from their tragic destination. At that stage, however, he acted with alarming promptitude; and the King was handled with a firmer touch than the King's enemies.

The House of Commons had its first intimation that anything was wrong on a Thursday afternoon; and Mr. Churchill promptly asked for an undertaking (which the Prime Minister refrained from giving) that no irrevocable step would be taken before a formal statement had been made to Parliament. On the next morning he still withheld the assurance for which Mr. Churchill asked, affording the unusual spectacle of an impetuous Baldwin unwilling to be delayed by a cautious Churchill. Here was a strange reversal of their rôles; but there might be cases in which good results could attend deliberation.

After all, the Prime Minister had contemplated German rearmament for at least four years without asking the country to do very much about it. Would it be unreasonable to devote as many months to the King's problem? That afternoon, however, he announced a summary decision that the Cabinet (to whom the problem had only just been put) was not prepared to ease the situation by special legislation. The King, a solitary figure at Fort Belvedere, asked to see Mr. Churchill as an old friend; and Mr. Baldwin raised no objection. It was a natural request. For he had been Home Secretary a quarter of a century before, when the Prince of Wales took his first timid steps in public. Friendship apart, there was a strong vein of chivalry in Mr. Churchill; and he had more reason than most men to know all that a happy marriage, which was the King's desire, means to a public man. Besides, there was a strong presumption that if Mr. Baldwin wanted anything, it could not be altogether right.

For once, however, time—as short a time as possible—was on Mr. Baldwin's side. Mr. Churchill issued a reasoned plea "for time and patience," arguing with perfect truth that Parliament had not yet been consulted and that his ministers were not entitled to advise the King to abdicate. Indicating that the sovereign had been faced with an ultimatum, he begged for "time and tolerance." But time was not vouchsafed. For, as one rueful chronicler records, "if Mr. Baldwin had been a little slow in dealing with the King, he was anything but slow in dealing with the people."

The House of Commons seemed to agree with him, since it practically shouted Mr. Churchill down when he rose on Monday with his usual request for an assurance that irrevocable steps would not be taken before they were consulted; and his subsequent attempt at argument upon the Constitution was ended prematurely by peremptory cries of "Speech" and "Sit down." For he was plainly on the losing side, and *The Times* gleefully recorded the proceedings under the headline, "Mr. Churchill's Bad Day." The issue was decided; and when Parliament, consulted at long last, was finally requested to confirm King Edward's abdication, Mr. Churchill left the field with dignity. For there was no controversy now; and after farewells at Fort Belvedere he turned with perfect loyalty to the new reign and to "a King and Queen" (as he wrote) "upon whose success British hopes are centered and British fortunes in no small measure depend."

But the episode had left its mark upon his prospects. For his intervention sharply depressed the rising scale of Mr. Churchill's fortunes, and the sad transaction gave Mr. Baldwin a new lease of life. A colleague stated proudly that nothing had interested the Prime Minister so much for years; and Mr. Churchill testified that "by his resolute and dexterous management of the abdication Mr. Baldwin regained at a bound the authority and regard which he had lost since the General Election. Indeed, a new vigour seemed to animate him. Physically as well as politically, he walked with decided step . . ." But this renewal of his powers and prestige ensured a further prolongation of his half-hearted ordering of international affairs and national defense, for which the price was to be paid in full by his successor and by all his fellow-countrymen; while Mr. Churchill's temporary eclipse, attributable to his honest advocacy of a straightforward course in circumstances of great difficulty, postponed to a more distant future his inevitable return to office. Without the tragedy of 1936 it might, perhaps, have come a good deal earlier; and in that event a firmer touch must have informed Britain's policy, a smarter pace accelerated her halting preparations for defense.

6

As 1937 opened and the dust subsided, the outlook from his watch-tower was no more inviting than before. But by this time Mr. Churchill's warnings had achieved a certain regularity which somehow diminished their effect, and the return of public confidence in Mr. Baldwin blunted their edge. For there was a growing feeling that if anything required attention, Mr. Baldwin would see to it; and Mr. Churchill's recurring intimations of the wrath to come were as familiar as the voice of a muezzin announcing the hour of prayer. After all, it was 1937, and nothing had happened to them yet.

The depressing prophet on the minaret informed them that "we are marching through that long dark valley of which I spoke to the House two years ago . . . We are for the time being no longer masters of our own fate. That fate no longer depends altogether on what we decide here or on what the Cabinet settle in Downing Street. It depends on what may happen in the world, on what other countries do, for good or ill.

It may be hard for our island people, with their long immunity, to realize this ugly, unpleasant alteration in our position . . ." That was the burden of his song, and he repeated it unweariedly in speech and print.

His anxieties gravely impaired his party orthodoxy, since the shortcomings of an easy-going Government were his constant theme; and he was willing to collaborate with any group which seemed equally aware of the impending danger. He had already appeared on the platform of the Albert Hall with Liberal and Labor speakers at an anti-Nazi demonstration; and it was significant that while Mr. Churchill was almost the only prominent Conservative to risk himself in such compromising company, Mr. Herbert Morrison, of the Labor Party, and Sir Walter Citrine, of the Trades Union Congress, many of whose political associates were more particular about the company they kept, were equally prepared to look outside the strict limits of their party wedding-rings by associating with Mr. Churchill in face of the German menace. For Mr. Churchill was still very much a Conservative in home politics. But his stand on national defense and foreign policy transcended party lines; and in 1937 it might almost have been said of him, as he had already written of the Duke of Marlborough in 1700, that a figure "with a non-party outlook, a Whig foreign policy, and a rather faded Tory coat, was found moving sedately along the central line of impending national requirements."

That was the key to all his utterances on the detail of defense and A.R.P. and the broad outline of a policy based on the League of Nations. He was emphatic on the high value of American sympathy and even advocated a declaration (which he lived to make himself after a famous voyage three years later) that "if the United States for their own purposes chose to take a lead in preserving peace and civilisation in and around the China Seas, they would be supported by Great Britain and the British Empire to the full limit of their strength." But his principal anxieties were European; and he continued to rely on the Royal Navy and the army of the Third Republic, on "salt water and the French fortress line." For the collaboration of the two Parliamentary democracies and, if necessary, of their armed forces seemed the one fixed star in a sadly dislocated firmament.

He was steadily losing his old misgivings about Russia, confining his anathema to "Trotskyite Communism," to the old evangelical variety which had preached world-revolution in 1919 and was now, to judge from his drastic treatment of its surviving representatives, as distasteful to Stalin as to Mr. Churchill. His sense of acute danger was indicated by a mild tone towards Germany, by more than one appeal that its autocrat "should now become the Hitler of peace," by references to his own credentials as a friend who had proposed a "naval holiday" in 1913, wished to send foodships into Hamburg in 1918, pressed for the raising of the blockade, liberated German prisoners before their time, and urged successfully that the Locarno treaties should afford the same protection to Germany

*HOME FROM THE SEA*—Fighting men of the British fleet get a smiling welcome from the Prime Minister. The crew of the destroyer *Hardy* after the battle of Narvik (above); and sailors from the *Ajax* and *Exeter* after the *Graf Spee* victory.

as to France. But nobody paid very much attention; and he confessed ruefully after King George's Coronation in the summer that "Parliament, which a year ago showed itself genuinely concerned about our defences, has now forgotten even that there could be such a fact as danger. Some say, 'How right the Government were not to be alarmed by the scaremongers! How right they were not to have a Ministry of Supply, and not to upset the ordinary business prosperity of the country! A whole year has passed and nothing has happened . . .' "

A year had passed, and Mr. Baldwin's sedative had been gratefully absorbed by large numbers of his fellow-countrymen, whom Mr. Churchill's stimulant failed to attract. For it was comforting to believe that everything possible was being done, that industry was not unduly dislocated by war preparations, that things, in fact, might be a good deal worse. That was the essence of the nation's outlook under Mr. Baldwin. The public mood was scarcely gay, but it was equable; and when Mr. Baldwin took his leave after the Coronation, it viewed with calm the substitution of Mr. Neville Chamberlain.

This statesman, whose earlier experience had been exclusively municipal, was admirably qualified to succeed Mr. Baldwin. His brief appearance as Mr. Lloyd George's Minister of National Service under the fierce stress of war had been disastrous. But in peace conditions he had filled the Ministry of Health with rigid competence, and as Chancellor of the Exchequer he had been Mr. Baldwin's leading colleague and heir-apparent through the decisive years, the fatal interlude when so much might have been done. His leading interests were in domestic politics; and his view of international affairs seemed to consist of a simple-minded certainty that all difficulties would evaporate before a few straightforward talks with the foreign principals. This method had been known to produce excellent results in business and on the City Council; and there was no apparent reason why it should not do the same in Europe, if the other parties were only as straightforward as himself. But were they? He learned the answer in the next two painful years.

So far as Mr. Churchill was concerned, Mr. Chamberlain had a high opinion of his ability; and it was his original intention to offer him a Cabinet appointment as soon as he had found his feet as leader of the party. But though his authority was soon established, the offer never came. For Mr. Chamberlain shared Mr. Baldwin's view that Mr. Churchill would prove a restless colleague who might form a most disturbing element in time of peace, although he was quite clear that, if it came to war, he would find room for Mr. Churchill. But until that calamity he preferred to follow his own course; and Mr. Churchill was left crying in the wilderness.

He might be haunted by unpleasant, apocalyptic visions, in which "dictators ride to and fro upon tigers which they dare not dismount. And the tigers are getting hungry." But the new Prime Minister, untroubled by such dreams, opened a hopeful correspondence with

Mussolini, and Lord Halifax enjoyed the privilege of Hitler's conversation.

Was this the new departure? Was the world to be re-built upon a clear-eyed recognition of things as they were—and irrespective of whether they were right or wrong? Early in 1938 Mr. Churchill was asking anxiously, "Is the new policy to come to terms with the totalitarian Powers in the hope that by great and far-reaching acts of submission, not merely in sentiment and pride, but in material factors, peace may be preserved?" If so, he could foresee the end—"I predict that the day will come when at some point or other, on some issue or other, you will have to make a stand, and I pray God that when that day comes we may not find that through an unwise policy we are left to make that stand alone."

He was still pressing for a Grand Alliance of the law-abiding nations, and he clung hard to Franco-British military unity. But, in default of these, his somber vision was of the abyss—"I have watched this famous island descending incontinently, fecklessly, the stairway which leads to a dark gulf. It is a fine broad stairway at the beginning, but after a bit the carpet ends. A little farther on there are only flag-stones, and a little farther on still these break beneath your feet . . ."

Presently the sheaves of Mr. Chamberlain's new policy began to arrive. First, he shed Mr. Eden, who had other views. Then he pursued negotiations with the Duce across the prostrate forms of Abyssinia and Spain. Encouraged by this melting mood, the Führer in

March, 1938, swallowed Austria at a single mouthful and with the customary German promise that nothing was intended against his next objective, Czechoslovakia. The grossness of his crime was aggravated for some students of deportment by the indelicacy of his ambassador, von Ribbentrop, in lunching with the British Cabinet on that very day; and Mr. Churchill, who was a slightly unexpected guest, remarked to somebody that evening, "Well, I suppose they asked me to show him that, if they couldn't bite themselves, they kept a dog who could bark and might *bite*."

The faithful watch-dog continued his warnings through 1938—on the need of a Peace Front in Europe, on the menace of political instability in France, on the threat to British trade-routes presented by the strange surrender of the Irish naval bases, on the aching void which might be filled by a Ministry of Supply, on the lengthening shadow across Czechoslovakia. But there were a few brighter elements. Franco-British unity was still unassailed; and Mr. Churchill, who crossed the Channel for the royal visit in the summer, walked about among the troops and felt the old confidence in their quality. American opinion was, within its limits, not unpromising; and he freely recognized "the services which Soviet Russia is rendering in the Far East to civilisation and also to British and United States interests . . . The Western democracies should recognise the part Soviet Russia, albeit for her own purposes, is playing in the Far East." He was pleading for national unity in face of danger and for international unity as well, from which he did not exclude the Russians, in order to "rally a peaceful Europe round a strong Britain and France."

But the scene darkened swiftly in the autumn, as the veils dropped from Germany's naked resolve to mutilate Czechoslovakia beyond hope of recovery. It sent Mr. Chamberlain skimming across the upper air to Berchtesgaden, to Godesberg, and finally to Munich. Here was his opportunity for straightforward talks with the Führer. But they hardly came up to his expectations, since the terms which he obtained at each successive interview were a little worse than those indicated in the last. Indeed, this Sibylline transaction was less a negotiation than a surrender; and when France and Britain surrendered Czechoslovakia's hopes of survival in the grinning presence of the dictators, they surrendered their own chance of aligning Europe against aggression. But the surrender had averted war; and in the sudden relief it was feverishly acclaimed as something in the nature of a victory. Had not the returning traveler triumphantly exhibited a piece of paper with a German signature at a cheering British air-port, announcing his belief that it meant "peace for our time"?

Mr. Chamberlain's insistence upon carrying an umbrella for air travel became a world-wide symbol of peace, of the peace that the world longed for; and his black-coated figure with its old-fashioned neckwear and unvarying smile was hailed as a civilian alternative to the perpetual menace of dictators' scowls and uniforms. There was a brief interval of universal gratitude, of cheering crowds and smiling sovereigns, of unsolicited thank-offerings and mountainous accumulations of enthusiastic correspondence from total strangers in every country of the world. The world's dream was of peace; and for a short time after Munich it clung deliriously to Mr. Chamberlain.

But the dream faded, as the grim outline of the consequences began to emerge; and Mr. Churchill told the House of Commons that "we have sustained a defeat without a war." He explained ungratefully that the settlement amounted to no more than "that the German dictator, instead of snatching the victuals from the table, has been content to have them served to him course by course." Nor could he resist a backward glance at "the last five years—five years of futile good intentions, five years of eager search for the line of least resistance, five years of uninterrupted retreat of British power, five years of neglect of our air defences."

Lord Baldwin, who emerged from his rusticity to sound a belated trumpet-call about rearmament, invited the cold repartee from Mr. Churchill that "it would have been much better if Lord Baldwin had said that two and a half years ago, when every one demanded a Ministry of Supply." But war-time ministries were not yet acceptable to Mr. Chamberlain and his colleagues, since a war-time ministry plainly implied a war-time minister—and that meant Mr. Churchill. Was he not the last Minister of Munitions of the Great War, who had been advocating something of the kind for years and was still making knowledgeable speeches about the practical detail of administrative and industrial organization, to say nothing of his revolutionary sentiments on "taking the profit out of war"? If they gave way and created a Ministry of Supply, there would be no logical alternative to Mr. Churchill as a minister; and that was something they were not prepared to face in 1938.

After all, there was a fundamental difference between his point of view and theirs. For Mr. Churchill wrote in "the grey aftermath of Munich" (as he termed it) that "the Prime Minister is pursuing a policy of a most decided character and of capital importance. He has his own strong view about what to do, and about what is going to happen . . . He believes that he can make a good settlement for Europe and for the British Empire by coming to terms with Herr Hitler and Signor Mussolini . . . By this time next year we shall know whether the Prime Minister's view of Herr Hitler and the German Nazi Party is right or wrong. By this time next year we shall know whether the policy of appeasement has appeased, or whether it has only stimulated a more ferocious appetite . . ." By this time next year Great Britain was at war.

As he surveyed the wreckage in the last weeks of 1938, Mr. Churchill began to feel his first doubts of the French, of "certain strata of the middle-class and the well-to-do"; and he underwent a somewhat belated conversion to the merits of the Spanish Republic. In the uncomfortable spring of 1939 his reading of the signs was that "the tendency upon the Continent is still towards a climax at no distant date," and he looked hopefully towards "the great counterpoise of Soviet Russia." Even Mr. Chamberlain began to lose his illusions, reminding himself strongly of the younger Pitt forced by a cruel destiny to turn from home politics to war, and watching Hitler with the first dawn of something like suspicion, aggravated by an angry sense that he had not been told the truth.

Suspicion became certainty when Czechoslovakia was wantonly eliminated in breach of Germany's last treaty and with the usual assurance this would be all; and Mr. Chamberlain turned mournfully to do in 1939 some of the things which Mr. Churchill had been pressing on them since 1934. There was a flurried effort to construct a Peace Front (the "Grand Alliance" of his frequent preaching) and an embryonic Ministry of Supply provided with a minister without portfolio—and without Mr. Churchill. His gaze was turning further east towards the Polish problem and the possibility of an "act of faith" in Soviet Russia. The Government followed without conviction and without visible results. But it was still unthinkable to find a place for Mr. Churchill.

They even found it easier to introduce conscription in the uneasy summer of 1939. For when a leading newspaper proprietor pressed Mr. Churchill's claims to office upon Mr. Chamberlain in June, the Prime Minister repeated the old litany of faults that Mr. Baldwin used to find with a restless colleague. If there was a war, of course he should be admitted; but until then the harmony of a peace-time Cabinet must not be endangered. Besides, most of its present members were opposed to Mr. Churchill's entry. Mr. Chamberlain, it seemed, could face it. But a large number of his colleagues would resign in preference to sharing their official dignity with Mr. Churchill; and as it was considered necessary to retain these thunderbolts of war, he still remained a private member.

He had become an emblem of the public will to resist further aggression, of the national anxiety about rearmament. Newspapers and politicians of all shades pressed for his admission to the Government. For his activities in isolation had made friends for Mr. Churchill who would never have supported him at other stages of his long career. Liberals and Labor recognized an ardent anti-Nazi, who could be relied upon to face aggression without a lingering desire to come to terms with it; dissatisfied Conservatives admitted that a high proportion of his predictions had come true; and Lord Beaverbrook turned gratefully towards the other thorn in Mr. Baldwin's side. As the sands of Mr. Chamberlain's experiment ran out, its failure became glaring. "No Prime Minister in modern times," as Mr. Churchill wrote, "has had so much personal power to guide affairs. Everything that he has asked of the nation has been granted; and when he has not asked what many thought necessary, no steps have been taken to compel him. There has never been in England such a one-man Government . . ." And when it ended in a public demonstration that it had been wrong at every point, it seemed natural to turn towards its most persistent critic.

As the danger deepened in the summer, Mr. Churchill was magnanimous—"It is no service to dwell upon the shortcomings or neglects of those who have been responsible. The time to be frightened is when evils can be remedied; when they cannot be fully remedied they must be faced with courage." Now there could be no turning back. Such time as might remain to them could only be employed in action, in the last preparations, in aligning all possible allies and the "hope that a full and solid alliance will be made with Russia without further delay." In the second week of August the French invited him to view the wonders, the slightly passive wonders, of the Maginot Line, which rendered the defense of France a mathematical certainty. (But modern science sometimes has an unsettling effect upon mathematics.) A private member still, he watched the Russian *volte-face* and the last agitated flutterings of Sir Nevile Henderson between London and Berlin. The war he had foreseen was on them now; and one Sunday morning in September the last of his unpleasant prophecies came true.

## MR. CHAMBERLAIN'S WAR

*"I wanted to go to Birmingham,
But they've sent me on to Crewe."*

OLD SONG.

WHEN the war came, Mr. Chamberlain's heart-
broken admission that his well-intentioned
effort to avert it had completely failed was not a trumpet-call. But Mr. Churchill could be counted on to set
the trumpet to his lips; and presently he got his opportunity. For the Prime Minister had always meant to
bring him back to office, if there was a war. He did not
succeed in modifying the composition of his Government by broadening its basis to include Opposition
Liberal and Labor elements; and his relations with the
Trade Unions continued to be almost as distant as before. But this was no time for perpetuating disagree-
ments between Conservatives, and he readmitted Mr.
Eden and Mr. Churchill. The first notion was to make
him a minister without portfolio in the War Cabinet;
but when he offered him the Admiralty it was decided
that all Service ministers should sit in the War Cabinet.
It was not far off thirty years since Mr. Churchill had
left the Home Office to become First Lord, and he returned to the Admiralty at sixty-four on the first day of
a new war. Within a month the country heard a ringing
denunciation of "Herr Hitler and his group of wicked
men, whose hands are stained with blood and soiled
with corruption." For he did not share his colleagues'
taste for public utterances in a minor key; and where

Mr. Chamberlain could only wring his hands, Mr. Churchill shook his fist.

That was how the country saw and heard him, though his main contribution was made in council and at the Admiralty. But a grateful public in the first gray winter of the war listened to a robust official utterance, which was not afraid to vilify what was vile and assessed the prospects with a broad, experienced outlook. Stoutly mispronouncing his country's enemies and all their misshapen appellations, he reported gaily on the Navy's hunt for lurking submarines "with zeal and not altogether without relish."

In Eastern Europe he refused to be discouraged by Russia's strange apostasy, insisting that the key to Russian policy was "Russian national interest. It cannot be in accordance with the interest or the safety of Russia that Germany should plant itself upon the shores of the Black Sea, or that it should overrun the Balkan States and subjugate the Slavonic peoples of South-Eastern Europe. That would be contrary to the historic life-interests of Russia." (Mr. Churchill's forecast of October, 1939, became Russian policy in June, 1941, when German appetites fulfilled his predictions and drove Soviet Russia to defend itself by arms.) In the next stage, as Russia moved along the Baltic, he recognized that "the Russian Soviet Government, embodied in the formidable figure of Stalin, has barred off once and for ever all Nazi dreams of an advance in the East. The left paw of the Bear bars Germany from the Black Sea; the right paw disputes with her the control of the

Baltic." For Mr. Churchill could always be relied upon to see the war in a large perspective.

That was a First Lord's duty with the seven seas in his charge; and he paid frequent tribute to the Navy's work. It bore the brunt of the first seven months of war. Indeed, as uneventful silence settled on the Western Front, it appeared to a slightly impatient audience that there was not much war and that what there was of it concerned the Navy and Mr. Churchill. Its casualties exceeded all other French and British losses by land, sea, and air (though he found time for a graceful compliment to French naval development "under the long care of Admiral Darlan"); and the skill and gallantry of Harwood's victory in the South Atlantic won the first laurels of the war.

Presently the yellow waters of the River Plate washed lazily round the bent plates that had once been a German pocket-battleship preferring suicide by scuttling in safe neutral waters to one more encounter with the lighter guns of British cruisers. Mr. Churchill was the nation's spokesman in the first pride of victory, and later when *Exeter* and *Ajax* sent their ship's companies to tramp through roaring London streets to Guildhall. His opportunities were not neglected on such occasions or in cheerful offers "to engage the entire German Navy, using only the vessels which at one time or another they have declared they have destroyed." But his utterances were not confined to Admiralty business. For in the fifth month of the war, as Europe cowered under German threats to break the military deadlock in the West by violating neutral territory, he spoke his mind with perfect candor to the neutrals:

> What would happen if all these neutral nations I have mentioned—and some others I have not mentioned—were with one spontaneous impulse to do their duty in accordance with the Covenant of the League, and were to stand together with the British and French Empires against aggression and wrong? At present their plight is lamentable; and it will become much worse. They bow humbly and in fear to German threats of violence, comforting themselves meanwhile with the thought that the Allies will win, that Britain and France will strictly observe all the laws and conventions, and that breaches of these laws are only to be expected from the German side. Each one of them hopes that if he feeds the crocodile enough, the crocodile will eat him last . . .

There, in January, 1940, was excellent advice conveyed in a farseeing parable of the course of European history for the next eighteen months. Its lucidity provoked nervous disclaimers; and Mr. Churchill's gallant effort to infuse reality into international relations was unrewarded. But his preference of fair-play to strict etiquette won wide popularity, when the destroyer *Cossack* slipped into a Norwegian fjord and liberated British seamen from the German prison-ship *Altmark* and from the technicalities of slightly argumentative neutrality. The First Lord announced without false refinements that "in the interpretation of the rules and conventions affecting neutrals humanity rather than legal pedantry must be our guide"; and his countrymen, remembering with gratitude a loud hammering

*BLITZ*—The Prime Minister surveying the ruins of the Debating Chamber of the House of Commons, scene of many of his triumphs and failures. For a decade before the war, these walls echoed his vehement but unheeded warning: "This cursed, hellish invention and development of war from the air has revolutionized our position."

in the winter night and a cheerful voice announcing, "The Navy is here!" agreed with him completely.

As the months went by, Mr. Churchill grew to be their spokesman more and more. His decided utterance said what they wanted said, whether he turned his scorn upon "a haunted, morbid being, who, to their eternal shame, the German peoples in their bewilderment have worshipped as a god," or dealt blandly with "thoughtless dilettanti or purblind worldlings who sometimes ask us: 'What is it that Britain and France are fighting for?' To this I answer: 'If we left off fighting you would soon find out'."

That was what England wished to hear, and at that time it rarely heard it except from Mr. Churchill. His colleagues were less invigorating, since the Prime Minister approached the war as a depressing duty rather than a fierce, exacting challenge. The public tone was low, and the nation's effort in the first winter of the war scarcely approximated to high pressure. The Trade Unions were unconvinced of the necessity for sacrifice; military operations seemed to halt at the French frontier; and war production barely passed a peace-time rate. The cold and darkness of the winter were not a tonic, and the war in general appeared to have been set to a dragging tempo. But the King's ships were at sea, and Mr. Churchill could always be relied upon to strike a rousing note. The Free Trade Hall at Manchester, where he had so often talked politics, heard him that winter in a more authoritative character:

Come, then: let us to the task, to the battle, to the toil
—each to our part, each to our station. Fill the armies,
rule the air, pour out the munitions, strangle the U-boats,
sweep the mines, plough the land, build the ships, guard
the streets, succour the wounded, uplift the downcast, and
honour the brave. Let us go forward together in all parts
of the Empire, in all parts of the Island. There is not a
week, nor a day, nor an hour to lose.

That was a leader's tone; and all that England had begun to ask in 1940 was to be led.

This need for leadership emerged sharply in the
spring, as Germany shattered the decencies of Danish
and Norwegian independence and struck north—first,
the professional leadership that Mr. Churchill knew so
well how to give, when the Admiralty "thought the
operation so hazardous that at one o'clock in the morning we told the captain of the destroyer flotilla that he
must be the sole judge of whether to attack or not, and
that we would support him, whatever he did and whatever happened." That intimation, which elicited the
cheerful answer "Going into action," sent the destroyers
into Narvik with excellent results. But a sterner call for
leadership sounded a few weeks later, when an Allied
military force had been landed in Norway and brought
off again without visible result.

Parliament was gravely critical; angry Conservatives
added their voices to the Opposition; and Mr. Chamberlain did little to assuage their feelings with an ir-
ritable exclamation that "even I have my friends in
the House, and we shall see what they think when the
vote comes." For he had had his own way for so long.

But the last word was with the House of Commons, with the excitable assembly which had danced so long to Mr. Baldwin's tune, watched him sacrifice a Foreign Secretary in 1935, dethroned a king in 1936, ignored Mr. Churchill's endless pleadings for rearmament year after year, empowered ministers to indulge in the unrewarding traffic of appeasement, and wept tears of thankfulness when Mr. Chamberlain set off for Munich in 1938. That was not much more than eighteen months ago. But their mood was changing now; and late one May evening Mr. Churchill rose to complete the Government's defense.

There was one compelling reason why the Navy had been unable to interrupt the flow of German troops across the sea to Norway or to facilitate the landing of artillery and reinforcements for the British expedition—"It is our failure in the last five years to maintain or regain air parity with Germany . . . The immense enemy air strength which can be brought to bear upon our patrolling craft had made this method far too costly to be adopted . . . The intense and continuous bombing of the bases at Namsos and Andalsnes prevented the landing at these small fishing-ports of any large reinforcements, even of the artillery and of the many supplies for the infantry we had already landed . . . There was no means by which their air superiority could have been overcome."

The facts were simple; and though they justified the action which the Government had just been forced to take, they were a vivid condemnation of five years of

285

Mr. Baldwin and two years of Mr. Chamberlain. The House confirmed it by a vote in which the Government's majority dwindled from something over 200 to a bare 81; Mr. Chamberlain, after consultation with Lord Halifax, asked Mr. Churchill if he would succeed him; then he went through the motions of inviting Labor to join his own Government; and after a refusal, Mr. Chamberlain resigned.

Now there was no alternative to the one leader who had pointed another road. All parties would agree to serve under him—Labor, Liberals, Trade Unions (he had already spoken in debate of "Mr. Bevin—who is a friend of mine, working hard for the public cause, and a man who has much help to give"), dissatisfied Conservatives who had rallied to him earlier, the Tory rank and file awakened to its leaders' errors a good deal after the eleventh hour, and Mr. Chamberlain himself if he were wanted. The way was clear at last; and in the ninth month of a war, for which he had not been permitted to prepare the nation, Mr. Churchill became Prime Minister.

# MR. CHURCHILL'S WAR

*"My Lord, I am sure that I can save this country, and that nobody else can."*

MACAULAY'S ESSAY ON CHATHAM.

# 1

THERE was a terrible simplicity about the order of events. Two days after the debate on Norway the war moved into its next stage. For that sunny Friday had been chosen by the Germans for the opening of their assault on Western Europe; and as neutral Amsterdam and Brussels heard bombs for the first time, French and British armies moved forward to the rescue, ominously undisturbed by any German bombing. The trap was nicely baited. But the uncanny symmetry of history supplied the antidote in the very instant of administering the poison. For the same evening in London Mr. Churchill was invited by King George to form a Government.

The coincidence was undesigned, though Nazi moves were often apt to coincide with the political crises of democracies. The German march was executed on the date and at the pace prescribed for it in the Great General Staff's time-table. While Britain in promoting Mr. Churchill from the Admiralty to 10 Downing Street acted on the unrehearsed impulses of democracy, the tanks were oiled, the dive-bombers were waiting, and the Dutch and Belgian traitors knew precisely what they had to do. Dutch and Belgian gallantry might prevent some of them and delay the military time-table by a few hours. But the assault on Western Europe proceeded with the smooth precision of all military movements in the absence of effective opposition;

and all through that bright Whitsun week-end England sat by its receivers listening to Dutch radio stations interrupting the incongruous gaiety of their recorded dance-music with grim announcements of the flight of German planes across the skies of Holland.

The German plan was beautifully premeditated: a German promise to respect Dutch and Belgium neutrality had been sufficient guarantee of that. There was nothing improvised about it. For the art of wars abhors impromptus; and as the plan unfolded, German forethought was rewarded by the punctual arrival of German troops at their objectives.

Three days afterwards a new Prime Minister informed the House of Commons, "as I said to those who have joined this Government: 'I have nothing to offer but blood, toil, tears and sweat'." Here was a striking variation on the muffled utterance of well-meaning old gentlemen, who had talked cautiously about an emergency when they meant a war. But if the public wanted someone with the courage to speak plainly, they had found him; and he stated their objective with the fierce simplicity of Clemenceau—"You ask, what is our policy? I will say: It is to wage war, by sea, land and air, with all our might and with all the strength that God can give us . . . You ask, What is our aim? I can answer in one word: Victory—victory at all costs, victory in spite of all terror, victory, however long and hard the road may be; for without victory, there is no survival."

That was Winston Churchill's Inaugural.

## 2

On the next day the Dutch ceased fire; the same afternoon the French along the Meuse gave way; and within a week the Germans reached the English Channel. But there was plainly worse to come. For the sweep of the German scythe down the valley of the Somme had severed the British and French forces on the Belgian front from the rest of the French armies standing before Paris and along the German frontier. The British Expeditionary Force and its allies were isolated with their backs to the North Sea, and Mr. Churchill braced his people for a shock.

There was still a hope of French recovery; and he reiterated his "invincible confidence" in their army and its leaders, if only they could "cast away the idea of resisting behind concrete lines or natural obstacles." That still remained to be seen, with General Weygand and (it might be hoped) the Foch tradition succeeding on that very day to the more mechanical Gamelin. But "after this battle in France abates its force, there will come the battle for our island"; and his voice was raised to hearten them against its coming. So far as operations on the Continent were concerned, he made no attempt to spare their feelings with the fatal tenderness of a blind censorship. (That deadly sedative had already sapped the nerves of France.)

One summer morning M. Paul Reynaud, speaking with more scorn than any human voice had ever held, announced that the Belgian king had capitulated on the left flank of the French and British forces, as they fell back towards the sea. Mr. Churchill passed no judgment at the time; but a week later he indicated a clear view of "this pitiful episode," precipitated "suddenly, without prior consultation, with the least possible notice, without the advice of his Ministers and upon his own personal act." Whatever the extenuation, the military consequences were indisputable. For Allied chances of escape towards Dunkirk were gravely compromised; and "the House," Mr. Churchill told the Commons, "should prepare itself for hard and heavy tidings." For he anticipated the elimination of almost the entire Expeditionary Force.

Those were the burning summer days, when England listened to the distant thunder of the Dunkirk beaches and one officer, as his ship drew in by the dim light of dawn, saw "what seemed to be vast black shadows on the pale sands . . . he could not think what they were. As it grew lighter he saw that the blacknesses were enormous formations of men standing, waiting. He saw them thus whenever he entered the pass, coming or going. They did not seem to change; they did not seem to sit, nor to lie down; they stood, with the patience of their race, waiting their turn." That fortitude and discipline reaped a miraculous reward, as the worst disaster was averted by the selfless gallantry of rearguards and the young men in the sky overhead and the little ships, the unforgotten, un-Homeric catalogue of *Mary Jane* and *Peggy IV*, of *Folkestone Belle, Boy Billy,* and *Ethel Maud,* of *Lady Haig* and *Skylark.* Just as another challenge in the Narrow Seas had once been met by the Elizabethans, when "from Lyme, and Weymouth, and Poole, and the Isle of Wight, young lords and gentlemen came streaming out in every smack and sloop" to face the Armada and to tear its threat to tatters, so the little ships of England brought the army home.

Mr. Churchill had not been a month in office, when the main British army was driven off the Continent with the loss of all its guns and transport; and the strange people whom he led had to be seriously warned that they "must be very careful not to assign to this deliverance the attributes of a victory. Wars are not won by evacuations . . ." True, a brilliant operation had retrieved 123,095 Frenchmen and 186,587 British troops, exclusive of their wounded in the hospital ships which (as he said) "being so plainly marked were a special target for Nazi bombs." But he was disinclined to boast.

The campaign was surveyed at length in his statement to the House of Commons—the "armoured scythestroke," followed by "a number of German divisions in lorries, and behind them again there plodded comparatively slowly the dull brute mass of the ordinary German Army and German people, always so ready to be led to the trampling down in other lands of liberties and comforts which they have never known in their own." He praised the Navy and the Royal Air Force and the splendid sacrifice of Calais, and gave thanks for the crowning mercy of Dunkirk. Then he turned to

293

face the future and the imminence of invasion. One phrase rang strangely in his hearers' ears, as he proclaimed Britain's ability "to defend our island home, to ride out the storm of war, and to outlive the menace of tyranny, if necessary for years, if necessary alone."

As the last word was spoken, it seemed a needless shadow on the picture, an improbable contingency in the first week of June; and the defiant intimation, with which his statement ended, that the country would fight on at all costs and at every point of its territory in the British Isles and beyond the seas appeared to be no more than an ornament of splendid rhetoric. But it was more, much more than rhetoric. For, one danger safely past, another supervened; and Mr. Churchill sounded the alarm bell once again. The phrase, as he confessed a fortnight later, was designed as a veiled warning to his countrymen that there might be even worse to come; and his harsh announcement of Britain's unchanged purpose gave notice to all quarters where other views might prevail that the end of the war was still a long way off.

For France was flagging; and nine days later Mr. Churchill was pleading the same cause to a mixed audience of French ministers at Tours. The German tide was running strongly across France. German strategy had not obliged by battering its armies against the carefully contrived and advertised marvels of the Maginot Line, which was now as irrelevant to the defense of France as a battleship at anchor in a quiet port. But it had fulfilled one fatal purpose by monopolizing

French attention at the expense of more active forms of warfare in the same degree as their defenses had once paralyzed Marlborough's allies by what Mr. Churchill termed "the dyke-mind of the Dutch." The static glories of the Line, with its magnificent elaboration of the requirements of the last war, had ignored the next. It had immobilized French military thought in an age when war was to be predominantly mobile once again.

France was fatally unready for the German rush. Its impact, which was little more than a fuller reproduction of the previous autumn's assault on Poland, seemed to come as a complete surprise to armies unprovided with the requisite equipment or (in some unhappy instances) with the will to meet it. General Weygand failed to develop any trace of Foch's genius for the offensive; and the war degenerated into a rearguard action. Its swift approach and a single touch of air attack put Paris out of action, and France receded southward.

For the moment they were all at Tours—all Paris, all the eager amateurs of politics, whose thrills had so long been to Paris what the bull-ring was to Madrid. They were all at lunch and the Prefecture was quiet, when Mr. Churchill arrived with Lords Halifax and Beaverbrook. But somebody was found; and presently he was telling M. Reynaud that he could not consent to a separate request by France for an armistice. There were no reproaches; they had quite enough to bear without that. But it was agreed that France should make one more appeal to the United States and that, if this was unproductive, they should meet again. It was a breathing-space; but Mr. Churchill seemed shaken, as he left for home.

The interval was fatal. For the tide of politics, advancing even faster than the Germans, submerged the last surviving fragments of the French will to resist. Equivocal performers, who had long played questionable parts in the *coulisses,* sidled towards the wings and even edged on to the stage. This unpleasing transformation-scene went forward with bizarre effects and gathering velocity when they all reached Bordeaux.

Behind the wide quays and the dusty boulevards the disheveled personnel of French politics and administration gathered in restaurants and hotel lobbies. But their purposes diverged in strange directions. For M. Reynaud, the Prime Minister, still adhered intermittently to the brave program outlined in their last appeal to President Roosevelt—"We will fight before Paris, we will fight behind Paris, we will shut ourselves up in one of our provinces, and if we are driven out we will go to North Africa, and, if necessary, to our possessions in America." Yet when the fighting before Paris went against them, there was none at all in Paris and not very much behind it. For Weygand's mind appeared to stray towards the preservation of an army for the defense of society against its enemies at home. (Seventy years earlier a bare suspicion of the same purpose had earned Marshal Bazaine the death-sentence from a French court-martial.)

But while the politicians wavered, there was one that knew his mind. Pierre Laval's strange Odyssey from Left to Right, from his extremist origins to his sedate position, from the Franco-Soviet pact which he had signed in Moscow to the Hoare-Laval agreement about Abyssinia of which he had been deprived by British scruples, hardly indicated any undue fixity of principle. But his opportunism lay at the moment in the direction of surrender; and he had already chosen an imposing partner. For Marshal Pétain was admirably qualified by his prestige, no less than by his apprehensions, to play the part.

A quarter of a century before his nerve had failed before a German break-through on the Western Front; but when Pétain wavered in 1918, France was sustained by Clemenceau and Foch. He was not much over sixty then. But at eighty-four, when skies were darker overhead and France was in still graver danger, it was easy to persuade him that the supreme duty was retreat, and that a soldier must conduct it. Besides, the old man had a muddled notion that the Germans would respect a soldier's honor and that a soldier's simple rule could redeem France from all the errors (as his little circle viewed them) of the Third Republic.

That was the fatal brew which simmered at Bordeaux, as Mr. Churchill waited for the news from France. The first development was a renewed request from M. Reynaud for release from the French obligation to fight on. The British Government consented to a French inquiry for the German terms of armistice, "provided that the French fleet is despatched to British ports and remains there while the negotiations are conducted." That was essential, since the addition of the French to the Italian Navy might gravely unbalance the situation in the Mediterranean.

The reply from Bordeaux was a fresh invitation to confer with M. Reynaud. But before Mr. Churchill started, a proposal was transmitted to the French Government which bore deeply the imprint of his strong feeling for France. This was nothing less than a declaration "that France and Great Britain shall no longer be two nations, but one Franco-British union" with common citizenship and joint organs of government under a single War Cabinet. It was proposed, in fact, that France and Britain should federate as the first two United States of Europe. Could friendship go further to sustain a fainting ally? But it was too late. Bordeaux was busy with the fascinating game of redistributing portfolios; and a proposal to fuse nine centuries of history was dismissed practically without discussion. Reynaud resigned, and there were smiling faces round the tables in the restaurants. For the Marshal was in office, and the war would soon be over.

Mr. Churchill heard the news as he was in the train on the first stage of his journey to Bordeaux. Now he plainly could not go himself. But the First Lord of the Admiralty and the Colonial Secretary were sent to safeguard the future of the French fleet and Colonial Em-

*INSEPARABLE*—Accompanied by his wife and the inevitable cigar and Homburg hat, the Prime Minister surveys the London dock areas after the great air-raid fires had laid the district waste. The British flag still waves free.

pire. As to the former, "every kind of private and personal promise and assurance" (in Mr. Churchill's words) were lavished on his naval colleagues by Admiral Darlan; and the two British ministers surveyed the dismal spectacle of Bordeaux. One of them brought back a gray picture of the Third Republic in collapse under its last President—*"ce misérable Lebrun qui pleure toujours."*

On the next day Marshal Pétain surrendered in the name of France, and four days later French officers re-entered Foch's railway carriage at Compiègne in the abasement of defeat. The terms of the surrender, which was complete, elicited "grief and amazement" from the British Government, while Mr. Churchill still reiterated his belief that "the genius of France will rise again." But for the moment, it had fallen low; and its present rulers showed every sign of holding it down. That left Great Britain without a single ally in the world except the exiled Continental governments, who were its guests, to face a military menace which had swept Western Europe in a month.

Now his countrymen could see what Mr. Churchill had meant a fortnight earlier by his fierce proclamation that "we shall defend our island, whatever the cost may be, we shall fight on the beaches, we shall fight on the landing grounds, we shall fight in the fields and in the streets, we shall fight in the hills; we shall never surrender."

3

In June, 1940, and the months that followed Great Britain, under Mr. Churchill, stood in greater peril than at any moment in its history, knew it, and rather liked it. The coastline of the Continent from the North Cape to the Pyrenees was in enemy control; and behind it an undefeated army with immense striking power and unlimited air strength waited its moment. The danger was no graver in the weeks before Trafalgar, when Nelson was decoyed to the West Indies and the *Grande Armée* lay waiting on the hills behind Boulogne, or in the breathless days that saw the vast crescent of the Armada draw slowly nearer to a silent island in a summer sea. For England in 1588 was not defenseless if Alva's men had landed; and England in 1805 had armed for years against a French invasion. But England in 1940? That question was never answered, because invasion never came. But it was plain that, in Froude's words, "a combination of curious circumstances, assisted by four and twenty miles of water, had protected England hitherto from sharing the miseries of the rest of Europe"; and that summer England wondered just how long the barrier would hold.

After years of gathering uncertainty about the future it was a relief to know precisely where they stood. There was not much room for doubting that in June, 1940; and it seemed preferable to the vague terrors of the unknown, which had hung over them during the inactive winter months, or the agonies they had experienced before the army was extricated from the Continent. Now they were all, or nearly all, at home; and they could face the worst together. Mr. Churchill had once written of "the genius of the English race in adversity."

But in those summer weeks they were braced by something more than adversity. For they had always valued their privacy. Their garden walls were higher, their railway compartments smaller than those of other people; and when all Continental aid fell away from them, they were inwardly sustained by a strange, consoling feeling that they had got the war to themselves. There were no more foreign complications now; and they could trust themselves to do whatever had to be done. It was somehow comforting to feel that their backs were to the wall, that there was nothing more for them to think about, and that henceforward action would determine the event. (That feeling was put into words by the Londoner who remarked sedately, "Well, we're in the final now.")

They could see clearly that they had not been very good at forecasting events or at making preparations to encounter them, and that they had been brought to the edge of the abyss by leaders who honestly supposed themselves to be traveling in the opposite direction. But all that was over, and life seemed infinitely simpler now that they could see the precipice in front of them. For they were free to concentrate on action, on immense increases of production, on improvising an entirely new defense force over a million strong.

They set about it in a mood of surprising cheerfulness. Indeed, they were unusually sociable that summer. Strangers actually spoke to one another, warmed by a sense that they were all in it together (and a comfortable feeling that nobody else was.) The Empire was with them, and sympathetic noises came from the United States. But the Empire was a long way off, except for an increasing number of its representatives in arms, who were comfortingly on the spot. If the blow fell it would fall on Britain. Their island was a stronghold; and as they walked about it they could see their own people and the large young men from the Dominions by whom it was to be defended. There were no heroics, because they all had far too much to do. But if their predicament that summer was Elizabethan, their temper was Elizabethan too.

One man's voice kept time to their steady pulse and occasionally made it beat a little faster. Indeed, it was not easy to say whether Mr. Churchill's mood was attuned to theirs or theirs to his, for they encouraged one another. He had begun at the darkest moment of the French collapse with a proud intimation that "we have become the sole champions now in arms to defend the world cause. We shall do our best to be worthy of this high honour. . . ." On the next day, surveying their situation "with a disillusioned eye," he enumerated as Great Britain's assets a large army, an unbeaten navy—"after all, we have a Navy. Some people seem to forget that we have a Navy. We must remind them"—

and an Air Force whose performance at Dunkirk gave promise of still better results nearer home.

With these resources his technical advisers had recommended that the war could be carried on with "good and reasonable hopes of final victory." This cool report was followed by an equally calm account of consultations with the Dominions, resulting in the decision of a united Empire to fight on. Then he permitted himself a final word of eloquent encouragement:

> The whole fury and might of the enemy must very soon be turned on us. Hitler knows that he will have to break us in this island or lose the war. If we can stand up to him, all Europe may be free and the life of the world may move forward into broad, sunlit uplands . . . Let us therefore brace ourselves to our duties, and so bear ourselves that, if the British Empire and its Commonwealth last for a thousand years, men will say, "This was their finest hour."

That was in June. A vivid sense that all of them were in it was reinforced by the inclusive composition of Mr. Churchill's all-party Government, in which Tory lions lay down with Trade Union lambs and Liberals of both complexions were on speaking terms, and by his unvarying refusal to reproach those responsible for past failings—"If we open a quarrel between the past and the present, we shall find that we have lost the future." (A few months later, on the death of Mr. Chamberlain, he became the chosen leader of the Conservative party, strange vindication of his chequered course. It was a posthumous success for Randolph

Churchill, and a triumph of unorthodoxy justified in action.)

His strong sense of urgency, of the "supreme hour," informed all his utterances. But there was no suggestion of the slightest strain. Indeed, a comfortable insularity began to creep into his surveys—"Here, in our island, we are in good health and in good heart. . . ." This was followed by a circumstantial forecast of defense in "every village, every town, and every city. The vast mass of London itself, fought street by street, could easily devour an entire hostile army . . ." and preparations for the purpose were becoming familiar objects of the countryside and of the urban landscape. For Mr. Churchill and his countrymen kept pace with one another. "Here," he had told them, "in this strong City of Refuge which enshrines the title-deeds of human progress and is of deep consequence to Christian civilisation; here, girt about by the seas and oceans where the Navy reigns; shielded from above by the prowess and devotion of our airmen—we await undismayed the impending assault." They knew precisely what he meant. Meanwhile, it was good to hear (as he told a later audience) that "the whole British Army is at home" and "the whole island bristles against invaders."

They were in August now. The summer weeks had passed, and they were still "erect, sure of ourselves, masters of our fate. . . . Few would have believed we could survive; none would have believed that we should to-day not only feel stronger, but should actually be stronger than we have ever been before." They had come a long way since midsummer, when very few outside the British Empire believed that they would have the courage to fight on, and cold-eyed neutral journalists composed judicial surveys at long range of what the world would be like "If Britain should lose." The statistics of defeat had seemed almost unanswerable then. But they were never very good at figures.

Logically the operations on the Continent, upon whose result the war had hitherto been staked, pointed to a German victory; and the French, always logical, succumbed. But the British mind impervious to logic, entirely failed to follow this disastrous reasoning. As they figured it out, it was palpably ridiculous for anybody to suppose (though nearly all the world supposed it) that the war was lost. Nothing was further from the truth, as they could see with their own eyes. Others might, perhaps, have lost it temporarily; for Oxford Street was full of foreign uniforms that summer. But they were quite convinced that nobody need feel the least anxiety about Great Britain.

They were helped to that conclusion by the cheerful voice of the Prime Minister; and no man ever rendered greater service to his people than their spokesman in those summer weeks of 1940. Perhaps it was his major contribution to their history. For they had never been articulate; and Mr. Churchill, by saying what they felt, enabled them to feel it still more strongly. He felt as they did about the things that they were fighting for, things that had sometimes been a trifle undervalued by sophisticated critics in the Twenties. But then Mr. Churchill had never been in sympathy with that enlightened decade; and neither, for that matter, were they. For when it came to it they found themselves insensibly aligned in defense of earlier ideals, of simpler standards well within their comprehension and Mr. Churchill's, of things that Englishmen had thought worth fighting for in 1914 and 1897 and 1815. (For they could see now that their history was not nearly so irrelevant as they had sometimes been inclined to think.)

He did not speak smooth words to them about an easy victory; and he said just what they wanted said about the enemy. His sturdy mispronunciation of foreign names appealed to them immensely; he would have his little bit of fun about the Italians, and the country roared. They were delighted when he offered Mussolini's navy a safe passage past Gibraltar to satisfy "a general curiosity in the British Fleet . . . whether the Italians are up to the level they were at in the last war or whether they have fallen off at all," no less than by his disrespectful word-pictures of the "little Italian accomplice trotting along hopefully and hungrily, but rather wearily and very timidly." But in his graver passages, his deeper notes, his invocation of "all that we have and are," his simple statement that "we may show mercy—we shall ask for none," he was the voice of England.

4

They had learned to know him as a voice. Careful articulation, a slight difficulty with the letter "s," judicious pauses, and a highly unusual vocabulary composed a personality in sound with which they were familiar by now. They knew when its lifting intonation savored a new and still less favorable portrait of "this evil man, this monstrous abortion of hatred and defeat" or lightly sketched "his tattered lackey Mussolini at his tail and Admiral Darlan frisking at his side." His utterance, unspoiled by the labored imitations of his junior colleagues, was quite unmistakable; and they all knew it after his broadcasts. For that summer the Prime Minister was more heard than seen by the great mass of his fellow-countrymen. When they saw him, thirty years of disrespectful effigies in political cartoons identified him plainly. (He was a little sensitive about it, explaining with some particularity in an essay upon the hardships of caricature that "my nose was not like a wart, and my hats were well fitted by one of the best hatters in London.") But they did not see a great deal of him at first. For there was too much to be done in Westminster for him to be seen very much outside.

Presently he began to get about a little. He had always liked to see things for himself, and there was so much for him to see—the new defense works, the expanding armies, the latest weapons introduced into the panoply of war from the gangster's repertory. It was not long before the watching cameras rewarded public curiosity with the image of a cheerful leader with a slightly unusual taste in hats and a way of fingering firearms with an air of brisk anticipation. Soon his cigar, his dogged mouth, his purposeful, gay eye were seen abroad; and England learned to know its leader's figure as well as the front line had once known Clemenceau's. There was a good deal of Clemenceau about him; and he confessed (as the old man had confessed to him one gusty day in 1918) a frank enjoyment of escape from Westminster to the realities of the front line.

In 1940 the front line was not so far away; and presently a square hat and a big cigar were seen ascending steep declivities in the neighborhood of coast defenses with considerable agility. The silhouette was unmistakable; and (unlike his elocution) it had no imitators. Guards of honor were inspected and new weapons viewed with an appraising eye, hunched shoulders, and a large Havana. His headgear varied from the agricultural to the marine. But the walking-stick and the cigar were quite invariable; and one wintry occasion in deep snow was honored with a magnificently hybrid costume—sea-boots planted wide apart and walking-stick erect in reefer pocket—which seemed to mark a definite attempt to introduce the long cigar into naval uniform.

They knew his figure now and cheered it to the echo, when they saw a busy, semi-naval presence hurrying at a hot pace up gangways into H.M.S. *Victory*, into unfinished warships, into whatever might be of interest to a Prime Minister who believed in seeing for himself. His life had scarcely brought him personal popularity on a wide scale till now. But there could be no mistaking what they felt about him, as the cheers rang out; and then the hat came off in a wide sweep, and a shy smile appeared. That, perhaps, was his reward after a long career in which he had so often stood alone.

After midsummer the war passed suddenly into a new phase. For the Germans snatched hungrily at command of the air above Great Britain in preparation for its final subjection. Their numerical preponderance was immense. But the attempt, watched by the quiet English fields in August and September, 1940, was unsuccessful. British gallantry, aided by superior design, beat off the German onslaught. German losses in the daylight air became unbearable, rising to 697 aircraft in the first ten days of their offensive and culminating in an autumn day when the Royal Air Force sent 185 enemy machines crashing into the country which they had failed to invade. Small wonder the Prime Minister's cigar remained unlit that morning as he watched the map in the Operations Room of a Fighter Group. He had already paid tribute to the gallantry of the few hundred men who stood between the country and defeat—"Never in the field of human conflict was so much owed by so many to so few . . ." and the event confirmed him, gloriously passing one more milestone in the long march towards victory.

A new experience awaited them that autumn, as the

Germans turned to a fresh expedient. The kindly German mind of Kaiser Wilhelm's day had already enriched the art of war with air bombardment of large cities, as with poison gas and promiscuous slaughter at sea by submarines; and no part of its inheritance was grasped more eagerly by the new Germany of the Third Reich. The swift destruction of civil populations from the sky by a preponderating airforce was a notion with a strong appeal to those who understood that they would be the bombers rather than the bombed; and the appalling prospect had played a large part in the unopposed ascent of Hitler's Germany to European power. Civilized susceptibilities, chilled by the filmed apocalypse of Mr. H. G. Wells' *Shape of Things to Come* and by press photographs of bombing at Shanghai, Madrid, and Barcelona, shrank from the terrible experience.

The bare threat had sufficed to cow France, Britain, and Czechoslovakia in 1938; the grim reality at Warsaw and Rotterdam was terrifying; and one touch of it was enough for Paris. If only they could break the nerve or shatter the huge fabric of London, Britain might be disorganized and defeated. So the attempt was duly made in force on fine autumn nights in 1940.

The daylight sky was now no place for German bombers. But each night the city learned to know the unpleasant music of their approach, the halting drone of enemy propellers, the swish and thud of bombs, the glare of fires, and the swift rush of automobiles through the empty streets. Each morning, as it picked its way to work across the broken glass, it counted the destruction; but each day it found that London was still there, if a little battered and with a disconcerting tendency to send its traffic round by unlikely routes. The night was past; and each misty autumn morning London turned to a new day of work. Its great pulse beat steadily, and it accepted Mr. Churchill's cheerful calculation that "it would take ten years at the present rate for half the houses of London to be demolished. After that, of course, progress would be much slower . . ." For the nightly siege of London failed to break their nerve or to destroy their city, and Londoners had met the challenge unafraid.

There was senseless killing, aimless destruction, silly savagery practiced upon unarmed people and their small belongings by a thwarted enemy. But they knew the German way by this time; and it led no further than a long vista of exasperated citizens vociferously informing Mr. Churchill that "We can take it" and (with more conviction) "Give it 'em back." He was out visiting them in the rubble of their shattered streets; and presently, when the scourge swept on into the provinces, they saw a swiftly pacing figure with which the Mayor occasionally had some difficulty in keeping up. The smile, the lifted hat (sometimes he lifted it on the end of his walking-stick to greet them, as he hurried by), swift handshakes, and a thrusting chin were all they saw of the Prime Minister; and sometimes he sat high on the back of an automobile so that they could see him better. That was how England greeted Mr. Churchill, as he went his rounds.

They rarely took him far afield. But once in the next year his duty sent him overseas to a quiet anchorage beyond the Western Ocean, where the misty hills looked down on a great British battleship at anchor beside an American cruiser. There he talked at ease with the President of the United States; and on a Sunday morning they sat smiling side by side, as two thousand men of two nations sang "Onward, Christian soldiers" under the silent English guns. Then he stood watching by the rail, as U.S.S. *Augusta* drew away. Homeward again across the Atlantic, with the sharp bows of his battleship curtseying to the mid-ocean swell, until they parted at the home port and a steel wall of cheering seamen sent him on his way. For Mr. Churchill had become his country's emblem.

5

Not that his duties were exclusively symbolic. For he had taken charge of a hard-pressed country and Empire in a dark hour in order to conduct a war. That was his element. He had been trained to war; the greater part of his official life had been devoted to war problems at the Admiralty, the Ministry of Munitions, and the War Office; nearly all his writings dealt with military subjects; even Lord Fisher in the moment of their deepest disagreement termed him "a War Man." On taking office as Prime Minister he became at the same time Minister of Defence; and the appointment was not merely decorative. For he assumed supreme charge of war direction. As he described the system to the House of Commons in May, 1941, "the Chiefs of Staff of the three Services sit each day together, and I, as Prime Minister and Minister of Defence, convene them and preside over them, when I think it necessary, inviting, when business requires it, the three Service Ministers. All large issues of military policy are brought before the Defence Committee . . ." The chairman there, as in the War Cabinet and the conference of Chiefs of Staff, was the Prime Minister; and, subject to the guidance of his professional advisers, the war in its conduct on the British side was Mr. Churchill's.

Its major operations bore the stamp of his capacity for taking necessary and profitable risks. With adequate support his Eastern enterprise in 1915 might well have changed the course of history; and it is impossible not to detect his touch in the judicious military speculation of 1940, which despatched valuable troops and still more valuable equipment to the East with a vivid sense of the high value of the Nile Valley and Suez Canal. The risk was great; but so were the rewards in the continued security of that pivot of the British Empire and the annihilation of the Italian counterpoise in Africa by Wavell's victories.

After he came to power, a more decisive touch became discernible in almost every act of British policy. The misappropriation of the French fleet by France's enemies was swiftly averted by firm action in which it is not easy to discern the hesitating touch of Mr.

313

Churchill's predecessors. The approach—"We are determined to fight on to the end . . . Should we conquer, we solemnly declare that we shall restore the greatness and territory of France"—had all his chivalry and his persistent love of France. The three alternatives of active service in the common cause, accommodation in British ports, or disarmament in the West Indies had all his resolution. And the swift culmination of the tragedy in action which preserved control of the Mediterranean for Britain—and for France as well—gave notice to the world of a great nation in deadly earnest. Tragic in the cruel contradictions of its first impact, no single act was more deeply impressive to a world of watching neutrals. For it was realized after Oran that Mr. Churchill's Britain meant business.

It was capable of prompt and salutary action, when menaced behind screens of artifice in Irak or Syria or Persia; and it was no less capable of prompt and generous reactions, when the German dementia of conquest hurled its armies at the throat of Soviet Russia. Here was a strange associate for Mr. Churchill. It was a moment of some delicacy. But he saw the broad issue and stated it at once without the least hesitation or insincerity. The challenge of a common enemy did not make him a Communist; but behind Communism he could see Russia, mile after mile of fields and villages and armies threatened by the "clanking, heel-clicking, dandified Prussian officers . . . the dull, drilled, docile, brutish masses of the Hun soldiery, plodding on like a swarm of crawling locusts." Against that threat

*ATLANTIC CHARTER*—Alone on the deck of H.M.S. *Prince of Wales*, Mr. Churchill watches the U.S. destroyer *McDougal* depart, bearing President Roosevelt to the U.S.S. *Augusta* after the historic meeting of August 23, 1941, which cemented the ties between their nations.

he stated plainly that "we shall give whatever help we can to Russia and to the Russian people"; and in the declaration, swift, effective, and sincere, Mr. Churchill spoke for England once again.

But there was one field of international relations in which his touch was still more badly needed. The European outlook of the United States in the early stages of the war might be defined as anti-Nazi without being pro-Ally. Hitler's absolute regime was obviously calculated to antagonize American opinion. But active sympathy with his opponents was severely limited. A good deal of muddled thinking on both sides of the Atlantic had attributed the European imbroglio to the supposed imperfections of the Treaty of Versailles rather than to that unhappy failure to apply it, which was due in no small measure to American repudiation of Woodrow Wilson.

On this foundation an imposing structure of misconception was erected, from whose summit large numbers of Americans looked down impartially upon both sets of European combatants, imagining that both were equally to blame and both contending for equally unworthy objects. The angularity of Mr. Chamberlain and his prolonged adherence to an injudicious policy of conciliation (profoundly unpopular in the United States, where eager onlookers vastly preferred heroic remedies) did little to repel this imputation; and even when it came to war, the spectacle itself was disappointing.

This frame of mind was stimulated by a small, but

active, group of which Colonel Lindbergh was the most widely known and Mr. Hoover the most experienced. The former had already rendered distinguished service to the Nazi cause by giving wide publicity to his opinion of the insignificance of the Russian air force in the decisive days of 1938, while the latter's experience in feeding hungry European countries during and after the last war inclined him strongly to favor a repetition of this gracious rôle regardless of its damaging effect on the Allied blockade of Germany. His anxiety to distract public attention from the war found its expression (as he stated candidly) in concentrated efforts to direct it towards the pressing needs of Finland; and his value as a judge of European statesmen was strangely illustrated by his favorable estimate, confided nine years earlier to Senator Borah, of M. Laval's "frankness and directness."

President Roosevelt and large numbers of his fellow-citizens had other views; and they were vastly reinforced by the events of 1940. The heroic spectacle of Britain facing the worst single-handed, of a whole nation under fire had its effect. Frank admiration kindled a desire to help. Besides there was a growing comprehension that the cause in which their help was needed was not exclusively British or even European. For as the German appetite expanded with success, its wider implications became apparent; and the Americas from the Great Lakes to Cape Horn surveyed the unpleasing outline of the German dream—a world dominated by the *Herrenvolk* (for the Jews' notion of a Chosen People

316

was oddly congenial to their oppressors) with tributary continents obediently furnishing their allotted quotas of raw material and manufactures for such payment and in such quantities as the requirements of a self-sufficient Europe and its African dependency allowed.

In this agreeable perspective the Americas would live on sufferance; and as the prospect made no appeal to them, they began to make their preparations for the defense of the New World against this evil exhalation of the Old. The first line was held by Britain; and Aid for Britain speedily became an American policy. But beyond the stark, material considerations of hemisphere defense they could see now that the American dream was not so different in essentials from the British aspiration to be free; and in the shadow of impending tyranny free peoples drew together.

This process was vastly facilitated by the ascendancy of Mr. Churchill. When his lively figure replaced the unresponsive Chamberlain, Anglo-American communications improved perceptibly. After all, he was Anglo-American himself. Here was a phenomenon with which Americans could sympathize. His vivid utterance, his combativeness, his political resilience, and above all his long campaign against the Nazis were elements in his career that roused friendly echoes on the further side of the Atlantic. Like the President's, his ruling passion was the Navy; and like another Roosevelt, he started life as a Rough Rider and was capable of "bull-moose" campaigns of solitary vehemence in the teeth of party orthodoxy. They always liked a fighter; and with Mr. Churchill at the helm they seemed to see the British Empire take its coat off to the fight.

That was the key to the immense and practical increase of American assistance which followed his accession. They could understand his easy-going statement, when he abandoned diplomatic ceremony in order to announce that "those two great organisations of the English-speaking democracies, the British Empire and the United States, will have to be somewhat mixed up together in some of their affairs for mutual and general advantage." Such informality was vastly preferable to the stiffness which they had been inclined (not without reason) to associate with British statesmen. He had always been a firm believer in Anglo-American association; and he went on to proclaim his faith—"No one can stop it. Like the Mississippi, it just keeps rolling along. Let it roll. Let it roll on full flood, inexorable, irresistible, benignant, to broader lands and better days."

It rolled to some considerable purpose as the months went by, to the transfer of American destroyers, to the lease of British bases for American defense, to the mounting flood—ships, food, munitions, planes, and guns—of material furnished to Britain under the elastic provisions of the Lease-Lend Act. There was a vivid comprehension of Britain's nexus with the New World in the lease of naval and air bases on British territory for the defense of the Americas. As Mr. Churchill said, "the army, air and naval frontiers of the United States have been advanced along a wide arc into the Atlantic Ocean" on coasts and islands owing allegiance to King George. But as King George was the sovereign of a great American Power, it was quite natural for the King of Canada and the British West Indies to play his part in hemisphere defense. For Great Britain stands as a corner-stone of the Atlantic world, of the great quadrilateral of peaceful life which runs from Liverpool and Cape Town to Buenos Aires and New York. That area is the center of modern civilization.

Its easy ways, its democratic government, its rich commerce all lie beneath the threat of barbarian invasion; and the significance of Anglo-American collaboration is in that broad circumstance. It underlay the growing intimacy of political relations and the fruitful informality of Mr. Churchill's meeting with President Roosevelt. What could be more American than their declaration of human rights "that all the men in all the lands may live out their lives in freedom from fear and want"? And what could be more British? For the same standards hold on both shores of the Atlantic; and their maintenance requires full service from both peoples. Their partnership, as Mr. Churchill said, is quite inevitable; and each partner knows his duty, as he defined it once in a voice that carried across three thousand miles of ocean—"We shall not fail or falter; we shall not weaken or tire. Neither the sudden shock of battle, nor the long-drawn trials of vigilance and exertion will wear us down. Give us the tools and we will finish the job."

6

Forty years ago a young author, writing his second book, reviewed a strange phase of the British destiny:

Year after year, and stretching back to an indefinite horizon, we see the figures of the odd and bizarre potentates against whom the British arms continually are turned. They pass in a long procession: The Akhund of Swat; Cetawayo, brandishing an assegai as naked as himself; Kruger, singing a psalm of victory; Osman Digna, the Immortal and the Irretrievable; Theebaw, with his Umbrella; Lobengula, gazing fondly at the pages of *Truth;* Prempeh, abasing himself in the dust; the Mad Mullah, on his white ass; and, latest of all, the Khalifa in his coach of state. It is like a pantomime scene at Drury Lane. These extraordinary foreign figures—each with his complete set of crimes, horrible customs, and "minor peculiarities"— march one by one from the dark wings of barbarism up to the bright footlights of civilisation. For a space their names are on the wires of the world and the tongues of men. The Sovereign on the Throne, the Minister in his Cabinet, the General in his tent, pronounce or mispronounce their styles and titles. A thousand compositors make the same combination of letters. The unusual syllables become household words. The street-boy bellows them in our ears. The artisan laughs over them at night in his cottage. The child in the nursery is cajoled into virtue or silence by the repetition of the dread accents. And then the world-audience clap their hands, amused yet impatient, and the potentates and their trains pass on, some to exile, some to prison, some to death.

There, in Winston Churchill's youthful prose, is a lively survey of Victorian encounters with hostile autocrats. But at longer intervals British forces have been measured upon larger issues with more powerful autocracies. For all autocrats who seek to dominate the whole of Europe are faced, sooner or later, with Britain's enmity; and their stately figures join the long procession—King Philip pacing slowly under the gray bulk of the Escorial and flinging the whole weight of Spain and the Indies against an island Kingdom; the *Roi Soleil* holding the Continent in fee among the terraces and mirrors of Versailles; Napoleon ruling from Seville to the Polish marshes and thwarted of his last success by British squares upon a trampled ridge in Belgium; Kaiser Wilhelm in vain pursuit of victory from the gates of Paris to the quiet woods of Doorn. Two died in exile, and two broken-hearted in the wreck of all that they had tried to build in despite of England. For England does not suffer one man to rule the Continent; and each attempt raises an English leader to oppose it—Cecil, Marlborough, Pitt . . .

Another Churchill joined the line to stand where Marlborough had stood, when a fresh challenge sounded and the maddest Mullah of them all essayed world-conquest with the drugged onset of a hypnotized community, dosed with a craving for revenge, with wounded pride at military failure in 1918, and with unpleasant outcrops of old tribal savagery. Is it Napoleonic? The French Empire grew in the air of easy growth that followed the great rains of the French Revolution. For the Revolution was its driving-power. But there is no trace of revolutionary impulse in the

sordid alternation of trickery and violence with which
Nazi showmanship imposed itself on Germany and
Germany on Europe. Freedom marched across the Continent behind the tricolor. But freedom is not enlarged
as the swastika flutters up to the masthead; and the German brings his own Inquisition in the shuttered automobiles of the Gestapo. Napoleon would not recognize
himself in Adolf Hitler.

Yet there are other individuals in history who have
attempted single-handed domination of the world.
Other barbarian raiders from the East—Attila, Genghis
Khan, Hulagu—leaped into the saddle of world-power
with a running start, as barbarism suddenly impinged
on settled civilization. Hitler's epiphany has far more
in common with the racing hordes of high-cheeked savages that broke in spray across the world than with the
steady tramp of the Old Guard, the pounding charge
of his cuirassiers rising in their stirrups with a roar
of *Vive l'Empereur!* as they swept past the small, great-
coated figure on the gray barb. For he was an eagle
among conquerors. But now we face a bird of prey.

## 7

Strange are the destinies of cavalry subalterns. Two,
at least, have been among their country's greatest war
ministers; and Macaulay's verdict on the first, whom
a baited Prime Minister once scouted as "that terrible
Cornet of Horse," may serve as a judgment of the second:

That the national spirit rose to the emergency, that the national resources were contributed with unexampled cheerfulness, this was undoubtedly his work. The ardour of his soul had set the whole kingdom on fire. It inflamed every soldier who dragged the cannon up the heights of Quebec, and every sailor who boarded the French ships among the rocks of Britanny. The Minister, before he had been long in office, had imparted to the commanders whom he employed his own impetuous, adventurous, and defying character. They, like him, were disposed to risk everything, to play double or quits to the last, to think nothing done while anything remained undone, to fail rather than not to attempt.

For Mr. Churchill is not far from Chatham.

*AUTHORITIES*

# AUTHORITIES

The best source of knowledge for Mr. Winston Churchill's life is afforded by his own writings and speeches, to which frequent reference is made.

The writer is also indebted to Mr. R. Sencourt's *Winston Churchill* (1940), Sir G. Arthur's *Concerning Winston Spencer Churchill* (1940) and Mr. H. Martin's *Battle: The Life Story of Winston Churchill* (1940) for their recent surveys of the field, and to "Ephesian's" *Winston Churchill* (1927) for an earlier study.

## VICTORIAN

### 1

The year 1874 may be recovered from the pages of *Punch* and Hansard, Vol. II of J. Morley's *Life of Gladstone* (1903), Vol. V of G. E. Buckle's *Life of Disraeli* (1920), Vol. II (Second Series) of *The Letters of Queen Victoria* (1926), the present writer's *The Queen and Mr. Gladstone* (1933), and Beeton's Christmas Annuals for 1872, 1873, and 1874, *The Coming K——, The Siliad,* and *Jon Duan.*

### 2

Mr. Winston Churchill's *Lord Randolph Churchill* (1906) supplemented by *Speeches of the Right Hon. Lord Randolph Churchill, M.P.* (1889), Lord Rosebery's *Lord Randolph Churchill* (1906), and Lady Randolph Churchill's *Reminiscences* (1908), furnish a full account of his parents; and the first twenty years of his life may be recovered from these sources and from his own account in *My Early Life* (1930), supplemented by his essay on *Cartoons and Cartoonists* in *Thoughts and Adventures* (1932). The writer is indebted to

Mr. E. A. H. Jay for fresh particulars of Mr. Churchill's life at his first school.

J. M. Barrie's sympathetic caricature of Lord Randolph Churchill is to be found in *Better Dead* (1891).

### 3

The year 1895 may be recovered from its periodicals and literature, especially *Punch, The Yellow Book,* and Rudyard Kipling's *The Seven Seas* (1896). Its antecedents and sequel are analyzed in the present writer's study of the Diamond Jubilee in *The Hundred Years* (1936), s.v. *St. Paul's.*

### 4

The facts of Mr. Churchill's career in 1895 and 1896 are narrated in *My Early Life,* and its social background is to be found in his mother's *Reminiscences* and *Life's Ebb and Flow* (1929), by Frances, Countess of Warwick.

### 5

Mr. Churchill has recorded his Indian experiences in *My Early Life* and *The Story of the Malakand Field Force* (1898), which may be supplemented by the writings of Rudyard Kipling *passim* and G. W. Steevens's *In India* (1899). His unpublished rejoinder to Bernard Shaw is referred to in his *Great Contemporaries* (1937), s.v. *George Bernard Shaw.*

### 6

*My Early Life* and *Savrola* (1900) supply the material for Mr. Churchill's later activities in India, and *The River War* (1899), supplemented by G. W. Steevens's *With Kitchener to Khartoum* (1899), and R. C. Slatin's *Fire and Sword in the Sudan* (1896), for his experiences in the campaign of Omdurman.

### 7

Mr. Churchill's career between the battle of Omdurman and the South African War is recorded by *My Early Life.* G. W.

# Authorities

Steevens's article about him is quoted in H. Martin's *Battle* (1940), and his speech about the Mahdi's tomb is referred to in W. S. Blunt's *Diaries* (1919), Vol. I, p. 397.

His meeting at sea with G. W. Steevens is placed by him before his arrival at Cairo in *My Early Life* (p. 227) and in "five days on a Mediterranean steamer, two in a Continental express" in the more nearly contemporary *London to Ladysmith via Pretoria* (p. 478).

## 8

Mr. Churchill's South African experiences and observations were recorded at the time in *London to Ladysmith via Pretoria* (1900) and *Ian Hamilton's March* (1900), supplemented later by *My Early Life* and a reference to General Botha's escape at Chieveley in his *Thoughts and Adventures,* s.v. *A Second Choice.* A full official record is to be found in L. S. Amery's *Times History of the War in South Africa* (1900-09), which may be supplemented by R. Kipling's *The Five Nations* (1903).

## 9

Mr. Churchill has recorded the events of 1900 following his return from South Africa in *My Early Life.*

## EDWARDIAN

### 1

Mr. Churchill's maiden speech on February 18, 1901, appears in *Parliamentary Debates,* Vol. LXXXIX. He re-issued his leading speeches on Army questions in *Mr. Brodrick's Army* (1903); and references to his political evolution appear in *My Early Life* and A. G. Gardiner's *Life of Sir William Harcourt* (1923), Vol. II, pp. 539, 591. His figure is included in *John Bull's* Parliamentary group of June 18, 1903. Wilfrid Blunt's impression of him in October, 1904, is in *My Diaries,* Vol. II

(1920), p. 77, and Joseph Chamberlain's estimate in *The Autobiography of Margot Asquith,* Vol. II (1922), p. 134.

## 2

Mr. Churchill's composition of *Lord Randolph Churchill* (1906) is referred to in his *Great Contemporaries,* s.v. *The Earl of Rosebery, Joseph Chamberlain,* and *John Morley* and in W. S. Blunt's *Diaries,* Vol. II, pp. 107, 311. His defense of Unionist Free Traders is in *The Autobiography of Margot Asquith,* Vol. II, pp. 60-1.

## 3

Mr. Churchill's impressions of the General Election of 1906 are in his *Thoughts and Adventures,* s.v. *Election Memories,* and Sir H. Campbell-Bannerman's report of local misgivings as to his prospects in 1904 in J. A. Spender's *Life of Sir Henry Campbell-Bannerman* (1923), Vol. II, p. 161.

Mr. Churchill's visit to the German maneuvers of 1906 is recorded in his *Thoughts and Adventures,* s.v. *The German Splendour,* and his first meeting with Sir J. Fisher at Biarritz in 1907 in his *World Crisis* (1923), Vol. I, p. 73, and Sir S. Lee's *King Edward VII* (1927), Vol. II, p. 534.

His leading speeches of 1906 and 1907 are collected in his *Liberalism and the Social Problem* (1909); and *My African Journey* (1908) gives an account of his visit to Uganda in 1907. Mr. Masterman's comment on his Transvaal speech is in L. Masterman's *C. F. G. Masterman* (1939), p. 84. Opinions of King Edward VII and Mr. Asquith in 1908 are in the *Life of Lord Oxford and Asquith,* by J. A. Spender and C. Asquith (1932), Vol. I, p. 195. Mr. Asquith's first suggestion of the Admiralty to Mr. Churchill is in his *World Crisis,* Vol. I, p. 67, and his objections to the Local Government Board in Sir E. Marsh's *A Number of People* (1939).

4

The North-West Manchester and Dundee by-elections of 1908 are recorded in Mr. Churchill's *Thoughts and Adventures,* s.v. *Election Memories* and J. Morley's *Recollections* (1917), Vol. II, p. 255; conversations with Mr. Masterman in L. Masterman's *C. F. G. Masterman.* Mr. Churchill's leading speeches of 1908 and 1909 are in his *Liberalism and the Social Problem* and *The People's Rights* (1910).

His marriage is referred to in *My Early Life* and W. S. Blunt's *Diaries,* Vol. II, p. 222.

The inner life of the Asquith Government in 1908 and 1909 is to be found in L. Masterman's *C. F. G. Masterman,* supplemented by the *Life of Lord Oxford and Asquith* by J. A. Spender and C. Asquith, Lord Haldane's *Autobiography* (1929), and Mr. Churchill's *Great Contemporaries,* s.v. *Herbert Henry Asquith* and his *Thoughts and Adventures,* s.v. *Personal Contacts;* Mr. Churchill's conversations recorded by L. Masterman and W. S. Blunt, and his visit to the German maneuvers of 1909 in *Thoughts and Adventures,* s.v. *The German Splendour* and *C. F. G. Masterman,* p. 166.

5

Mr. Churchill's service as Home Secretary in 1910 and 1911 may be recovered from L. Masterman's *C. F. G. Masterman,* who was his Under-Secretary, supplemented by conversations in W. S. Blunt's *Diaries,* J. Galsworthy's *Justice* (1910), and Max Beerbohm's *The Succession* in Leicester Galleries' catalogue, April-May, 1911, and *The Bookman,* August, 1911. The Sidney Street episode is recorded in his *Thoughts and Adventures,* s.v. *The Battle of Sidney Street,* supplemented by H. Martin's *Battle;* the Agadir crisis, railway strike, and Mr. Churchill's transfer to the Admiralty in his *World Crisis,* Vol. I, supplemented by D. Lloyd George's *War Memoirs,* Vol. I (1933), Lord Grey's *Twenty-five Years* (1928), Vol. I, Lord Hal-

dane's *Autobiography,* Sir F. Maurice's *Haldane,* Vol. I (1937),
Sir C. E. Callwell's *Field-Marshal Sir Henry Wilson* (1927),
Vol. I, the *Life of Lord Oxford and Asquith,* by J. A. Spender
and C. Asquith, Vol. I, and *C. F. G. Masterman,* by L. Masterman.

## War

### 1

Mr. Churchill's tenure of the Admiralty between 1911 and
the outbreak of war in 1914 is recorded in his *World Crisis,*
Vol. I, supplemented by the *Life of Lord Oxford and Asquith,*
Vol. II, by J. A. Spender and C. Asquith, *Haldane,* Vol. II, by
Sir F. Maurice, *Adventure* (1930), by J. E. B. Seely, and con-
versations in W. S. Blunt's *Diaries* and L. Masterman's *C. F. G.
Masterman.* For his early contributions to air warfare the
writer is indebted to his *Thoughts and Adventures,* s.v. *In the
Air* and to information furnished by Air Commodore A. W.
Bigsworth, C.M.G., D.S.O., A.F.C.

The events of July and August, 1914, are recorded in Mr.
Churchill's *World Crisis,* Vol. I, supplemented by the *Life of
Lord Oxford and Asquith,* Vol. II, Lord Morley's *Memorandum on Resignation* (1928), and *The Autobiography of Margot Asquith,* Vol. II.

### 2

Mr. Churchill's work at the Admiralty from the outbreak of
war to the end of 1914 is narrated in his *World Crisis,* Vol. I,
supplemented by the *Life of Lord Oxford and Asquith,* Vol.
II; C. E. Callwell's *Field-Marshal Sir Henry Wilson,* Vol. I;
Lord Grey's *Twenty-five Years,* Vol. II; Lord French's *1914*
(1919); Sir G. Arthur's *Life of Lord Kitchener* (1930), Vol. III;
and Lord Riddell's *War Diary* (1923).

For the Antwerp expedition, a summary of facts is to be
found in the official *Military Operations: France and Belgium,*

*1914,* Vol. II (1925), and a critical appreciation in B. H. Liddell Hart's *World War* in *Encyclopædia Britannica, 14th Edition* (1929), vol. xxiii.

### 3

The initiation and conduct of the Dardanelles expedition down to May, 1915, may be studied in *Dardanelles Commission: First Report* (1917) and Vol. I of the official *Military Operations: Gallipoli* (1929); from Mr. Churchill's point of view in Vol. II of his *World Crisis* (1923); from Lord Fisher's point of view in his *Memories* (1919) and Vol. II of Sir R. H. Bacon's *Life of Lord Fisher* (1929); from Mr. Asquith's point of view in Vol. II of his *Memories and Reflections* (1928); and from the military point of view in Vol. III of Sir G. Arthur's *Life of Lord Kitchener* and Vol. I of Sir I. Hamilton's *Gallipoli Diary* (1920).

Material as to the political crisis of 1915 exists in the preceding works, supplemented by D. Lloyd George's *War Memoirs,* Vol. I; Lord Riddell's *War Diary;* and Lord Beaverbrook's *Politicians and the War, 1914-1916* (1928).

### 4

Mr. Churchill's narrative of his interlude as Chancellor of the Duchy of Lancaster between May and November, 1915, is in Vol. II of his *World Crisis,* supplemented by his *Thoughts and Adventures* s.v. *Painting as a Pastime,* Sir E. Marsh's *A Number of People,* Lord Riddell's *War Diary,* and Vol. I of Sir I. Hamilton's *Gallipoli Diary.*

His statement on resignation on November 15, 1915, is in *Parliamentary Debates,* Vol. LXXV.

### 5

Mr. Churchill's military career in France may be recovered from his *Great Contemporaries* s.v. *Sir John French,* and his *Thoughts and Adventures* s.v. *With the Grenadiers* and "*Plugstreet,*" supplemented by J. E. B. Seely's *Adventure* and Lord

Birkenhead's *Contemporary Personalities* (1924) s.v. *Right Hon. Winston Spencer Churchill.* His memorandum on "Variants of the Offensive" is in his *World Crisis,* Vol. II.

His speeches in March and May, 1916, are in *Parliamentary Debates,* Vols. LXXX and LXXXII; the social and political scene may be recovered from C. à C. Repington's *First World War* (1920), Vol. I.

The facts as to his omission from the Government in December, 1916, are in Lord Beaverbrook's *Politicians and the War,* Vol. II (1932); Lord Riddell's *War Diary;* and his own *World Crisis,* Vol. III; and the circumstances of his appointment in July, 1917, are recorded by Mr. Lloyd George in Vol. III of his *War Memoirs.*

6

Mr. Churchill has narrated his tenure of the Ministry of Munitions from July, 1917, to the end of the war in his *World Crisis,* Vol. IV, which may be supplemented by C. à C. Repington's *First World War,* Vol. II; Sir E. Marsh's *A Number of People;* and Lord Riddell's *War Diary.*

His activities in France in 1918 are recorded in his *Thoughts and Adventures* s.v. *A Day with Clemenceau;* C. E. Callwell's *Field-Marshal Sir Henry Wilson,* Vol. II; and D. Lloyd George's *War Memoirs,* Vol. V.

POST-WAR

1

Mr. Churchill's activities in the interval between the Armistice and his departure from the Ministry of Munitions in January, 1919, are recorded in Vol. V of his *World Crisis: the Aftermath* (1929), supplemented by Lord Riddell's *Intimate Diary of the Peace Conference and After* (1933); Coventry strike of July, 1918, in Vol. IV of *The World Crisis.*

## 2

Mr. Churchill has recorded his tenure of the War Office during 1919 and 1920 in his *World Crisis: the Aftermath*, supplemented by Vol. II of C. à C. Repington's *First World War*, Vol. II of C. E. Callwell's *Field-Marshal Sir Henry Wilson*, Lord Riddell's *Intimate Diary of the Peace Conference*, and Sir E. Marsh's *A Number of People*.

## 3

Mr. Churchill's occupation of the Colonial Office in 1921 and 1922 is recorded in his *World Crisis: the Aftermath*, supplemented by his *Great Contemporaries* s.v. *Lawrence of Arabia* and *George Nathaniel Curzon;* Sir E. Marsh's *A Number of People;* Lord Riddell's *Intimate Diary of the Peace Conference;* Dundee election, 1922, in his *Thoughts and Adventures* s.v. *Election Memories*.

## 4

The interval between Mr. Churchill's defeat at Dundee in 1922 and his return to office in 1924 is referred to in his *Thoughts and Adventures* s.v. *A Second Choice* and *Election Memories*, supplemented by Vols. I and II of his *World Crisis;* Vol. II of B. E. C. Dugdale's *Arthur James Balfour;* and *H.H.A.: Letters of the Earl of Oxford and Asquith to a Friend*, Second Series (1934); comment by Mr. H. G. Wells in his *Men Like Gods* (1923); and an article quoted by the present writer in *The Missing Muse* (1929) s.v. *The Buccaneer*.

## 5

Mr. Churchill's term of office as Chancellor of the Exchequer from 1924 to 1929 can be reconstructed from press and Parliamentary reports; Lord Oxford's comments in *H.H.A.: Letters of the Earl of Oxford and Asquith to a Friend*, Second Series; and Lord Baldwin's criticism of Mr. Churchill's Cabinet methods in *Neville Chamberlain as He Was,* by Lord Camrose (*Daily Telegraph,* November 15 ,1940). The writer is indebted to Mr. H. A. Gwynne for recollections of Mr. Churchill in action on the *British Gazette,* and to his own essay *General Strike* in *The Missing Muse* for a contemporary view of these events.

## JEREMIAD

Mr. Churchill's Romanes Lecture, 1930, on *Parliamentary Government and the Economic Problem* is reprinted in his *Thoughts and Adventures.*

### 1

Mr. Churchill's leading speeches on Indian topics were reprinted in his *India* (1931).

### 2

Mr. Churchill's publications between 1930 and 1939 were: *My Early Life* (1930); *The World Crisis: The Eastern Front* (1931); *Thoughts and Adventures* (1932); *Marlborough: His Life and Times,* Vol. I (1933), Vol. II (1934), Vol. III (1936), Vol. IV (1938); *Great Contemporaries* (1937); *Step by Step* (1939).

*Arms and the Covenant* (1938) was edited by his son, Randolph S. Churchill.

### 3

Mr. Churchill's leading speeches on foreign affairs and defense between 1932 and 1936 were reprinted in *Arms and the Covenant,* and his fortnightly commentary on events, beginning in March, 1936, in *Step by Step, 1936-1939* (1939). The background of international affairs is portrayed from another point of view in *A Great Experiment* (1941), by Viscount Cecil, and the events of 1936 are studied in detail by the present writer in *The Hundredth Year* (1940).

## 4

The circumstances of King Edward's abdication are fully narrated by the present writer in *The Hundredth Year;* Mr. Churchill's comment in *Step by Step* s.v. *Mr. Baldwin's Revival.*

## 5

Mr. Churchill's leading utterances between 1937 and the outbreak of war in 1939 are reprinted in *Arms and the Covenant, Step by Step,* and *Into Battle* (1941), edited by Randolph S. Churchill; Mr. Chamberlain's intentions about Mr. Churchill in Lord Camrose's *Neville Chamberlain as He Was;* and Mr. Churchill's comment on Government lunch to Ribbentrop, March 11, 1937, in J. C. Wedgwood's *Memoirs of a Fighting Life* (1941).

The feeling of events may be recovered from D. Low's *Low Again: A Pageant of Politics* (1938) and *Europe Since Versailles* (1940).

### Mr. Chamberlain's War

The documentation of the war is still fragmentary and journalistic. Mr. Churchill's leading speeches are reprinted in *Into Battle;* the circumstances of his appointment to the Admiralty in September, 1939, and of Mr. Chamberlain's resignation in May, 1940, in Lord Camrose's *Neville Chamberlain as He Was.*

### Mr. Churchill's War

Mr. Churchill's speeches prior to November, 1940, are reprinted in *Into Battle.* Provisional narratives of the military operations in France and Belgium and the evacuation from Dunkirk are available in *The Diary of a Staff Officer (Air Intelligence Liaison Officer) at Advanced Headquarters, North B.A.F.F., 1940* (1941); J. Masefield's *The Nine Days Wonder*

(1941); and E. Keble Chatterton's *Epic of Dunkirk* (1940); of the course of French politics in Elie J. Bois's *Truth on the Tragedy of France* (1940); and of the air war from August to October, 1940, in *The Battle of Britain* (1941); D. Low's *Europe at War* (1941) and *War Cartoons* (1941) contain invaluable reminders of current events.

Mr. Churchill's statement on Defense procedure in the House of Commons, May 7, 1941; Mr. Hoover's high opinion of M. Laval in C. D. Johnson's *Borah of Idaho* (1936), p. 445. The quotations in the two final notes are from Mr. Churchill's *River War*, Vol. II, pp. 217-8, and Macaulay's first essay (1834) on William Pitt, Earl of Chatham.

The writer is indebted to the kindness of British Movietonews Ltd. for his study of the most vivid and authentic of all documents, the newsreels recording Mr. Churchill's public appearances in 1940 and 1941.

He was in England throughout the period described and in London during the air-raids of September and October, 1940.

# *INDEX*

# INDEX

# Index

# Index

# Index

344

# Index

## Index

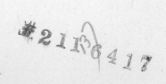